INNOVATION AND CREATIVITY IN ELT METHODOLOGY

EDUCATION IN A COMPETITIVE AND GLOBALIZING WORLD

Additional books in this series can be found on Nova's website under the Series tab.

Additional e-books in this series can be found on Nova's website under the e-book tab.

EDUCATION IN A COMPETITIVE AND GLOBALIZING WORLD

INNOVATION AND CREATIVITY IN ELT METHODOLOGY

HANDOYO PUJI WIDODO

AND

ANDRZEJ CIROCKI

EDITORS

New York

For permission to use material from this book please contact us:
Telephone 631-231-7269; Fax 631-231-8175
Web Site: http://www.novapublishers.com

NOTICE TO THE READER

The Publisher has taken reasonable care in the preparation of this book, but makes no expressed or implied warranty of any kind and assumes no responsibility for any errors or omissions. No liability is assumed for incidental or consequential damages in connection with or arising out of information contained in this book. The Publisher shall not be liable for any special, consequential, or exemplary damages resulting, in whole or in part, from the readers' use of, or reliance upon, this material. Any parts of this book based on government reports are so indicated and copyright is claimed for those parts to the extent applicable to compilations of such works.

Independent verification should be sought for any data, advice or recommendations contained in this book. In addition, no responsibility is assumed by the publisher for any injury and/or damage to persons or property arising from any methods, products, instructions, ideas or otherwise contained in this publication.

This publication is designed to provide accurate and authoritative information with regard to the subject matter covered herein. It is sold with the clear understanding that the Publisher is not engaged in rendering legal or any other professional services. If legal or any other expert assistance is required, the services of a competent person should be sought. FROM A DECLARATION OF PARTICIPANTS JOINTLY ADOPTED BY A COMMITTEE OF THE AMERICAN BAR ASSOCIATION AND A COMMITTEE OF PUBLISHERS.

Additional color graphics may be available in the e-book version of this book.

Library of Congress Cataloging-in-Publication Data

Innovation and creativity in ELT methodology / editors, Handoyo Puji Widodo, Andrzej Cirocki.
p. cm.
Includes bibliographical references and index.
ISBN: 978-1-62948-146-3 (softcover)
1. English language--Study and teaching--Foreign speakers--Cross-cultural studies. 2. Creative teaching--Cross-cultural studies. I. Widodo, Handoyo Puji. II. Cirocki, Andrzej.
PE1128.A2I536 2011
428.0071--dc22
2011010176

Published by Nova Science Publishers, Inc. † New York

CONTENTS

PREFACE

Innovation and Creativity in ELT Methodology comprises a collection of pedagogical articles, giving language teachers a fascinating insight into the way different teaching approaches, methods, procedures, and techniques can be explored in the language classroom. Written by established and emerging scholars, this edited volume covers current key issues in teaching, including four macro language skills like listening, speaking, reading, and writing; three micro language skills such as pronunciation, vocabulary and grammar, as well as English through content areas and technology—CALL. This is a valuable resource book for language teachers, language materials developers, pre-service language teachers, and language teacher educators who would like to explore and creatively craft their own teaching practices to help language learners become competent users of the target language.

ACKNOWLEDGMENTS

The authors would like to express their deepest appreciation to the following contributors: Larry Vandergrift, Willy A. Renandya, Jonathan Newton, Joseph A. Foley, Osman Z. Barnawi, Rob Waring, Jayakaran Mukundan, Mary J. Curry, Hee-Jeong Oh, Lynda Yates, Beth Zielinski, Stuart Webb, Paul Nation, Jeannine M. Fontaine, Rachael Shade, Adriadi Novawan, Tom Salsbury, John Spiri, Tilly Harrison, and Sharon Deckert for having been fully committed to writing the chapters for this much-needed volume. Without their contributions, this edited work would not have been possible.

The authors also wish to express their special gratitude to Frank Columbus, Maya Columbus, Nick Longo, and Stephanie Gonzalez for encouraging us to complete this volume and getting this work published.

NOTES ON EDITORS AND CONTRIBUTORS

HANDOYO PUJI WIDODO

Handoyo Widodo is Chair of the Department of Language, Communication, and Tourism at Politeknik Negeri Jember based in East Java, Indonesia. He has published extensively in international journals and co-edited two ELT books. He is a regular presenter at international conferences and workshops. He is Editor-in-Chief of the *International Journal of Innovation in ELT* and *Research* and Associate Editor of *Journal of Language Teaching and Research*. He is also currently on the Editorial Board of *Asian ESP Journal*, *TESL Canada Journal*, *TESL-EJ*, and *TESOL-Spain Newsletter*. His areas of specialization include ELT ... development, English for Specific Purposes (ESP), ... e can be contacted at *handoyopw@yahoo.com*.

...ZEJ CIROCKI

...fessor of English as a Foreign Language at the ...isk, Poland. He holds an MA in English philology ...ed linguistics from Adam Mickiewicz University in ...icate in English Language Teaching to Adults (St. ...3. His research interests include second language ...sm in glottodidactics, learner autonomy, language ...nd communicative language teaching. His latest ...nguage Teaching* and *Observation of Teaching*: ...arch on Teaching* (with Gloria Park and Handoyo ...incom in Germany. His email address is

... NOVAWAN

...Novawan is a lecturer at Politeknik Negeri Jember based in East Java, Indonesia. He teaches writing, speaking, and ESP courses like English for Clinical Nutrition. He is currently involved in a collaborative ASEAN project on *Capability-Building of English*

Language Curriculum Developers for Professional Communication for University Faculty in ASEAN Universities in collaboration with CELC, National University of Singapore (NUS) funded by the Temasek Foundation based in Singapore. His professional and research interests lie in language teaching methodology, ELT media, and language materials development. He can be contacted at *a_novawan@yahoo.com*.

BETH ZIELINSKI

Beth Zielinski's research interest is in the area of pronunciation and intelligibility, and her doctoral thesis investigated "the features of pronunciation that have an impact on intelligibility in speakers of English as a second language." She has conducted pronunciation classes for international university students, private consultations for corporate clients, and professional development sessions for teachers, as well as publishing and lecturing in the area. She can be contacted at *beth.zielinski@mq.edu.au*.

HEE JEONG OH

Hee Jeong Oh is a doctoral student at the Margaret Warner Graduate School of Education at University of Rochester, New York. Her research focuses on "responses among Korean families to the growing dominance of English and the pressure to learn English." Before beginning her PhD, she taught English at a Hanwool Middle School in Seoul for three years. She can be contacted at *blue0502@hotmail.com*.

JAYAKARAN MUKUNDAN

Jayakaran Mukundan is Associate Professor at the Faculty of Educational Studies, Universiti Putra Malaysia. He has developed software Retrotext-E and Retrotext E 2.0 for evaluating ELT textbooks. He won gold medals at the British Invention Show, UK (2009) and at IEANA, Germany in 2010 respectively. He is involved in teaching and researching in two main areas: ELT materials and writing. He has been involved with the Asia Teacher-Writers Group from the very beginning. He is Director for the Extensive Reading Board and Visiting Fellow, Leeds Metropolitan University, UK. He can be contacted at *jaya@educ.upm.edu.my* or *jaya284@gmail.com*.

JEANNINE M. FONTAINE

Jeannine Fontaine is Associate Professor in the PhD Program in Composition and TESOL at the Indiana University of Pennsylvania where she has taught courses in second language acquisition and literacy, linguistics, and cognitive studies for over twenty years. She has taught at Middlebury College and the University of North Carolina and has presented extensively at international conferences. Her research interests have ranged over several applied linguistic areas, but her current interest is in aspects of linguistic stylistics, metaphor, and linguistic devices supporting humor. She can be contacted at *jfontain@iup.edu.*

JOHN SPIRI

John Spiri is Associate Professor in the Education Department at Gifu Shotoku Gakuen University in Japan. In addition to academic articles, he has published two EFL/ESL textbooks and self published four others. As a part-time journalist, he has written for *The Japan Times*, *The Boston Globe*, and a number of other publications. His research interests include autonomy, computer assisted language learning, and global issues in language education. In addition to teaching at several universities in Japan, he has taught EFL in Taiwan and at colleges in Vermont, USA. He can be contacted at *spiriatwork@gmail.com.*

JONATHAN NEWTON

Jonathan Newton is Senior Lecturer in the School of Linguistics and Applied Language Studies, Victoria University of Wellington, New Zealand. He has been involved in language teaching and language teacher training for more than twenty years in both New Zealand and China where he began his teaching career. His research and teaching interests include task-based language teaching, classroom-based second language acquisition research, intercultural language learning and teaching, and workplace-related intercultural pragmatics. He has published in books on language teaching methodology and in journals including *Second Language Research, System, Journal of Pragmatics, English Language Teaching Journal* and *Modern English Teacher.* He recently co-authored a book with Paul Nation, *Teaching ESL/EFL Listening and Speaking* (2009) through Routledge. He can be contacted at *Jonathan.Newton@vuw.ac.nz.*

JOSEPH A. FOLEY

Joseph Foley is Professor and Director of the Doctoral Program in the Graduate School of English at Assumption University of Thailand, Bangkok. Previously, he was Head of English Language in the Department of English Language and Literature at the National University of Singapore where he taught for more than 25 years. More recently, he was a Language Specialist with Southeast Asian Ministers of Education Organization (SEAMEO), Regional Language Centre (RELC) in Singapore. His research interests are mainly in the area of systemic linguistics and its application to education and World Englishes. He can be contacted at *jfoley@au.edu.*

LARRY VANDERGRIFT

Larry Vandergrift is Professor at the Official Languages and Bilingualism Institute at the University of Ottawa where he teaches courses in French, English, and Second Language Acquisition. He conducts research in the teaching of second language listening and has published in many journals: *Applied Linguistics, Annual Review of Applied Linguistics, Language Learning, Language Teaching, Modern Language Journal, Canadian Modern Language Review,* and *Foreign Language Annals*. His book, with Christine Goh, *On the Teaching of L2 Listening*, will be published in 2011. He is a previous editor of the *Canadian Modern Language Review*. He can be contacted at *lvdgrift@uottawa.ca*.

LYNDA YATES

Lynda Yates has been involved with TESOL and teacher education for over 30 years and has taught in a wide range of settings and countries. Her research interests focus on adult language learning and teaching, pronunciation, intercultural communication, language in the workplace, and issues for transnational and immigrant learners. She is currently Associate Professor in Linguistics at Macquarie University, Australia. She can be contacted at *Lynda.Yates@ling.mq.edu.au*.

MARY JANE CURRY

Mary Jane Curry is Associate Professor of Language Education at the Margaret Warner Graduate School of Education at University of Rochester, New York. She is a co-author of *Teaching Academic Writing: A Toolkit for Higher Education* (Routledge, 2003). With Theresa Lillis, she has co-authored *Academic Writing in a Global Context: The Politics and Practices of Publishing in English* (Routledge, 2010) as well as articles on scholarly publishing in *TESOL Quarterly, Written Communication, International Journal of Applied Linguistics*, and *English for Specific Purposes Journal*. In addition, she has published in *Studies in the Education of Adults, Literacy*, and *Numeracy Studies* and *Community College Review*. She can be contacted at *mjcurry@Warner.Rochester.edu*.

OSMAN ZAKARIA BARNAWI

Osman Barnawi is Assistant Professor at the English Language Center, Yanbu Industrial College, Saudi Arabia. He has published extensively in international journals such as *International Journal of Teaching and Learning in Higher Education, English Language Teaching*, and *Journal of Language and Linguistic Studies*. He is a reviewer of *Educational Research and Reviews* and *Journal of Teacher Education*. He is a regular presenter at international conferences and workshops. His research interests include second language writing, second language learners' identities, critical pedagogy, crisis leadership in higher education, performance assessment in higher education, extensive reading, ESP program evaluation, educational technologies, philosophy of social science, and language teacher education. His email address is *albarnawim@hotmail.com*.

PAUL NATION

Paul Nation is Professor of Applied Linguistics in the School of Linguistics and Applied Language Studies at Victoria University of Wellington, New Zealand. He has taught in Indonesia, Thailand, the United States, Finland, and Japan. His specialist interests are language teaching methodology and vocabulary learning. A four book series *Reading for Speed and Fluency* appeared from Compass Publishing in 2007. His latest books on vocabulary include *Learning Vocabulary in Another Language* (2001) published by Cambridge University Press, *Focus on Vocabulary* (2007) through NCELTR—Macquarie University, and *Teaching Vocabulary: Strategies and Techniques* published by Cengage Learning (2008). Two books, *Teaching ESL/EFL Listening and Speaking* (with Jonathan Newton) and *Teaching ESL/EFL Reading and Writing*, have recently appeared from Routledge. His email address is *Paul.Nation@vuw.ac.nz*.

RACHAEL SHADE

Rachael Shade is a doctoral student at the Indiana University of Pennsylvania. Her research interests include how motivation affects language learning and how motivations vary across cultures, intercultural communication, gender studies, and applied linguistics. She has taught at the University of Maryland, College Park, and has presented her work at national and international levels. Her email address is *r.p.shade@iup.edu*.

ROB WARING

Rob Waring teaches English and Language Education at Notre Dame Seishin University in Okayama, Japan. He has written, co-written, and been a series editor for about 170 graded readers. He is actively involved as a Board Member of the Extensive Reading Foundation (www.erfoundation.org). His email address is *waring_robert@yahoo.com*.

SHARON K. DECKERT

Sharon Deckert is Assistant Professor in the Composition and TESOL program at Indiana University of Pennsylvania. Her research interest includes questions of how individuals construct identities that function for particular purposes. She has examined how children co-construct identities with adults in forensic interviews. She has published in *Corpus Analysis: Language Structure and Language Use* (Rodopi Publishers, 2003) and in *ESL Writers: A Guide for Writing Center Tutors* (2nd ed., Boynton/Cook Publishers, 2009). Her work has been presented nationally and internationally. Her email address is *sdeckert@iup.edu*.

STUART WEBB

Stuart Webb is a Senior Lecturer and the MA Program Director in the School of Linguistics and Applied Language Studies at Victoria University of Wellington. His research interests include vocabulary studies and extensive reading and listening. He has published in journals like *Applied Linguistics*, *Language Learning*, *Studies in Second Language Acquisition*, and *TESOL Quarterly*. His email address is *stuart.webb@vuw.ac.nz*.

TILLY HARRISON

Tilly Harrison is Senior Teaching Fellow at the University of Warwick where she teaches on the Masters in English Language Teaching with a specialty in ICT and Multimedia. Her research interests are the uses of technology (wikis, corpora, online peer review, etc.) to enhance the writing of second language learners. She has organized and given many CALL related workshops and teacher training sessions and is a long-standing member of the International Association of Teachers of English as a Foreign Language (IATEFL) where she was Coordinator of the Computer (now Learning Technologies) Special Interest Group from 2000 to 2004. Her email address is *Tilly.Harrison@warwick.ac.uk*.

TOM SALSBURY

Tom Salsbury is Assistant Professor in the Department of Teaching and Learning, College of Education at Washington State University, Pullman. He is a pre-service and in-service K-12 teacher educator, specializing in linguistically diverse content area classrooms. He was a classroom ESL teacher for 17 years in the U.S., Taiwan, Spain, and Mexico. His current research is in second language vocabulary acquisition, particularly with English language learner populations in content area learning. His email address is *tsalsbury@wsu.edu*.

WILLY A. RENANDYA

Willy Renandya is a Language Teacher Educator with extensive teaching experience in ASEAN countries, including Indonesia, Malaysia, Singapore, the Philippines, and Vietnam. He currently teaches applied linguistics courses at the National Institute of Education, Nanyang Technological University (NTU), Singapore where he also serves as Head of the Teachers' Language Development Centre. Prior to his current position, he taught at SEAMEO-RELC, Singapore where he also served as Head of the Department of Language Education and Research. He has published articles and books on various topics, including an edited book entitled *Methodology in Language Teaching: An Anthology of Current Practice* with Jack C. Richards, published by Cambridge University Press (2002, 2008). He is also co-editor (with Jack C. Richards) of a language teacher resource series, called *the RELC Portfolio Series*, which has been translated into Portuguese and Spanish. His latest publication *Teacher, the Tape is too Fast–Extensive Listening in ELT* (co-authored with Thomas S.C. Farrell) appeared in the *ELT Journal* in 2011. His email address is *willy.renandya@nie.edu.sg*.

INTRODUCTION

Handoyo Puji Widodo and Andrzej Cirocki

The field of foreign or second language teaching (e.g., TEFL, TESL, or TESOL) has undergone many fluctuations and shifts over the years. For instance, in English language teaching (ELT), there have been changing demands for best practices in needs analysis, instructional goals and objectives, syllabus and lesson planning, language teaching methodology, instructional materials, and assessment and evaluation.

In particular, over the decades, in the area of methodology in ELT, numerous approaches, methods, techniques, and procedures of teaching English have been proposed. Each of them has imposed a dogmatic idea on the *best* language teaching practices that language teachers could adopt to help learners become competent users of the target language.

However, as the postmethod language emerged, the idea of practicality, particularity, and possibility (Kumaravadivelu, 2006) encourages language teachers to situate their own teaching practices in a particular context that is referred to as particular learner characteristics and needs, learner learning styles and strategies, learning and teaching resources, as well as sociocultural and institutional factors.

Given this notion, this volume on *Innovation and Creativity in ELT Methodology* is trying to offer more methodical frameworks of teaching English as a mediating or transnational language where language learners are regarded to have their own cultural and linguistic resources. With these resources, language learners are better able to acquire the skills needed so that they can communicate with other people who do not share the same language. Driven by this notion, this book aims to:

- offer a resource book on current practices of English language teaching that bridge the gap between theory and practice. In this regard, theory informs practice, and vice versa;
- suggest well-crafted methods of language learning and teaching as well as an alternative to the conventional question-and-answer approach to language classroom activities and tasks;
- provide novice English teachers with theoretical and practical guides to teaching English classes as a starting point for exploring more teaching approaches, methods, techniques, and procedures in the language classroom;

- foster a scholarly discussion on the issue of *innovation* and *creativity* in English language instruction at different levels;
- promote approaches methods in language learning and teaching that are deeply rooted in the notion that teaching language is an art of exploration and creativity where there is no best approach to and method of language teaching that is best suited for all classroom settings;
- provide a valuable guide to developing innovative and creative language programs by examining various factors (e.g., learners and socio-institutional contexts) in order to better design such programs; and
- produce exemplary and grounded work that promotes the idea that language teachers should "theorize what they practice and practice what they theorize" (Kumaravadivelu, 2006, p. 173).

Written by established and emerging scholars, this volume puts more emphasis on addressing recent critical issues in teaching: (a) four macro language skills like listening, speaking, reading, and writing; (b) micro language skills such as pronunciation, vocabulary, and grammar; (c) English through content area and technology (e.g., CALL); and (d) English through CALL and corpora. The volume also presents a perceptive insight into how a task-based framework can be used as an approach to English language teaching. Specifically, the entire volume consists of seventeen chapters, including:

- Chapter 1 discusses the importance of interactive listening and examines social and cognitive challenges that listeners face in interactive listening contexts.
- Chapter 2 deals with the role of extensive listening in foreign and second language teaching. It also explains language learning benefits and provides practical activities, which promote extensive listening in the language classroom.
- Chapter 3 provides three principles to guide teachers and materials designers in integrating an intercultural dimension into language materials and lessons based on communicative language teaching.
- Chapter 4 offers a discussion on key issues in teaching speaking from a linguistic perspective, *corpus linguistics*, and it argues that textbooks tend to emphasize *transactional* conversation rather than *interactional* one, which may result in a stilted form of speaking in adult learners of English.
- Chapter 5 presents theoretical and empirical accounts of metacognitive strategy training in ESP reading programs, aiming at assisting language learners in becoming independent and fluent L2 readers.
- Chapter 6 introduces the idea of extensive reading and explains why it is necessary in language instruction. Also, it shows how to set up an extensive reading program and suggests ways to run it effectively.
- Chapter 7 demonstrates ideas how teachers can realize their writing potential, and thus become more confident in teaching the skill of writing.
- Chapter 8 displays an approach to teaching about genres in circulation, describing various activities, and suggesting ways L2 students can expand their awareness of the issue in question.

- Chapter 9 explores different aspects of learning and teaching pronunciation and provides insights into why learners might find this aspect of learning English challenging.
- Chapter 10 examines vocabulary learning activities and sheds light on what teachers need to consider when designing, selecting, and modifying activities.
- Chapter 11 looks at learners' needs for vocabulary learning in an early speaking course. Additionally, it examines various activities and gives special attention to the design of vocabulary focused communicative tasks.
- Chapter 12 advocates a flexible approach to the teaching of grammar. The authors make an attempt to bring grammar back to its rightful place by encouraging language teachers to help learners appreciate the wonders of English, including its subtle tricks.
- Chapter 13 argues for visually-based approach to teaching grammar, discussing various possibilities of using visuals to make grammar teaching more attractive and effective.
- Chapter 14 overviews the teaching of English through content areas, emphasizing the importance of contextualized instruction and scaffolding in the development of content-based language learning activities.
- Chapter 15 discusses the use of corpora for materials writing and accessing online corpora for language study and research. It aims to demonstrate how corpora can be effectively exploited in language learning and teaching.
- Chapter 16 presents the concept of affordance in the history of CALL and looks at ways technology can be employed to enhance the learning of English in a classroom setting.
- Chapter 17 provides language teachers with a set of questions that can be used to evaluate whether a proposed activity has the qualities of a well-developed task.

By addressing the critical key issues above, language teachers can become aware that they play crucial roles as teaching explorers and innovators in the classroom. This notion suggests that classrooms should be viewed as a site for exploring and crafting any teaching approaches, methods, techniques, and procedures in order to meet students' needs for learning English and help them become successful learners and users of the target language. Thus, the volume pulls together theory, research, and practice in ELT methodology and fosters postmethod language pedagogy where language teachers are encouraged to self explore and create best English teaching practices in their own teaching context. Informed by current empirical and theoretical accounts, language teachers can view theory and practice as "mutually complimentary entity" to build and expand practically, theoretically, and empirically grounded ideas or knowledge of English language teaching (ELT).

REFERENCES

Kumaravadivelu, B. (2006). *Understanding language teaching: From method to postmethod.* Mahwah, NJ: Lawrence Erlbaum. Chapter 1

In: Innovation and Creativity in ELT Methodology
Editors: H. P. Widodo and A. Cirocki

ISBN: 978-1-62948-146-3
© 2013 Nova Science Publishers, Inc.

Chapter 1

TEACHING INTERACTIVE LISTENING

Larry Vandergrift
University of Ottawa, Canada

ABSTRACT

A desired goal for many L2 learners is the ability to develop competence in interactive listening, that is, the ability to converse with speakers of the target language. Interactive listening competence, however, is rarely researched or developed explicitly in L2 classrooms. This chapter begins with a discussion of the importance of interactive listening and an examination of the social and cognitive challenges faced by listeners in interactive listening contexts. This is followed by a description and discussion of research-based strategies that listeners can use to participate more meaningfully in interaction with another speaker. The chapter concludes with a number of pedagogical activities for teaching L2 interactive listening in classroom settings. The underlying premise of this chapter is that language learners can be given tools to negotiate meaning and become better conversational partners. These tools can help learners obtain language input made comprehensible to them by their interlocutors, thereby facilitating language acquisition.

> Sometimes I can catch the whole sentence, but I can't understand the true meaning of the words. Because I haven't the same culture as the speaker, I couldn't give the accurate response to it. When I couldn't understand the speaker's words, I give a smile in response to it. Maybe I look a little wooden, but I have no choice. If I always ask the speaker to say again, he or she'll feel too boring with me (Li Chen).

INTRODUCTION

Most foreign and second language (henceforth L2) listening instruction focuses on the development of one-way listening; that is, listening to aural texts and answering comprehension questions. A desired goal for many L2 learners, however, is the ability to develop competence in interactive listening; that is, the ability to hold a conversation with speakers of the target language. The objective of interactive listening can be either transactional, to give and/or receive information, or social, to participate meaningfully in conversation.

However, negotiating this social interaction competently can be particularly challenging, as suggested by Li-Chen. In order to become competent listeners, L2 learners need to learn how to handle both the cognitive and social demands of interactive listening. I argue that language learners can be given the tools by which they can better capitalize on these listening events and learn to become better conversational partners.

This chapter discusses the teaching of interactive listening, interwoven with references to pertinent research. After examining the importance of this kind of listening for language learning, I will discuss some of the social and cognitive challenges faced by listeners in interactive listening contexts. I will, then, describe and discuss specific strategies that listeners can use as tools to participate meaningfully in interaction with another speaker. Finally, based on the premise that interactive listening can be taught, I will present a number of possibilities for teaching L2 interactive listening in classroom settings.

IMPORTANCE OF INTERACTIVE LISTENING

Interactive listening plays an important role in language learning since it provides learners with opportunities to (1) seek language input that can be made comprehensible through the process of meaning negotiation and (2) learn how to be good conversation partners through the use of appropriate receipt tokens that convey participation in the discourse and move it forward. Vandergriff (2006) refers to this as "establishing common ground;" that is, meaning negotiation and use of appropriate receipt tokens can lead interlocutors to share more and more information, thereby establishing more common ground and greater intersubjectivity.

Negotiating Meaning

Listening is probably the most critical skill for L2 learning, and interactive listening contexts can be ideal events for language learning. When listeners confront a comprehension problem and maximize opportunities to negotiate meaning with their interlocutor (initiated perforce by some kind of interactive listening strategy), they solicit further language input. The interlocutor responds by repeating or restating the message in a different way, thereby tailoring the language input to a level comprehensible to the listener. If the restated information is still not adequately understood, both interlocutors can continue to negotiate meaning until an adequate level of comprehension has been realized for the interaction to move forward.

The importance of interactive listening strategies for negotiating meaning cannot be underestimated. In addition to allowing interaction between interlocutors (of which at least one is not sufficiently proficient in the target language) to move forward, these strategies have the potential to provide comprehensible input to language learners. For example, Pica, Young, and Doughty (1987) demonstrated how comprehension checks and clarification requests used by non-native speakers in interaction with a native speaker (NS) on directions to complete a task prompted the NS to modify input through repetition and rephrasing of input content. These modifications played a critical role in facilitating comprehension. When listeners have the opportunity to negotiate meaning, language input can be made comprehensible to them at their current level of understanding, and this can have salutary effects on language acquisition (Lightbown and Spada, 2006).

Moving Discourse Forward

Interactive listening involves more than comprehension clarification and verification, however. Good listeners must also work with their interlocutor to move the discourse forward. To do this, they use receipt tokens, often referred to as uptakes or backchannel cues (e.g., *hm hm*, etc.), to signal comprehension as well as engagement with their interlocutor.

As noted by Gardner (1998), these tokens have a core functional meaning that suggests alignment with the interlocutor (much like the establishment of common ground referred to earlier pointed out by Vandergriff) and encourages the speaker to continue. Garcia Mayo (2001) found that with advanced level learners this could also take the form of one speaker completing the other's utterance. For example, when the primary speaker describes coffee preparation and states "I found the coffee but could not find any ..." and the listener, now in a speaking role, interjects with "... filters," the listener demonstrates engagement with the meaning of the communication. Consequently, the response of the interlocutor may well take the form of another receipt token, such as *yeah*, before the interaction moves on. Receipt tokens can also take the form of repetition, as noted by Greer, Andrade, Butterfield, and Mischinger (2009), particularly if a new piece of information has been added; e.g., *a new car, OK*. In this way, listeners acknowledge comprehension of a new element and signal that the interaction can go on.

This type of interactive listening strategy may transfer from L1, which is advantageous if both languages share similar conversational norms. However, backchannel cues can be culturally bound and used incorrectly, thus affecting the quality of the interaction and leading to negative perceptions of the other. For example, Japanese learners of English, to be polite and to avoid confrontation, used backchannels ("nod," "hm hm") that frustrated their English L1 interlocutors who were not certain to what degree their partners really understood them (Cutrone, 2005).

Furthermore, the placement of these cues in the interaction and their prosodic shape can determine how they are received by the interlocutor. Gardner (1998) found that the core meaning of receipt tokens such as *yeah* and *hm hm* changed significantly by the intonation contour of the utterance; e.g., a rising contour suggesting a question and a falling contour suggesting agreement. Obviously, this has important implications for pedagogy if listeners wish to accurately convey a message to their interlocutor how they are being understood.

In sum, use of appropriate interactive listening strategies can enhance L2 learning by helping learners to obtain necessary comprehensible input and to become better conversation partners. This is important because the listener's response not only informs the interlocutor of how a prior utterance has been understood, but also of how subsequent utterances can be designed. Interactive listening, thus, entails a constant back and forth acknowledgement of understanding by which the participants interactively construct meaning and move the conversation along (Brouwer, 1999).

CHALLENGES OF INTERACTIVE LISTENING

Interactive listening is constrained by both social and cognitive challenges. The status relationship between interlocutors may limit the degree to which listeners will intervene to seek clarification and negotiate meaning (Carrier, 1999). Listeners are more likely to intervene in interaction contexts where the status relationship between speakers is equal (like with a friend) than during a job interview where the relationship is unequal. Furthermore, the nature and type of interactive listening strategies used will be constrained by language proficiency since low-level listeners lack the vocabulary for any complex intervention. This will limit both the degree of intervention possible and the nature of the interaction strategies used.

Social Challenges

An important variable in the success of interactive listening is the social dynamic. When listeners face a comprehension problem, how they deal with it will depend on a number of affective variables such as willingness to take risks, fear of losing face, assertiveness, and motivation. The degree to which these variables will influence the interaction will depend on the relationship between the interlocutors since status relationships can affect comprehension and the freedom to negotiate meaning. Differences, for example, in age, gender, language proficiency, and power relationships (employer-employee), often turn interactive listening events into contexts where the disadvantaged listener feels powerless. These feelings of inferiority often affect how much is understood (due to increased anxiety) and the degree to which listeners will dare to clarify comprehension in order to save face. Furthermore, the face-to-face nature of these events also requires listeners to attend to non-verbal signals (e.g., furrowed eyebrows), body language, and culturally-bound cues (e.g., certain gestures), which can add to or change the literal meaning of an utterance.

On the other hand, the contextual nature of interactive listening can also facilitate comprehension for the listener. Whether the context is formal or informal, listeners in interactive situations often have a common communicative goal that facilitates interpretation—e.g., the job description, the applicant's curriculum vitae, and the job interview protocol between the job applicant and the interviewer; the "script" for selling/buying shoes shared by salesperson and customer looking to buy a pair of shoes; or the common life experiences shared by friends and the understood assumptions that underlie their conversation.

In each of these situations, the context provides the backdrop against which to predict the information heard, question types used, routines followed, or in the case of conversation between friends, common understandings without stating things explicitly. The highly contextualized nature of these interactive situations will facilitate more rapid word recognition, allowing listeners to process the interlocutor's message more efficiently. When they confront something unexpected, cannot resolve the comprehension problem internally, or simply do not understand, listeners can intervene and ask their interlocutor to clarify, repeat, or speak more slowly provided that their relationship with the primary speaker is sufficiently informal.

Cognitive Challenges

The cognitive challenges of interactive listening are particularly demanding for low proficiency language learners. Listeners at beginning levels of language learning are incapable of efficiently processing rapid speech. Their limited vocabulary and experience with the target language force them to pay attention to the individual words they hear. Because they are not yet capable of automatically processing much of what they hear, low proficiency listeners must, perforce, engage in controlled processing of the individual words they recognize. This has consequences for how much they can process because working memory (WM) resources are limited. As their language proficiency increases, listeners are able to process more information at once; this allows them to grasp more information and to think more about what they hear. Research by Rost and Rost (1991) and Vandergrift (1997) observed that more advanced listeners were not frustrated by the cognitive constraints that limited what beginning listeners could attend to in real time. With prolonged language exposure, these listeners internalized more language, allowing them to process words as thought groups. This left them with room in WM to think about responding to their interlocutor and to moving the discourse forward.

The obligation to respond is another major cognitive challenge of interactive listening. As listeners attend to their interlocutor, they must not only process the content of the message in real time, but also clarify their understanding when comprehension is uncertain and respond appropriately. This increases the cognitive load significantly because listeners must allocate their limited WM resources to both comprehension and production in swift succession. This may, sometimes, lead listeners to fake understanding using a backchannel cue to encourage their interlocutor to continue with the hope that additional cues in the developing discourse will clarify understanding. Although the contextualized nature of interactive listening can facilitate comprehension, as suggested above, the cognitive demands made on listeners can, sometimes, be heavier. In these contexts, in addition to attending to what their interlocutor is saying, listeners must attend to and understand any paralinguistic signals or other gestures that may add meaning beyond the literal meaning of a word or phrase. Because these cues need to be processed along with the speech, they add to the cognitive load of interactive listening. Furthermore, when the social and affective demands of the listening task are high; for example, the interlocutor is in a power relationship over the listener and the stakes of the interaction are high (e.g., an immigration interview), WM resources are even more constrained. The consequence is that listeners will be even more limited in how much of the interlocutor's utterance they will be able to process.

The cognitive and social challenges of interactive listening can be alleviated somewhat by equipping listeners with appropriate interactive listening strategies, tools that can help them make best use of their WM resources and the contextual cues at their disposal.

TOOLS FOR INTERACTIVE LISTENING

In a classroom study on interactive listening strategies used by students during seminar discussions, Lynch (1995) observed two broad categories of moves made by the listener. The first includes old information questions for clarification of an earlier comprehension difficulty, moves characterized by a backward orientation. The second includes new information questions or receipt tokens that carry the discourse forward or ask the interlocutor to elaborate further, moves characterized by a forward orientation. Table 1 highlights a number of interactive listening strategies identified through research with L2 listeners engaged in an interactive task, contexts where they alternated in both speaking and listening roles (Dörnyei and Kormos, 1998; Rost and Ross, 1991; Vandergrift, 1997). Evidence for these strategies was corroborated in subsequent studies (Farrell and Mallard, 2006; Vandergriff, 2006).

Strategies with a Backward Orientation

The first three types of strategies describe efforts by listeners to clarify understanding. When listeners do not understand or wish to clarify understanding with their interlocutor, they may use a strategy with a backward orientation to the discourse. These strategies include using (1) a global reprise, a request for repetition or a signal that conveys non-understanding; (2) a request for clarification or a specific lexical reprise; and (3) a hypothesis-testing technique to either verify or confirm comprehension. These types of strategies are also referred to as repair strategies (e.g., Dornyei and Kormos, 1998) since they constitute a response to problems encountered and, therefore, have a backward orientation.

The most basic interactive listening strategies involve a minimal signal of non-understanding. When listeners do not understand, cannot hear, or are uncertain about what they have heard, they can (1) use a global reprise (e.g., *pardon?*); (2) ask their interlocutor to repeat what he or she said (e.g., *What did you say?*); or (3) suggest lack of comprehension through some voluntary or involuntary non-verbal signals (e.g., a confused look). The first two signals are explicit requests for help that require the interlocutor to rephrase or simplify what he or she just said. The third signal, however, is more subtle and may or may not be noticed unless the interlocutor is sympathetic and/or has a vested interest in the listener's collaboration. In these cases, the interlocutor may be required to do a considerable amount of rephrasing or even resort to gestures before the utterance is understood, and the interaction can move forward. Research shows that beginning level listeners tend to use these kinds of strategies because their linguistic repertoire is limited (Rost and Ross, 1991; Vandergrift, 1997). They have few other linguistic resources to signal lack of understanding and, due to cognitive constraints, can only focus on the few words they know rather than the overall meaning of the utterance.

Second, on a less global level of misunderstanding, when listeners have not understood a particular word or fragment that appears to be critical for understanding, they can use a specific reprise.

Table 1. Interactive listening strategies: Definitions and examples

Strategy		Definition	Examples
Backward Orientation	1. Global reprise/ask for repetition/ convey non-understanding	Listeners either ask for outright repetition, rephrasing or simplification of preceding utterance, or indicate non-understanding in non-verbal ways.	What was the question? Pardon? Confused looks, blank looks, furrowed eyebrows...
	2. Ask for clarification /specific lexical reprise	Listeners ask a question referring to a specific word, term or fragment that was not understood in the previous utterance.	Where? ...le souper? Is that dinner? ...he is going ...?
	3. Hypothesis testing/ask for Confirmation	Listeners ask specific questions about facts in the preceding utterance to verify that they have understood and/or what they are expected to do.	...after finishing his homework? ...the last book?
Forward Orientation	4. Uptaking/back-channelling	Listeners use kinesics and verbal or non-verbal signals to indicate to their interlocutor to continue and that they understand.	Nods, uh-huh oui, ah, oh, laughing at the appropriate time
	5. Forward inference/interpretive summary	Listeners overtly indicate current understanding by asking questions using previously understood information.	If he is chosen, do you think he will go?
	6. Faking/feigning understanding	Listeners send uptaking signals or non-committal responses in order to avoid seeking clarification and admitting to their interlocutor that they have not understood.	comme ci, comme ça. (So so). Yes (smile). Je pense (I think so).

Source: Vandergrift and Goh (in press), based on Dörnyei and Kormos (1998), Rost and Ross (1991), Vandergrift (1997). Reproduced with permission.

In this case, listeners ask for clarification by underscoring the word or fragment not understood (e.g., *He is going where?*). This kind of strategy is used by listeners who understand much more can hold more words in memory and are then able to help their interlocutor by pinpointing what they did not understand more precisely. This situation involves much less work by the interlocutor in order to move the interaction forward.

The third type of interactive listening strategy with a backward orientation involves a subtle shift from seeking clarification to seeking confirmation. To ensure that they have understood correctly, listeners seek any needed clarification through a process of hypothesis testing; that is, they ask a specific question about what their interlocutor has just said to verify that they have understood and/or what they are expected to do. With the help of this kind of strategy, listeners signal their desire for verification of comprehension, prompting their interlocutor to confirm or clarify. This kind of move by listeners requires very little work from the interlocutor and allows the interaction to move ahead relatively fluently. Although this strategy is classified among the strategies with a backward orientation, it is actually a transition to a forward orientation, allowing listeners to verify and/or signal understanding so that the interaction can move forward.

Strategies with a Forward Orientation

Interactive listening involves more than comprehension clarification. The next three strategies, those with a forward orientation, focus more on the moves listeners make consciously or unconsciously to signal their engagement and turn taking in the interaction to move it forward. Listeners can do this by (1) using culturally acceptable receipt tokens (uptakes or backchannels) to simply signal understanding; (2) asking their interlocutors to elaborate further through forward inferencing; and (3) faking understanding.

Among the strategies used by listeners to move the interaction forward, the most common and natural tactic is uptaking or backchanneling. To signal to their interlocutor to continue, listeners use kinesics (e.g., nods) and verbal (e.g., *yes, really?*) or non-verbal signals (e.g., *uh-huh, hm hm*) that convey their interest and their comprehension so far. The verbal cues are particularly important in telephone conversations where interlocutors have no other way to gauge whether the other is listening. However, the types of backchanneling cues, when and how often to use them, are often culturally bound, as noted earlier. Nevertheless, backchanneling cues remain the most simple and natural way for listeners to be good conversation partners and to develop intersubjectivity with their interlocutor.

A higher level of backchanneling is the forward inference where listeners overtly indicate their current understanding by asking questions that include an interpretive summary based on previously understood information. This strategy is used by more advanced level listeners who can demonstrate active listening skills by rephrasing what they have understood and then encouraging their interlocutor to continue. It suggests a genuine level of intersubjectivity with the interlocutor that leads him/her into the next logical step in the interaction.

The final tool, faking understanding, can be strategic in intention; however, it has mixed usefulness, depending on the context. Listeners may feign understanding in situations where their intervention may be construed as disruptive or discourteous, particularly if the interlocutor is not well-known to them. In these contexts, listeners may hope that lack of understanding will be clarified through some contextual clues or the developing interaction or that they will not be obligated to respond. Listeners may initiate a global or specific reprise at that time, depending on their relationship with the interlocutor. Sometimes, however, listeners will continue to fake understanding, just to save face. For example, in a qualitative analysis of negotiation of meaning in a classroom task, it became clear that interlocutors in each dyad, in order to save face, actively supported each other in accomplishing the task even when meaning may not have been entirely clear (Foster and Ohta, 2005).

TEACHING INTERACTIVE LISTENING

Given the desire of L2 learners to converse in the target language and the potential of interactive listening strategies to foster L2 learning and good conversation skills, instruction in interactive listening strategies deserves to be promoted in L2 classrooms. It is difficult, however, to provide authentic practice because this skill is best learned through interaction with native speakers in real life contexts. All the same, there are some things that classroom teachers can do to sensitize language learners to appropriate responses and to provide useful tools to successfully negotiate listening in interactive contexts. This final section of the chapter will present and discuss a number of pedagogical activities that will help language learners negotiate this type of listening: (1) learning to request clarification; (2) in-class practice activities; (3) observing and discussing videos; and 4) individual practice with multimedia.

Learning to Request Clarification

An initial step of preparing language learners for interactive listening is to provide them with expressions that they can use in any situation where they are conversing or seeking information. The following represent a sample of expressions to repair misunderstanding or non-understanding that can be practiced in class with fellow students, using activities as suggested in the next section.

Pardon me?
Would you please repeat that?
I don't understand.
What was that (last) word?
Could you speak more slowly, please?
What did you say?
What do you mean?
Can you give me an example, please?
I'm sorry. I didn't get that.

Listeners need to exercise discretion in using repair strategies, however. As suggested by Harder (1980) and Li-Chen (at the opening of this chapter), listeners who continue to persist in clarifying meaning in situations far beyond their level of language competence risk being perceived as "pests." Unless an emergency (e.g., being lost) dictates continued clarification until comprehension has been achieved, beginner-level language learners should limit their interactions to simple requests and interactions with a sympathetic native speaker.

In-Class Practice Activities

Interactive listening practice is relatively easy for L2 teachers to incorporate if they already engage their students in group work and cooperative learning activities. In these types of activities, students can learn to question their interlocutor when they do not understand or when they think that they do not understand, using the expressions given above. These interactive activities should give all participants an equal opportunity to share information and to seek clarification so that they can negotiate meaning. Not only will this practice provide listeners with opportunities to practice clarification strategies, but the resulting interaction can also have salutary benefits for comprehension. Pica (1991) demonstrated that this could have particular benefits for beginning level language learners in understanding teacher directions. Three different groups of students were asked to either: (1) directly negotiate meaning through clarifications, repetitions, and confirmations; (2) observe the negotiators; or (3) do the listening task away from the other groups. Results demonstrated that comprehension was higher for the lower level learners in the negotiator group than for those in the observer and simply listening groups.

Students may need some guidance and encouragement in explicit use of these expressions. Based on my own classroom experience, teachers need to circulate among the groups and remind students to use these tools for negotiating meaning. Lam and Wong (2000) found that although students were aware of interactive listening strategies for clarifying and verifying comprehension during a discussion, they became bogged down in linguistic problems, especially when group members did not support each other in clarification efforts. Teacher monitoring and support is obviously an important component of teaching interactive listening.

The following activities are examples of the types of tasks that involve interactive listening where language learners can practice negotiation of meaning, using the clarification and verification expressions provided above.

- *Information gap* (Farrell and Mallard, 2006): The fundamental premise underlying information gap tasks is that each participant has some of the information needed for the group to complete the task successfully; each participant needs to speak and understand what the others are saying. This could involve putting various parts of a story together to create the whole, or describing a picture where each member of a dyad has a slightly different version of the same picture. In all cases, the pictures are prompts only, and participants must rely totally on speaking and understanding in order to complete the task. Problems in comprehension and misunderstanding are clarified through negotiation. These tasks usually work best with dyads where both partners are actively engaged in speaking and listening.
- *Jigsaw listening* (Field, 2008): These tasks are somewhat similar to information gap activities in that each participant begins by listening to part of a recording in group (often called the "expert" group) as often as necessary so that all members have all the necessary information to bring back to their home group. Members, then, return to their home group (composed of one member from each of the expert groups) to relate what they understood so that the home group can reconstruct the basic content of the text as a whole. The amount of information to be brought from the expert group to the home group needs to be limited so as not to overtax memory.
- *Contradict the speaker* (Willing, 1989): The teacher or student gives a short presentation on a familiar topic related to the current theme of study; however, the text has a number of obvious errors in it. Students (or interlocutor, in the case of

dyads) are expected to detect the errors and then intervene with an appropriate clarification request. In this case, some additional expressions such as *Did I hear you say . . .?* or *What was that again?* may need to be provided in addition to those listed above.

- *Picture dictation* (Pattison, 1987): The teacher or another student gives a detailed description of a scene (that uses some of the vocabulary the class has been learning recently), speaking slowly enough for students to be able to draw what they hear. Students are encouraged to ask questions to clarify the position or size of items, for example. In order to force students to seek clarification and verification, items can be situated where they would not normally be found. This activity can also take the form of following directions on a map.

Observing and Discussing Videos

Teachers can also use videos where language learners observe the use of listening strategies in native-non native speaker interactions. This is probably the best way to bring interactive listening with native speakers into the classroom. These videos can be viewed a number of times, with the focus of each observation changing so that listeners can attend separately to repair strategies, backchanneling cues, turn taking signals or forward inferencing, and summarizing. With beginning level language learners, teachers can periodically stop the tape to discuss the strategies observed or, at a more advanced level, stop the video at points where the non-native partner is having difficulty and discuss the most appropriate strategy to use in that situation. The advantage of videos to observe interactive listening strategy use allows language learners to observe and reflect on strategy use privately without losing face in front of the class. Having observed strategy use, however, listeners should practice these strategies, using activities as suggested above. Through the use of training videos, Rost and Ross (1991) demonstrated that low proficiency listeners learned how to ask for specific lexical clarifications, concluding that this strategy was the most viable for students at that level, given the cognitive and social challenges of interactive listening.

Individual Practice with Multimedia

The potential of multimedia for teaching the use of backchannels in interactive listening has been successfully demonstrated by Ward, Escalante, Al Bayyari, and Solorio (2007). Language learners who knew no Arabic were taught to listen for prosodic cues in Arabic and use appropriate backchanneling cues at the appropriate time. Listeners heard examples of the cue, observed correct visual representations of voice pitch for the cue, received auditory and visual feedback on their attempts to produce the cue and, finally, received feedback on their performance on simulated dialogs where they took on the role of listener. The importance of this study lies in the potential of multimedia for teaching language learners to respond appropriately to speech by native speakers. In order for this training to be meaningful for language learners, however, it should be introduced using speech samples that are comprehensible to listeners so that they can become good conversation partners who are also meaningfully engaged in the message conveyed by their interlocutor.

CONCLUSION

Interactive listening is an important part of language competence, but difficult to develop. Learners need authentic practice with sympathetic interlocutors, which is not always easy to find outside the classroom. Language learners can be given tools to negotiate meaning and become better conversational partners in interactive listening contexts, however. Learners like Li Chen, whose experience with interactive listening opened this chapter, can be supported in their comprehension efforts. Practice with a range of appropriate interactive listening strategies can begin in the classroom, particularly with beginner level learners. Once practiced, these strategies can help language learners negotiate meaning more efficiently and effectively to further the interaction and to solicit additional comprehensible input in appropriate, acquisition-friendly contexts outside the classroom.

REFERENCES

Brouwer, C. (1999). A conversation analytic view on listening comprehension: Implications for the classroom. *Odense Working Papers in Language and Communication, 18*, 37-48 (ERIC Document Reproduction Service No. ED460642).

Carrier, K. (1999). The social environment of second language listening: Does status play a role in comprehension? *The Modern Language Journal, 83,* 65-79.

Cutrone, P. (2005). A case study examining backchannels in conversations between Japanese-British dyads. *Multilingua, 24*, 237-274.

Dörnyei, Z., and Kormos, J. (1998). Problem-solving mechanisms in L2 communication: A psycholinguistic perspective. *Studies in Second Language Acquisition, 20*, 349-385.

Farrell, T. C., and Mallard, C. (2006). The use of reception strategies by learners of French as a foreign language. *The Modern Language Journal, 90*, 338-352.

Field, J. (2008). *Listening in the second language classroom. Cambridge:* Cambridge University Press.

Foster, P., and Ohta, A. (2005). Negotiation for meaning and peer assistance in second language classrooms. *Applied Linguistics, 26*, 402-430.

Garcia Mayo, M. del Pilar. (2001). Repair and completion strategies in the interlanguage of advanced EFL learners. *ITL Review of Applied Linguistics*, 139-168.

Gardner, R. (1998). Between speaking and listening: The vocalisation of understandings. *Applied Linguistics, 19*, 204-224.

Greer, T., Andrade, V., Butterfield, J., and Mischinger, A. (2009). Receipt through repetition. *JALT Journal, 31*, 5-34.

Harder, P. (1980). Discourse as self-expression: On the reduced personality of the second language learner. *Applied Linguistics, 1*, 262-270.

Lam, W., and Wong, J. (2000). The effects of strategy training on developing discussion skills in an ESL classroom. *ELT Journal, 54*, 245-255.

Lightbown, P., and Spada, N. (2006). *How languages are learned.* Oxford: Oxford University Press.

Lynch, T. (1995). The development of interactive listening strategies in second language academic settings. In D. J. Mendelsohn and J. Rubin (Eds.), *A guide for the teaching of second language listening* (pp. 166-185). San Diego, CA: Dominie Press.

Pattison, P. (1987). *Developing communication skills.* Cambridge: Cambridge University Press.

Pica, T. (1991). Classroom interaction, negotiation, and comprehension: Redefining relationships. *System, 19,* 437-452.

Pica, T., Young, R., and Doughty, C. (1987). The impact of interaction on comprehension. *TESOL Quarterly, 21,* 737-758.

Rost, M., and Ross, S. (1991). Learner use of strategies in interaction: Typology and teachability. *Language Learning, 41,* 235-271.

Vandergriff, I. (2006). Negotiating common ground in computer-mediated versus face-to-face discussions. *Language Learning and Technology, 10,* 110-138.

Vandergrift, L. (1997). The Cinderella of communication strategies: Receptive strategies in interactive listening. *The Modern Language Journal, 90,* 338-352.

Vandergrift L., and Goh, C. (in press). *Teaching and learning second language listening: Metacognition in action.* New York: Routledge.

Ward, N. G., Escalante, R., Al Bayyari, Y., and Solorio, T. (2007). Learning to show you're listening. *Computer Assisted Language Learning, 20,* 35-51.

Willing, K. (1989). *Teaching how to learn: Learning strategies in ESL.* Sydney: National Center for English Language Teaching and Research.

In: Innovation and Creativity in ELT Methodology
Editors: H. P. Widodo and A. Cirocki

ISBN: 978-1-62948-146-3
© 2013 Nova Science Publishers, Inc.

Chapter 2

EXTENSIVE LISTENING IN THE LANGUAGE CLASSROOM

Willy A. Renandya
Nanyang Technological University, Singapore

ABSTRACT

This chapter discusses the role of extensive listening in foreign or second language learning and teaching. It explains the language learning benefits of extensive listening, explores the kinds of material that are suitable for extensive listening, and provides practical activities that promote extensive listening in the foreign or second language classroom.

INTRODUCTION

Jeremy Harmer (2003) has this familiar advice for teachers of English who are really interested in helping their students acquire the language: "Students need to be exposed to the English language if they want to learn it, and one of the best ways of doing this is through listening" (p. 29). Harmer is not alone as other methodologists have expressed the same view, saying that extensive exposure to comprehensible language, either through reading or listening, helps enhance students' general proficiency in the target language. People now agree that providing large amounts of comprehensible oral language is considered to be one of the best ways to teach a second language. Some second language researchers (e.g., Krashen, 1982; Krashen and Terrell, 1983) have even gone so far as to suggest that comprehensible input is the only way in which people learn a second language. Krashen's view is perhaps a bit too strong and dogmatic, and many researchers tend to disagree with him. But to my knowledge, no second language researchers or pedagogists would consider large amounts of meaningful language input to be harmful for language acquisition. All seem to agree that comprehensible input is extremely valuable, especially at the early stages of language learning.

One way of providing large amounts of comprehensible input is through extensive listening, defined here to mean "all types of listening activities that allow learners to receive a lot of comprehensible and enjoyable listening input" (Renandya and Farrell, 2010, p. 5).

In this chapter, I will provide a more elaborate definition of extensive listening, explain the benefits of extensive listening, describe the kinds of material that are suitable for extensive listening, and offer practical suggestions for teachers who want to know how to incorporate extensive listening in their teaching. But first, to set the context for the discussion on extensive listening, I will describe a more familiar approach to teaching listening, known as *intensive listening*.

INTENSIVE LISTENING

One approach that is still widely used in foreign or second language classrooms today is what has been termed *intensive listening*. In intensive listening, the main objective of the lesson is often to teach students new grammar or vocabulary. The format of the lesson normally consists of a three-step sequence:

1. *pre-listening* in which the teacher does some warm-up activities to prepare learners for the passage. Pre-teaching of new vocabulary and grammar often occurs at this phase of the lesson;
2. *while-listening* in which students are asked to fill out some worksheets as they listen to the passage. The purpose of the worksheet is usually to get students' attention focused on some aspects of the passage; and
3. *post-listening* in which students do some language analysis exercises, answer comprehension questions, and other follow-up activities.

This lesson format is now considered to be too rigid and reflects the structuralist view of audiolingualism. The listening lesson has now been considerably revised to reflect current thinking about the roles of bottom-up and top-down processing. Listening activities in current ELT practice include those that clearly link bottom-up and top-down listening. Figure 1 reflects the current format of a listening lesson (Field, 2002, p. 245).

Despite the considerable modifications that have been made to the lesson procedure, the amount of listening practice that takes place in a typical listening lesson is normally quite minimal. Not much time is actually spent on getting students to listen to the passage. Depending on the difficulty level of the passage and the type of tasks students are asked to do in the while-listening stage, they are usually asked to listen to the passage twice, and only occasionally, three times.

In a typical 50-minute listening lesson, students listen to a two- or three-minute passage twice or three times – a total of about nine minutes of listening, which is less than 1/5 of classroom time. Students spend a bigger chunk of classroom time on tasks and activities that do not involve meaningful listening to the text.

> *Pre-listening*
>> Set context
>>
>> Create motivation
>
> *Listening*
>> Extensive listening* (followed by questions on context, attitude)
>>
>> Preset task/present questions
>>
>> Intensive listening
>>
>> Check answers
>
> *Post-listening*
>> Examine functional language
>>
>> Infer vocabulary meaning

*Extensive listening here simply means listening quickly for general understanding. The purpose of extensive listening at this phase is slightly like when one skims through a reading text in order to get the gist.

Figure 1. Current Format of a Listening Lesson

An inspection of two teacher resource books on listening confirmed my observation above. The first one is teacher resource book entitled *New Ways in Teaching Listening* edited by David Nunan and Lindsay Miller (1995). This book contains more than 130 classroom activities that address various aspects of listening intended for learners of different proficiency levels. These activities were contributed by experienced classroom teachers from many parts of the world.

However, a quick tally on the number of times students are encouraged to listen to the passage for each activity confirms my suspicion that not much time is actually given to the listening itself. Overall, the activities involve fewer than two listening passages. Only a handful requires listening to the passage more than twice or three times.

Similarly, Goodith White's (1998) book entitled *Listening* contains some 70 highly interesting classroom activities. But, like Nunan and Miller's, these activities do not encourage listening to the passage more than twice. More interestingly, activities intended for beginning level students in both books require an average listening of less than 1.5 times per lesson.

There is no doubt that recent classroom tasks and activities have been designed to deal with problems in the listening classroom that teachers will find very useful. Teachers, however, need to be mindful when selecting listening activities for classroom use. They should, first of all, be clear about the aims of their listening lessons and select those that are most appropriate for achieving these aims.

If they are working with beginning level learners, and the main goal of the program is to build up learners' general level of proficiency in the language through exposure to listening, activities that do not support the attainment of the goal should not be given too much emphasis. Instead, the listening lesson should be organized around tasks and activities that allow multiple or repeated listening, either listening to the same passage repeatedly or listening to a set of similar passages a number of times.

The challenge is that the tasks should be designed in such a way that students become motivated to listen to the passage as often as possible. This means that the tasks should be:

- purposeful,
- motivating,
- fun to do, and
- sufficiently challenging.

In a later section, I describe how tasks with these characteristics can be used to motivate students to listen to the passage as often as is pedagogically possible.

EXTENSIVE LISTENING

Reading specialists have now confirmed the key role that extensive reading plays in the acquisition of reading skills, declaring that the best way to learn to read is by reading (Day and Bamford, 1998). The evidence of extensive reading is strong: It can improve students' word recognition skills, vocabulary, reading comprehension, fluency, and general language proficiency (see *Summaries of Research on the Impacts of Extensive Reading* at www.extensivereading.net). What is amazing is that students obtain all these benefits by simply doing something pleasurable. They just read anything that they find enjoyable. The only condition is that they should choose reading materials that they can understand on their own and that they read a lot of these materials.

A number of writers have recently suggested that the idea behind extensive reading can be applied to listening (e.g., Ridgway, 2000). Ridgway, who is particularly critical of the strategy based approach to teaching listening, argues that "in listening, working from text, or from texts in general, may be a more productive way of approaching comprehension than working from the notion of strategies" (p. 179). He maintains that what students need most is ample practice in actual listening so that they develop skills and automaticity in processing oral language. If we accept the idea that extensive listening is the oral version of extensive reading, by extension, we can also say that listening is best learned through listening.

There is now a growing body of evidence that shows that simply listening to comprehensible materials through simple and familiar classroom activities such as dictation and reading aloud can improve EFL/ESL students' listening skills. For example, Kiany and Shiramiry (2002) conducted an experiment that investigated the effect of frequent dictation on the listening comprehension of elementary EFL learners in Iran. Two groups of 30 students received the same number of listening materials based on the *Headway Elementary Series*. The experimental group who received dictation exercises made significantly larger learning gains in the listening test than the control group. The book flood study in the Fiji Island conducted by Elley and Mangubhai (1983) provides further evidence on the positive impact of an interactive reading aloud activity (called the shared book methodology in the study) on the experimental students' listening, speaking, and reading skills. Given the results of Elley and Mangubhai's study, it is surprising that the shared book approach has not been particularly popular in foreign or second language listening classrooms.

In another study, Zhang (2005) provided her lower proficiency middle school students in China with extensive listening activities in which they listened to a large number of comprehensible and interesting stories read aloud by the teacher. During the read-aloud sessions, the teacher made sure that the speed was appropriate to beginning levels of English and that the language was comprehensible so that the students could follow the stories fully. At the end of the six-week long experiment (approximately 42 hours of listening sessions), Zhang's extensive listening students performed significantly better in the cloze and recall listening tests than the control students who received intensive and systematic listening strategy training. Not only did the extensive listening students outperform the strategy based students on the receptive measures, but they also outscored the control students on the picture storytelling test – a measure that required a productive use of the language.

BENEFITS OF EXTENSIVE LISTENING

The language learning benefits of extensive listening are many. First and foremost, it provides learners with a cognitive map, i.e., a network of linguistic information from which learners can "build up the necessary knowledge for using the language" (Nation and Newton, 2009, p. 38). This knowledge, according to Nation and Newton, allows for the development of the other language skills. The importance of listening in the earlier stages of language learning is highlighted by Nord (1980, p. 17, cited in Nation and Newton, 2009, p. 38):

> Some people now believe that learning a language is not just learning to talk, but rather that learning a language is building a map of meaning in the mind. These people believe that talking may indicate that the language was learned, but they do not believe that practice in talking is the best way to build up this "cognitive" map in the mind. To do this, they feel, the best method is to practice meaningful listening.

The other benefits of extensive listening include the following:

- It can enhance learners' ability to cope with the speech rate. Students often report having difficulty understanding spoken language, not because the content is difficult or the language is too hard, but because it is too fast. What we consider *normal* speech is often perceived as being too fast, especially by our lower proficiency students. We cannot simply ask them to listen faster; what we can do is to give them repeated listening practice so that they gradually become used to listening to normal speech.
- Extensive listening can improve student word recognition skill. Students may recognize words when they see them, but not when they hear them on tape. This phenomenon is quite common among lower proficiency students. Repeated exposure to spoken language can help students develop automaticity in sound-script relationships.
- It can enhance student bottom-up listening skills. In speech, words often take on different forms from when they are said in isolation. Speech phenomena such as assimilation (e.g., *in class – ing class*), contractions (e.g., *going to – gonna*), and resyllabification (e.g., *went in – wen tin*) are common in speech and known to cause

listening problems. Sensitizing students to these phenomena is the first step to help students deal with them, but unless they have had enough practice in hearing these features in connected speech, they will not develop sufficient facility to deal with these speech features.

- Extensive listening can improve student listening vocabulary. Spoken language is different from written language. Spoken language often contains language features not found in written language such as fillers (e.g., *er*, *well*, or *ok*) or stock phrases (e.g., *do you know what I mean?* or *got it?*). Spoken language also tends to be less formal or colloquial, and often colored by the presence of slang or non-standard grammar and vocabulary (e.g., *what do you got? I ain't got nobody*). Extensive listening provides the kinds of practice that improve our students' listening vocabulary.
- It can help students become more fluent listeners. Intensive listening gives a lot of emphasis on accuracy, often at the expense of fluency. We, now, know that listening fluency – the ability to recognize spoken words, phrases, and sentences smoothly, quickly and effortlessly – is equally, if not more, important than accuracy. Fluent listening can develop only after learners have a lot of experience with meaning focused listening practice.
- Extensive listening can give students a lot of opportunities to experience a high level of language comprehension. What we want our students to experience is a higher and deeper degree of comprehension when they listen to spoken text because it is this type of comprehension that is more likely to lead to acquisition. With lower proficiency learners, repeated listening of the same material (called *narrow listening*) does lead to greater understanding. Dupuy (1999) reported that for her lower proficiency learners of French as a foreign language, a higher degree of comprehension (95% and above) is possible only after the third or fourth listening.
- It can enhance student general proficiency in the language. Students who engage in extensive listening have reported improvements not only in their listening comprehension, but also in their vocabulary, speaking, reading skills as well as higher confidence in the language (Dupuy, 1999; Elley and Mangubhai, 1983; Zhang, 2005).

CHOOSING THE RIGHT MATERIALS

The main goal of extensive listening is to give students a lot of practice in understanding spoken English. Because of this, one key consideration when choosing listening material is that it must contain information that attracts the students' attention. If the content is interesting, the students may want to listen to the same text a number of times, thus giving them repeated listening practice. If the content is not attractive, they will not be motivated to listen to the material again. We must remember, however, that our students have diverse interests. What is interesting for one student may not be appealing to another student. A good way to start is to ask our students about the kinds of listening material they want to listen to. Then, we can select materials that cater to our students' varied interests.

It is of utmost importance that the listening materials are at the right level. Unlike in intensive listening where the materials are pitched above the students' proficiency level, in extensive listening, the materials should be pitched at or even below their current level. To use an SLA jargon, the students should be listening to materials at an *i* or *i-1* level; *i* refers to students' current level. The principle that we need to remember is that it is better that they listen to easier texts than more challenging ones. For students who have had minimal exposure to meaningful language and who lack confidence in their listening, we may use materials at an *i-2* level. Once the students have built up sufficient listening fluency, they can move on and work with the more challenging materials. The key here is that the students can listen and comprehend the materials on their own, ideally without any external help from the teacher. Ridway (2000) argues convincingly that our students "need to practice listening comprehension, not listening *in*comprehension" (p. 184) as is often the case in intensive listening. The use of easier materials will ensure that our students receive large amounts of practice in listening comprehension.

The following questions can be used as a guide for teachers when choosing listening materials (adapted from Nation and Newton, 2009, p. 43):

- Is the material a piece of meaningful communication?
- Does the material contain interesting information that attracts the learners' attention?
- Can the students comprehend the material without any external help?
- Are there language features (e.g., words, idiomatic expressions, collocations) that can engage learners' attention?
- What learnable language, ideas, skills, or text types will learners meet through the listening experience?

Waring (2008, pp. 7-8) provides practical tips for students to choose the right extensive listening materials for their independent practice. Students should ask themselves the following questions:

- Can I understand about 90% or more of the content (the story or information)?
- Can I understand over 95-98% of the vocabulary and grammar?
- Can I listen and understand without having to stop the CD or tape?
- Am I enjoying the content of the listening material?

A "yes" answer to all these questions means that the students have picked the right materials. Any "no" answer to these questions means that the material is probably too hard (beyond their level), thus resulting in low or poor comprehension. If the materials are not appealing, the students will not enjoy the content and soon get bored.

AUTHENTIC MATERIALS

Current practice in ELT strongly promotes the use of authentic materials, which are considered to be natural, interesting, and motivating, and which teachers believe can help prepare students to deal with the natural, unscripted, spontaneous nature of real world speech.

Some suggest that teachers should use only authentic materials in the classroom. Non-authentic materials, on the other hand, are considered unnatural, uninteresting, and unmotivating, and should, therefore, not be used in the classroom as they can hinder the learning process. The perceived superiority of authentic material and its indiscriminate use in the classroom has recently been questioned. Day (2003), for example, points out that the key consideration when choosing teaching materials is not whether they are authentic or non-authentic. What is important is whether the materials are appropriate for the students who are learning the language, i.e., whether the materials are at the right level, whether they contain rich and meaningful language, and whether the content is suitable and interesting. Day, further, points out that criticism against non-authentic materials is often misplaced and based on unfounded evidence. He maintains that while there are non-authentic materials that are poorly written and of appalling quality, the same can be said about authentic materials. There are badly written authentic materials out there that are absolutely uninteresting.

Does this mean that we should abandon the use of authentic materials in the classroom? The answer is "no." We just need to use it more judiciously. For the more advanced students, authentic materials may just be the kind of materials they need to further develop their proficiency. But, with lower proficiency learners, we can use carefully selected abridged materials. For learners who are still struggling with basic elements of the language, simplified or graded materials can be an excellent source of listening practice.

EXTENSIVE LISTENING ACTIVITIES

As mentioned earlier, extensive listening refers to all kinds of listening activities that give students a lot of opportunities to comprehend a lot of meaningful and enjoyable input. These activities can be teacher directed dictations or read-alouds or self directed listening for pleasure that students can do outside the classroom (Renandya and Farrell, 2010). The key thing to remember is that our students get the opportunity to listen in quantity and have fun doing it. In this section, I will describe three activities that we can do to give our students a lot of meaningful listening practice.

Narrow Listening

Narrow listening is an excellent way to provide our beginning level students with short conversational language that focuses on familiar contents. Narrow listening, according to Dupuy (1999, p. 351), refers to "the repeated listening of several brief tape-recorded interviews of proficient speakers discussing a topic both familiar and interesting to the acquirers." Because the topics are familiar to the students, and they can choose to listen to the tapes of the same topics as many times as they like, they are likely to receive a large amount of comprehensible aural input. Also, the students can proceed at their own pace and without the pressure of testing. The following can be used as a general guideline to carry out narrow listening activities:

1. Materials: Identify a set of very familiar topics such as food, travel, music, sports, or leisure activities. Ask some five or six proficient speakers to talk about each topic using conversational language for 1 or 2 minutes and have this recorded. Multiple copies of the tapes can be placed in the classroom for students to practice during the break, or in the library or self access centre for students to practice during their free time.

2. Procedures:

   a. Tell students that the focus of the activity is on meaning, not on form. They should try to understand the speakers' ideas about the topics and not concentrate too much on how the speakers express these ideas.

   b. Tell them that they should listen to the tape as often as possible and that the more they listen, the greater their understanding will be.

   c. Tell them that they can choose to listen to the topics that are interesting to them. They do not have to listen to the topics that they do not find interesting.

   d. Tell them that initially they may find it difficult to listen to different speakers who speak with different speaking rates, accents, and styles. After listening several times, they will become used to these.

   e. Tell them that they can do their listening practice at their convenience – during recess, during their library time, or any other free time. They can, also, borrow the tape to bring home so that they listen at their leisure time.

Teacher Read-Alouds or Storytelling

Teacher read-alouds can be a valuable strategy for improving students' listening skills. Reading experts suggest that the benefits of teacher read-alouds go beyond improving listening skills. Some of the most important language learning benefits of reading aloud by teachers include:

- It can increase students' vocabulary;
- it can build up students' background knowledge;
- it exposes students to different types of text genres;
- it models fluent reading and word pronunciation; and
- it helps students develop more positive attitudes towards language learning.

There are many ways of conducting read-alouds. The following can be used as general guidelines:

- The selection of materials should ideally meet the following criteria:
  o The materials (usually short stories) are highly interesting and appropriate for the age level of the students and
  o The language is just right for the students' levels and of appropriate lengths.
- Use a variety of materials so that students are exposed to different topics, text types, and language styles.

- The speed of reading should not be too fast so that students can follow fully what is happening in the story.
- Use appropriate tone of voice, facial expressions, gestures, and props to make the story more exciting and more importantly comprehensible.
- Do interactive read-alouds where the teacher pauses at strategic points in the story to engage the students in a short, collaborative meaning making dialog. This type of reading is more engaging and appealing than when the students just listen to the story throughout the read-aloud session.
- It is better to read aloud daily for 5 minutes or so than rarely and for a longer period of time.

Repeated Listening: A Sample Lesson

Let us look at a listening lesson for beginning level students in an EFL context that focuses on getting them to listen to a passage repeatedly and enjoyably. The purpose here is to give students repeated exposure to the passage so as to develop their general aural recognition and comprehension skills. Asking students to listen to the same text a number of times may be problematic as students tend to lose interest in the content after a set of listening. Thus, it is important that the tasks designed for each listening session should be enjoyable and provide reasons for repeated listening.

Let us say we have decided to use an animal story *The Fox and the Crow,* which has been rewritten to make it more lively and comprehensible for a read-aloud session (see a story in Appendix). What sort of tasks can be designed to encourage repeated listening? Renandya and Zhang (2003) suggest the following activities:

1. Do a quick warm-up to get students interested in the story. In pairs, students can be asked to talk about what they know about foxes and crows and how they are usually depicted in fables. This should not take more than 5 minutes.
2. In order for students to listen for general understanding, before students listen to the passage, you can ask general comprehension questions such as *What did the fox do to get the meat? Why did the crow want to sing for the fox?* Questions that require some kind of personal response would be good, too (e.g., *Which of the two characters do you like better? If you were the crow, what would you do?*)
3. Read aloud the story in ways that help students comprehend the content. You should use whatever resources are available to ensure comprehension. These include using slower than normal speed of reading; pausing at important points in the story; repeating some lines that students may have difficulty understanding; and using gestures, pictures, and other visual aids if necessary.
4. Randomly select students to answer the questions posed earlier, but do not tell students if their answers are correct or incorrect. Instead, read aloud the story again, this time at a slightly faster speed.
5. Ask the class if the answers given earlier were correct. A brief discussion may, then, ensue in which the class tries to reach a general agreement on the main points of the story.

6. Tell/Check. Tell the class that you will be reading aloud the story one more time, pausing at certain points in the story. At each pause, you ask the students to take turns telling and checking the main points of what they have just heard:
    • Read aloud the story up to the second paragraph.
    • Students work in pairs. One student will be the teller and the other the checker. The teller tells the main points of what has just been read to the checker. The checker checks if the teller got the main points right.
    • Read aloud the rest of the story.
    • The students change roles. The checker is now the teller and vice versa.
    • Call on one or two checkers to tell the class what their teller said.

1. Tell the class that you have changed certain parts of the story (e.g., the ending of the story) and you want the class to listen to you again. Their job is to spot the part that has been changed. A brief discussion can, then, follow in which students compare the original story with the new version.
2. In small groups, students take turns reading aloud the story. Each group will, then, select a group representative to read aloud to the whole class. The class, then, casts their vote on the best reader. This activity gives students countless listening opportunities.
3. If time permits, you can do a dictation exercise, which gives students another opportunity to listen to the story. If students find dictation not too exciting, you can instead do a dictogloss exercise. The procedures for this exercise are:
    • The teacher reads the text, and the students listen.
    • The teacher reads the text again, and the students write down some key words or phrases (normally about five to ten words/phrases depending on the length of the passage).
    • In pairs, students compare their lists and try to agree on a common list.
    • Students, then, use the key words to reconstruct the text either orally or in writing.
    • The teacher reads the story one more time, and the students check if their reconstructed piece matches the original story.

In this sample lesson, we can see clearly that students are given ample listening practice. In addition, they do not listen passively as the passage is read a number of times. On the contrary, each listening requires a different type of processing that not only helps students develop a better understanding of the passage, but also enhances their perception skills, i.e., the ability to perceive spoken language effortlessly.

CONCLUSION

This chapter suggests earlier that listening is best learned through listening. One excellent way of providing our students with a lot of listening practice is through extensive listening where students are encouraged to listen to a huge amount of interesting and comprehensible material. Extensive listening provides a lot of language learning benefits. It gives the students just the right kind of language practice that allows them to develop a cognitive map of meanings upon which the other language skills can be built up. Repeated exposure to language through extensive listening also enhances students' ability to develop fast and automatic word recognition skill, to increase their listening vocabulary, to better cope with fast speech rate, to comprehend language at a much deeper level, to develop facility in processing oral language features (e.g., contractions, assimilation, and resyllabication), and to process oral language more fluently and accurately.

It has been suggested that exposure to input alone may not be sufficient to develop listening competence and that some focused language practice that targets key speech features is required. Field (2009), for example, has suggested that listening teachers devote some instructional time in order to help students become more aware of speech features that often cause comprehension difficulties. I agree that sensitizing students to their problems and teaching them how to deal with these problems is indeed a very useful first step, and I submit that all good teachers should do this.

However, the next step, which involves turning declarative knowledge into procedural and fully automatized knowledge, requires more than just engaging students in some consciousness raising activities. This step requires hundreds of hours of practice, something which has been confirmed by research. Drawing on years of second language acquisition research, Ellis (2002, p. 175), for example, states that:

> The real stuff of language acquisition is the slow acquisition of form-function mappings and the regularities therein. This skill, like others, takes tens of thousands of hours of practice, practice that cannot be substituted for by provision of a few declarative rules.

Extensive listening, which provides students with a lot of meaningful and enjoyable listening practice, is one excellent way of helping students develop automaticity in processing aural language input.

REFERENCES

Day, R. (2003). Authenticity in the design and development of materials. In W. A. Renandya (Ed.), *Methodology and materials design in language teaching: Current perceptions and practices and their implications* (pp. 1-11) [Anthology Series 44]. Singapore: SEAMEO Regional Language Centre.

Day, R., and Bamford, J. (1998). *Extensive reading in the second language classroom.* Cambridge: Cambridge University Press.

Dupuy, B. C. (1999). Narrow listening: An alternative way to develop and enhance listening comprehension in students of French as a foreign language. *System, 27,* 351-361.

Elley, W. B., and Mangubhai, F. (1983). The impact of reading on second language learning. *Reading Research Quarterly, 19*(1), 53-67.

Ellis, N. C. (2002). Frequency effects in language processing. *SSLA, 24,* 143-188

Field, J. (2002). The changing face of listening. In J. C. Richards and W. A. Renandya (Eds.), *Language teaching methodology: An anthology of current practice* (pp. 242-247). Cambridge: Cambridge University Press.

Field, J. (2009). More listening or better listeners? *English Teaching Professional, 61,* 12-14.

Harmer, J. (2003). Listening. *English Teaching Professional*, *26*, 29-30.

Kiany, G. R., and Shiramiry, E. (2002). The effect of frequent dictation on the listening comprehension ability of elementary EFL learners. *TESL Canada Journal*, *20*(1), 57-63.

Krashen, S. (1982). *Principles and practice in second language learning.* Oxford: Pergamon.

Krashen, S., and Terrell, T. (1983). *The natural approach: Language acquisition in the classroom.* San Francisco, CA: Pergamon.

Nation, I. S. P., and Newton, J. (2009). *Teaching ESL/EFL listening and speaking.* New York: Routledge.

Nord, J. R. (1980). Developing listening fluency before speaking: An alternative paradigm. *System*, *8*(1), 1-22.

Nunan, D., and Miller, L. (1995). *New ways in teaching listening.* Bloomington, IL: TESOL.

Renandya, W. A., and Farrell, T. S. C. (2010). "Teacher, the tape is too fast" – Extensive listening in ELT. *ELT Journal*, 1-8. (doi:10.1093/elt/ccq015)

Renandya, W. A., and Zhang, Wenfang. (2003). Where's the listening? *Guidelines*, *25*(1), 12-16.

Ridgway, T. (2000). Listening strategies: I beg your pardon? *ELT Journal*, *54*, 179-185.

Waring, R. (2008). Starting extensive listening. *Extensive Reading in Japan*, *1*(1), 7-9.

White, G. (1998). *Listening.* Oxford: Oxford University Press.

Zhang, Wengfang. (2005). *An investigation of the effects of listening programmes on lower secondary students' listening comprehension in PRC.* Unpublished MA dissertation, SEAMEO Regional Language Centre, Singapore.

APPENDIX: SAMPLE LISTENING TEXT

The Fox and the Crow

A crow was sitting in a tree enjoying a big piece of meat when a fox passed by. "That meat looks so good," the fox said to himself. "Hmm … I can't climb trees, so I'll have to use my brain to get the meat."

The fox thought for a moment and then said to himself, "I've got an idea!" He looked up at the crow in the tree and said, "Good morning, Ms. Crow, how are you this morning? You look great! You look beautiful too in the sun. And your mouth!! Oh, … it's so pretty!! I think your voice must be as beautiful as you are! I'm sure no one in this world can sing better than you."

The crow was so happy to hear this. No one had ever said a nice thing about her voice. So, she opened her mouth and began to sing for the fox. But, as soon as she opened her mouth, the meat fell to the ground. She tried to pick it up, but it was too late. The fox had already taken it and run away.

"Your voice is ugly," he cried over his shoulder. "I've never heard anyone singing that badly and you are very foolish, too."

The crow was really hurt. She couldn't do anything, but cry.

In: Innovation and Creativity in ELT Methodology
Editors: H. P. Widodo and A. Cirocki

ISBN: 978-1-62948-146-3
© 2013 Nova Science Publishers, Inc.

Chapter 3

TEACHING ENGLISH FOR INTERCULTURAL SPOKEN COMMUNICATION: FROM CLT TO iCLT

Jonathan Newton
Victoria University of Wellington, New Zealand

ABSTRACT

This chapter presents a set of three principles to guide teachers and materials designers in integrating an intercultural dimension into materials and lessons based broadly on communicative language teaching (CLT). These principles include (1) that learning is based on opportunities to experience socially situating communication; (2) that learners have guided opportunities for metacognitive reflection on intercultural experiences and observations; and (3) that through the processes of comparing and connecting cultures, they have opportunities not only to explore the culturally shaped worlds and perception of others, but also to see their own culture(s), behaviors, and identity from the perspective of others. Three practical applications of these principles, covering a range of teaching approaches and settings, are presented and discussed.

INTRODUCTION

In this chapter, I propose a framework for intercultural communicative language teaching (iCLT) in which an intercultural stance is integrated into CLT in three main ways: through socially situating communication activities; through metacognitive reflection on intercultural experiences and observations; and through guided analysis of their own culturally shaped perceptions and those of others.

In its various manifestations, communicative language teaching (CLT) has been adopted in English language textbooks, national curricula, and classroom language teaching practices worldwide. Simply put, CLT prioritizes the goal of communicative competence (e.g., grammatical or linguistic competence) and achieves this through engaging learners in active language use; learning *through* communication rather than learning *about* communication. However, as noted by Byram (1997), the model of communicative competence on which this methodology is based (Hymes, 1974) is largely acultural; cultural influences on how we communicate and how we perceive the communicative practices of others are usually ignored.

The implicit assumption seems to be that these matters will take care of themselves. On the contrary, research suggests that without explicit guided attention to the cultural dimensions of communication, they are easily overlooked. This blind spot becomes a glaring weakness in the face of a growing demand for interculturally competent English speakers who can work and communicate effectively in increasingly multicultural workplaces and communities.

INTERCULTURAL LANGUAGE TEACHING AND LEARNING

Teaching interculturally involves using classroom activities to raise awareness of the cultural influences on our lives. It focuses on the awareness and skills necessary to navigate crosscultural encounters and experiences, and to successfully participate in a world in which intercultural communication in English is becoming ever more widespread.

Intercultural language teaching differs from communicative approaches that treat culture as an assumed backdrop to communication, which may, incidentally and haphazardly, be bought into focus as the need arises.

Rather, intercultural teaching recognizes the intertwined and inseparable nature of language and culture and so treats culture learning as an integral part of all language learning. It is, however, most emphatically not just about transmitting information about culture. Instead, it focuses on raising awareness of culture and culture-in-language in the lived experience of the students as well as in the lives of people in the target language community.

As such, intercultural teaching is a vehicle for developing language learners, firstly a deeper and more reflective understanding of their own cultural world(s) and identity, and secondly, an understanding of and the skills to accommodate the cultural differences they experience in their lives and interactions.

The desired outcome of this approach is learners who can confidently navigate intercultural interactions and relationships, not just because they have achieved a certain level of linguistic or even communicative competence, but because they are *interculturally* competent (Byram, 2006). There has been an intercultural paradigm shift in foreign or second language education in a growing number of education settings over the past 10-20 years. *The Common European Framework of Reference for Languages* (Council of Europe, 2001), probably the most influential and widely cited language policy document internationally, identifies intercultural awareness and intercultural skills as core competencies to be achieved through language education. It expands on intercultural awareness to include:

- openness towards, and interest in, new experiences, other persons, ideas, peoples, societies, and cultures;
- willingness to relativise one's own cultural viewpoint and cultural value-system;
- willingness and ability to distance oneself from conventional attitudes to cultural differences. (p.105)

Underlying these statements is a view of language learning as inextricably tied up with learning about culture, and in the process, learning about the culturally constructed nature of one's own world.

The Finnish scholar, Pauli Kaikkonen (2001) identifies three key characteristics of intercultural language teaching. First, it focuses on the inseparable relationship between culture and language and on the power of language as both a carrier of culture and a tool for constructing our taken-for-granted cultural worlds.

Second, it encourages learners to construct their understanding and awareness of culture through observation, experience, and reflection. Third, it values learners' subjectivity by involving learners "with their whole personality: as knowing, feeling, thinking and acting individuals" (p. 64). These themes are threaded through the framework for iCLT that I introduce below.

A FRAMEWORK FOR INTERCULTURAL COMMUNICATIVE LANGUAGE TEACHING (iCLT)

You will notice that in discussing intercultural teaching I choose not to use terms like *approach* or *method*. Instead, I use the term *an intercultural stance*. I do this to avoid the notion that this is a new method or approach that supersedes older alternatives. This is a mistaken view of how to teach interculturally.

An intercultural stance in not methodologically constrained; it sees opportunities for intercultural learning wherever texts, interactions, or cultural information are available. With this in mind, I discuss three key principles for adopting an intercultural stance in communicative language teaching.

Each is well supported in the rapidly growing research literature on intercultural language learning, and, while they are well suited to teaching spoken communication interculturally, they apply also to reading, writing, and listening. These principles, expressed from a learner-action perspective, are that learners will:

1. engage in genuine social interaction;
2. explore culture in language, communication, behavior, and ways of being; and
3. compare and connect languages and culture and reflect on differences and similarities.

In discussing the three principles below, I illustrate each with a practical application. Although each practical application is linked to a single principle, all three principles are outworked in each example.

Principle 1: Engage Learners in Genuine Social Interaction

Socially situated interaction is an obvious starting point for developing intercultural competence. Social interaction forces us to take culture into account in the linguistic and behavior choices we make and to consider the effect of these choices on others.

Conversational talk, including talk generated through tasks (Ellis, 2003) and role plays (Morgan, 1993), provides important opportunities for learners to notice and explore culture-in-language and to develop flexibility and communicative awareness, two elements of intercultural competence identified by Byram (2006).

Email and internet based interactive spaces and tools such as Skype and Facebook are increasingly popular ways for learners to interact in (and about) the target language (e.g., Belz, 2003; Bretag, 2006; Kramsch and Thorne, 2002; O'Dowd, 2003, 2007; Ware, 2005).

iCLT approaches interaction in two ways. First, it treats any interaction involving the target language and/or culture as an opportunity to explore linguistic and cultural boundaries and to engender awareness of one's own as well as the other's ways of communicating and maintaining relationships and of dealing with crosscultural misunderstandings and communication breakdowns.

Second, interactions can be used to directly and explicitly explore the cultural worlds, beliefs, values, and attitudes of others through topics, which provide opportunities for explicit discussion of cultural comparisons. Thus, learners experience culture, firstly through the *way* communication proceeds, and secondly through the *content* of *what* is discussed or written about. And so from an intercultural perspective, interaction is not simply a tool for developing fluency; it provides opportunities for learners to confront their culturally constructed worlds and cultural assumptions, and so to learn more about themselves.

Unfortunately, many language learning activities involve learners in manipulating or practicing language in a kind of social vacuum so that language use is only superficially communicative and is even less likely to involve opportunities for intercultural learning. Here is one such task from a recently published textbook:

> Work in pairs. Look at the people below and describe their physical characteristics (followed by pictures of four people).

Readers may be able to identify communication tasks from their own experience, even ones which hold more communicative potential than this rather limited one, which offer few opportunities for learners to situate the communication in a real-world setting where social and cultural considerations play an important role in shaping language choices.

One way to improve the quality of social interaction is to adapt such activities, so they emerge out of what I shall call *communicative events*. In a communicative event, learners communicate valued meanings or information to someone for a real or imagined purpose. As soon as learners engage in not just activities, but in communicative events, opportunities for intercultural language learning open up. This is because people involved in a communication event have to make choices about language and content that are deeply influenced by their cultural background and require attention to who they are talking to and why.

Following is an outline of the process involved in transforming a pedagogic exercise into a communicative event, which involves genuine social interaction. This example assumes the context of an EFL class in a school in a country where English is a foreign language (say, for example, Japan).

Practical Application 1. From Language Exercise to Communicative Event

Step	Example
1. Identify topic area and language goals	Food Lesson: learn the English names of common food items and practice using this vocabulary in sentences.
2. Establish communicative setting How can the exercise be placed in a setting that is familiar or relevant to students?	Ask students to think about food available on school campus.
3. Establish communicative event What kind of scenarios might involve the students in talking about the food on their campus to someone from another cultural background?	A group of English speaking exchange students will visit your school for one month. The class is responsible for looking after them and introducing them to school life.
4. Establish target task(s)	Interview, chat, Skype, or write an email to a student in an English speaking country about food on their campus and their food preferences. Role play: In pairs, one student acts as campus tour guide, and the other acts as an exchange student asking questions about [Japanese] food. The goal is to identify what the exchange students' preferences are in the school canteen, and how these are different or similar to their usual diet at school.
5. Pre-task preparation	View authentic stimulus for communicative event (teacher provides or students research/find/choose). Group and whole class work on language resourcing for the tasks. One half of the class develops food descriptions and recommendations as campus tour guides. The other half develops questions about [Japanese] food and practices expressing food preferences.
6. Perform target tasks	Role-plays are performed two-three times with different partners.
7. Post-task reflection	Students discuss issues and attitudes that have emerged from cultural connections made before and during the task.

The following questions illustrate the kinds of prompts that can be used for encouraging reflection on intercultural interaction. In the model above, they would fit into steps 5 and 7.

a.   What similarities and differences did you notice in food options on your campus and that of the interviewee (as obtained in Step 4a)?
b.   What judgements did you form about these options? Why?
c.   Should the visiting students just "fit in" and eat what we eat?
d.   How would you feel if the visiting students were critical of the food on campus? How could you respond?

Exploring such questions becomes part of the intercultural learning experience afforded by involvement in the communicative event. These kinds of questions can be used to guide the learners' engagement in the communicative event as well as to generate further discussion before and after main tasks. The following two principles expand on the reflective approach to culture that emerges through these kinds of questions.

Principle 2: Encourage and Develop an Exploratory and Reflective Approach to Culture and Culture-In-Language

The second principle stands in contrast to the static descriptions of cultural facts typical of traditional approaches to culture in language teaching. Culture defies easy description and involves much more than facts. Just as with an iceberg, what is unseen is much larger than what is seen, so also visible forms of culture are underpinned by a much larger body of less visible, but more subtly pervasive forms of culture; by hidden values, attributions, and interpretations of the world. Consider, for example, how much culture pervades such everyday uses of language as forms of address, the marking of formality and interlocutor status, uses and types of humor, and the non-verbal behaviors that accompany language (e.g., gesture, facial expressions, and the culturally shaped daily life rituals in which language is embedded). As Claire Kramsch (1993) has pointed out, every time we speak we perform a cultural act. Greeting routines provide a further example. These can be realized in various observable ways including a handshake, raised eyebrows, a kiss, or a nod of the head. However, lying beneath these behaviors are non-observable values, attitudes, expectations to do with status, relationships, and social distance; all of which are uniquely structured and perceived within different cultural contexts (Finkbeiner and Koplin, 2002).

Thus, teaching that focuses on learning about visible culture overlooks important dimensions of culture. For this reason, intercultural language teaching shifts the focus from *transmission* of objective cultural knowledge to *exploration* by learners of dynamic aspects of culture *in* and *around* everyday language use. The word *exploring* fits well with *discovery learning* in which learners observe, analyze what they observe, and construct understanding from this process. It is also synonymous with constructivist views of education. Exploration allows learners to *construct* their understandings from firsthand experience and reflection, and thereby to engage more deeply in the learning process. Four simple rules of thumb can help teachers develop an exploratory approach to culture:

1.   Focus on the dynamic and lived experience of culture.
2.   Encourage reflective dialogue alongside experience.
3.   Guide students as they interpret their experience of the target culture and language, especially in regard to less visible aspects of culture such as values and beliefs.

4. Provide a metalanguage for discussing intercultural experience, for example: *culture, invisible culture, same, different, self, identity, stereotypes,* and *prejudice*.

The following practical application of this principle is part of a unit on *making complaints and criticizing* in a textbook (Riddiford and Newton, 2010) designed for English language learners who are employed or are seeking employment in an English speaking workplace. The series of activities in the sample below are all based around a transcription and recording of an authentic workplace interaction involving a manager reprimanding her team for errors in their written reports. The activities emphasize reflecting on one's own ways of communicating as well as on the strategies used by the native English speakers in the transcribed interaction. As such, the unit offers rich opportunities for intercultural dimensions of communication to be foregrounded.

Practical Application 2. Workplace Talk in Action (from Riddiford and Newton, 2010)

Making complaints and criticising
The context
Sara is the manager of a team within a government department. Rebecca, Ella, Simon and Mary are all members of the team. The team has worked together for about one year. Sara has noticed an increasing number of writing errors in documents produced by the team.

1. Thinking about context
    Working with a partner, use the context information and complete the table.

Sara and the team	High	Medium	Low
Status difference			
Level of familiarity			
Level of difficulty (how hard is it to make the complaint?)			

2. Thinking about communication
    Here is one way that Sara could raise the problem: "Look, I'm very unhappy with the quality of your writing. It's full of mistakes, and I'm really embarrassed by it. It gives us all a bad name. You need to do something about it or else there might be consequences."
    What is wrong with this approach? Find at least three problems with this communication.

3. Role-play
    The first part of the conversation between Sara and the team is provided below. Work with a partner to role-play the conversation. When you have role-played, write down your conversation.

    The conversation:
    Sara: …which leads me on to one other item which I haven't got on the agenda, um, is it all right if I…?
    Rebecca: Yep, yeah, sure
    Sara: … um, and that's the, the issue of writing [deep breath].

4. Comparison and analysis
   a. Comparing the conversation
      Compare your conversation with the original conversation between Sara and her team (see below). What differences do you notice?
   b. Analyzing the conversation
      Underline words or phrases that Sarah and her team use to make the conversation go smoothly. Note:

      - The phrases they use to agree and acknowledge each other's comments
      - The way Sara phrased the complaint
      - The words or phrases used to soften the force of the complaint
      - Whether Sara and her team are trying to be co-operative. How can you tell?
      - Whether humor is used. Why or why not?

      Listen to the way the complaint is expressed. Listen in particular to:

      o The volume of Sara's voice (loud or soft)
      o The stress pattern of the complaint. Which words are stressed?
      o The use of pauses
      o The use of any sighs or inhaling and exhaling (noticeable breathing in and out)
      o The intonation pattern of the complaint. Is it a falling, rising or mixed falling and rising pattern?
   c. Evaluating the conversation
      Rate Sara's communication using the scales below (circle a number in each scale). Discuss the evidence you used to make your rating.

   (i) How *polite* was Sara?

Polite			Impolite
1	2	3	4

   (ii) How *direct* was Sara?

Direct			Indirect
1	2	3	4

   (iii) Overall, how *effective* was Sara's communication style? Effective communication involves achieving your purpose efficiently while also maintaining good relationships.

Very effective			Not at all effective
1	2	3	4

   d. Focus on turn-taking
      Read the conversation again and focus on the steps taken in the dialogue.

      - How does the dialogue begin? Brainstorm some other useful openers.
      - Where in the conversation does the complaint come?
      - How is the complaint responded to? What other responses would be appropriate?

    e.   Cross-cultural comparison

Compare this communication style with the style used in your country. Are there any differences or similarities?

    f.   Work with a partner to identify some ways to communicate effectively based on your analysis of Sara's communication. Can you think of situations when it is appropriate to be more direct and not use these softening words or phrases?

    g.

5.   E-mail and telephone communication

    a.   Imagine that this communication takes place via e-mail. Write Sara's initial e-mail to her team. How might a team member reply?

    b.   Write what Sara would say to a team member if she telephoned him or her about this matter.

    c.   What changes, if any, have you made to the communication in a and b compared to the face-to-face version?

The Original Conversation between Sara and the Team

1 2	Sara	…Which leads me on to one other item which I haven't got on the agenda, um, is it all right if I…?
3	Rebecca	Yep, yeah, sure
4 5 6 7 8 9 10 11	Sara	… Um, and that's the, the issue of writing [deep breath]. Um when, um whenever you – well, we're drafting, well, I've noticed a couple of mistakes creeping into our work. That's stuff that … that even I've looked at. I notice them because the letters go through - all the letters that go out of the ministry go through what's called the day file. They also go through ... each manager as well as our own staff. But suddenly sometimes as I'm re-reading, I spot a spelling mistake that I didn't see the first time or a grammatical mistake.
12	Simon/Rebecca	… mm, yeah
13 14 15 16 17 18 19 20	Sara	I really ask for all of you to make sure that you take it to one other person, okay?, At least to look at before you, before you post it. Even when you send it to me to look at, it must also be checked by others. Of course when you're doing a big chunk of work then that's normal for us, we'll always, we always do that checking. But even with just simple letters make sure that they're looked at. It's so easy to overlook just a simple mistake and the less mistakes we send out the better.
21	Simon	Yeah,
22 23 24	Rebecca	I'd, I'd like to take that a bit further too 'cos, um, if we're going to use other languages in the letter, I think we should make sure that they're checked as well.
25	Simon	Mm

As with the other two practical applications discussed in this chapter, this unit exemplifies all three principles equally well. Principle 1 is outworked in a number of places: in Steps 3 and 5; in the expectation that many of the other steps would be carried out in discussion groups or pairs; and in the authentic piece of interaction on which the unit if based.

Comparison and contrast, as presented in *Principle 3*, are also important learning processes throughout the unit.

Thus, the three principles work naturally in tandem with one another: the processes of experiencing, exploring, reflecting, and comparing or making connections all draw on one another to create a rounded expression of interculturally informed learning.

Principle 3. Foster Explicit Comparisons and Connections between Languages and Cultures

The third of the three principles involves opportunities to compare and connect languages and cultures. Language learning positions learners between languages and between cultures in what is referred to as a third place between the learners' own cultural identity (the First Place) and the target language culture(s) (the Second Place). This can be confusing and disorientating for the learner, and can lead him or her to withdrawal back into the first place where they become more resistant to an intercultural understanding of cultural difference. For learners to successfully enter and embrace this third space requires some care on the part of the teacher as she or he guides the learners in exploring cultural similarities and differences (Kramsch, 1993).

In resources developed by the Department of Education in Tasmania (2005), the journey to the third space is seen as involving four steps: identify, investigate, reflect, and describe. I discuss these steps below and exemplify them with a series of prompt questions adapted from the Tasmanian resource, which are designed to guide teachers and learners on the journey of cultural discovery. The first step, *Identify,* involves exploring the *First Place* (a learner's own cultural world) using the following kinds of prompt questions:

- How do these things work in my world?
- How is this situation handled in my culture?
- How would my family and friends react to this situation? (Department of Education, Tasmania, 2005)

One of the challenges in teaching culture is that knowledge of one's own culture is largely implicit and so not easily available for conscious reflection. We are often unaware of the cultural values, which allow us to communicate within our own culture, let alone those that underpin behavior in another culture with which we come in contact. And yet, as Byram (1997, 2006) argues, recognizing personally held cultural systems is a necessary precondition for identifying these systems in others.

For this reason, interculturally informed language teaching encourages learners to reflect on their own culture as the starting point for intercultural awareness. The second step, *Investigate,* involves exploration of the *Second Place*, that is, the cultural worlds of others. The following prompt questions are designed to guide students in their exploration of this second place:

- How do these things work in your world?
- How is this situation handled in your culture?

- How would your family and friends react to this situation?
- How does learning your language help me get to know you better? (Department of Education, Tasmania, 2005)

The third step, *Reflect*, involves a journey to the *Third Space*, that is, to a hybrid space in which identity and awareness are no longer constrained by simple dualities, but emerge from deeper understands of self and others, of commonalities and difference; a dynamic space in which cultural givens are open to dialogue and negotiation (Kramsch, 1993). Learners can be guided towards this space with questions such as the following:

- How do similarities/differences between us affect our responses to this situation?
- How does language help us engage and negotiate effectively in this situation?

The fourth and final step, *Decide*, offers opportunities to explore the *Third Space* through prompt questions such as:

- How will I decide to behave/respond to this situation?
- What practices will I adopt or reject?
- What attitudes will I consciously cultivate? (Department of Education, Tasmania, 2005)

As these steps show, comparing cultures is a practical focus for language teaching, which allows learners to develop more sophisticated concepts of culture. It helps undermine notions of the immutability of one's own cultural values and cross-cultural prejudices by revealing the constructed nature of our ways of being in the world. Thus, gradually, the learner decentres from his or her own culture, viewing it from the perspective of members of other cultures.

As Byram (1997) notes, an intercultural approach leads to "the relativisation of what seems to the learner to be the natural language of their own identities, and the realisation that these are cultural and socially constructed" (p. 22). The end result, as described by Tomlinson and Matsuhara (2004), is "a gradually developing inner sense of the equality of cultures, an increased understanding of your own and other people's cultures, and a positive interest in how cultures both connect and differ" (p. 5). An important goal of iCLT is learning not only about a new language and culture, but also about what constitutes culture in general. One of the most important ways that this can be achieved is through guided comparison of one's own culture with other cultures.

Our cultural identity and background acts as a lens through which we view and interpret other cultures. Through comparison, students can shift the focus of this lens and gain greater understanding of their own culture and language as well as an appreciation of and sensitivity towards different cultural and linguistic practices. Thus, the development of positive attitudes towards difference and a readiness to accept and adapt are important aspects of iCLT.

Furthermore, in any new situation, attempting to communicate in a different language and behave appropriately does not entail hiding one's own linguistic and cultural identity, but requires the ability to observe and interpret differences and similarities and a readiness to modify one's behavior to suit the circumstances and achieve one's communicative goals. The principles for adopting an iCLT that I have discussed above are neatly exemplified in the ABC's activity designed by Claudia Finkbeiner (2006) and presented below. This activity is a good example of how learner's firsthand intercultural encounters provide the basis for a communicative task that explores cultural differences and similarities and that ensures learners' reflections on experience are central to the task rather than peripheral or incidental.

Practical Application 3. The ABC's Approach to Intercultural Language Learning

(Learners are paired with learners or people from different cultural background, including pairing over the Internet with learners or English speakers from other parts of the country or world)
A as in *Autobiography*
Each learner writes or narrates relevant aspects and/or key events from his or her autobiography.
B as in *Biography*
Learners interview a partner from a different cultural background (audio or videotaped). The interviewer will, then, construct a biography describing the key events in that person's life.
C as in *Cross-Cultural Analysis* and *Appreciation of Differences*
Learners study their autobiographies and compare them to the biographies they have written. They note down similarities and differences and discuss these with their partner. They share their findings with other pairs of learners or with the class.

Source: Finkbeiner, 2006.

I have presented, here, only the bare bones of the ABC activity. Obviously, each step needs to be carefully scaffolded, language structures and vocabulary supplied, and guidelines given for interacting and comparing. More important for the purposes of this chapter are the features of interculturally informed pedagogy that this activity so neatly exemplifies:

- the starting point is awareness of self and of one's own culturally shaped reality;
- learners are engaged in genuine communication in which authentic meanings are talked about;
- learners construct intercultural understandings through exploration and discovery, rather than through teacher's talk;
- guided comparison is used to connect cultures;
- culture is treated as dynamic, lived experience rather than static knowledge; and
- instruction seeks to develop interculturally tuned communicative competence.

CONCLUSION

The goal of iCLT is intercultural communicative competence. This includes learners being able to:

- construct intercultural knowledge and understanding from experience and guided reflection;

- *interrogate* cultural facts rather than taking them at face value, i.e., engage in critical enquiry;
- notice the language used in particular situations and how native speakers behave, and examine their (the learners') feelings and reactions in relation to what they notice;
- experiment with the language in communication, and analyze their difficulties or feelings (e.g., embarrassment in making new sound or doing something, which feels *unnatural*);
- identify a range of culture based causes of miscommunication and describe appropriate strategies to deal with these.

Becoming interculturally competent is not an automatic outcome of second language learning (e.g., Schulz, 2007; Sinicrope, Norris, and Watanabe 2007). Dellit (2005) makes this point succinctly: "Ignoring culture does not leave a vacant cultural place which can be filled in later. Rather, it leads to a cultural place which is filled in by uninformed and unanalysed assumptions" (p. 7). To cultivate intercultural sensitivities in learners requires teachers to adopt an intercultural stance towards culture and language. Culture is no longer ignored or treated incidentally through cultural anecdotes and casual observations or through transmission of cultural information. Instead, an intercultural stance produces an integrated and consistent focus on culture as an inseparable part of all language and communication.

An interculturally informed pedagogy adds value to the teaching and learning goals of linguistic and communicative competence rather than detracting or subtracting from them. By relying on a communicative methodology to achieve the goal of interculturally competent learners, it ultimately enriches this methodology. Therefore, I consider it timely to propose reframing and revitalizing the familiar term "communicative language teaching" (CLT) so that it embraces an intercultural dimension. The alternative term, *intercultural Communicative Language Teaching* (iCLT) which I have discussed in this chapter, provides one way of giving the intercultural stance its due weight in the theory and practice of contemporary language teaching.

REFERENCES

Belz, J. A. (2003). Linguistic perspectives on the development of intercultural competence in telecollaboration. *Language Learning and Technology*, 7, 68-117.

Bretag, T. (2006). Developing 'Third Space' interculturality using computer-mediated communication. *Journal of Computer-Mediated Communication*, 11, 981-1011.

Byram, M. (1997). *Teaching and assessing intercultural communicative competence.* Clevedon, PA: Multilingual Matters.

Byram, M. (July, 2006). *Language teaching for intercultural citizenship* [Keynote address]. Presented at the NZALT Conference, University of Auckland, 4-6 July 2006.

Council of Europe. (2001). *Common European framework of reference for languages.* Cambridge: Cambridge University Press.

Dellit, J. (2005). *Getting started with intercultural language learning: A resource for schools.* Melbourne: Asian Languages Professional Learning Project, Asia Education Foundation.

Department for Education [Tasmania, Australia]. (2005). *Report on supporting intercultural language learning in secondary schools project.* Hobart, Australia: Department of Education.

Ellis, R. (2003). *Task-based language learning and teaching.* Oxford: Oxford University Press.

Finkbeiner, C. (2006). Constructing the third space together: The principles of reciprocity and cooperation. In P. R. Schmidt and C. Finkbeiner (Eds.), *The ABCs of cultural understanding and communication: National and international adaptations* (pp. 19-42). Greenwich, CT: Information Age Publishing.

Finkbeiner, C., and Koplin, C. (2002). A cooperative approach for facilitating intercultural education. *Reading online.* Retrieved July 9, 2007, from http:www.readingonline.org/ newliteracies/lit_index.asp?HREF=finkbeiner/index.html

Hymes, D. H. (1974). *Foundations in sociolinguistics: An ethnographic approach.* Philadelphia, PA: University of Pennsylvania Press.

Kaikkonen, P. (2001). Intercultural learning through foreign language education. In R. Kohonen, P. Jaatinen, P. Kaikkonen, and J. Lehtovaara (Eds.), *Experiential learning in foreign language education* (pp. 61-105). Harlow, UK: Longman.

Kramsch, C. (1993). *Context and culture in language teaching.* Oxford: Oxford University Press.

Kramsch, C., and Thorne, S. (2002). Foreign language learning as global communicative practice. In D. Block and D. Cameron (Eds.), *Globalization and language teaching* (pp. 83-100). London: Routledge.

Morgan, C. (1993). Attitude change and foreign language culture teaching. *Language Teaching, 26,* 63-75.

O'Dowd, R. (2003). Understanding the "other side": Intercultural learning in a Spanish-English e-mail exchange. *Language Learning and Technology, 7,* 118-144.

O'Dowd, R. (2007). *Online intercultural exchange: An introduction for foreign language teachers.* Clevedon: Multilingual Matters.

Riddiford, N., and Newton, J. (2010). *Workplace talk in action: An ESOL resource.* Wellington, NZ: Victoria University of Wellington.

Schultz, R. (2007). The challenge of assessing cultural understanding in the context of foreign language instruction. *Foreign Language Annals, 40*(1), 9-26.

Sinicrope, C., Norris, J., and Watanabe, Y. (2007). *Understanding and Assessing Intercultural Competence: A Summary of Theory, Research, and Practice.* University of Hawai'i at Mānoa. Retrieved February 23 2009, from http://www2.hawaii.edu/~jnorris/

Tomlinson, B., and Matsuhara, H. (2004). Developing cultural awareness: Integrating culture into a language course. *Modern English Teacher, 13*(1), 1-7.

Ware, P. (2005). "Missed" communication in online communication: tensions in a German-American telecollaboration. *Language Learning and Technology, 9,* 64-89.

In: Innovation and Creativity in ELT Methodology
Editors: H. P. Widodo and A. Cirocki

ISBN: 978-1-62948-146-3
© 2013 Nova Science Publishers, Inc.

Chapter 4

ISSUES IN TEACHING SPEAKING FOR ADULT LEARNERS OF ENGLISH

Joseph A. Foley
Assumption University, Thailand

ABSTRACT

Adult learners bring a level of experience and maturity to their language learning as well as diversity in terms of culture, education, and exposure to English. To be a successful user of English involves both linguistic and communicative competence. In this chapter, the focus will be mainly on linguistic competence based on what we know of spoken language from corpus linguistics. The argument put forward here is that textbooks tend to emphasize "transactional" conversation rather than "interactional." Although these forms of conversation have overlapping features, "interactive" conversation is dominated by being spontaneous, interpersonal where participants have symmetrical rights. These characteristics may not be sufficiently highlighted in the lexical and grammatical features of the often "scripted" conversations found in textbooks. This can result in what may sound like a stilted form of speaking in adult learners.

INTRODUCTION

Teaching speaking to adult learners is very different from teaching children and adolescents. This is mainly because adults bring a level of experience and maturity, and this is reflected in their expectations and motivations. The adult classroom presents a great deal of diversity in terms of cultural background, age education, and previous exposure to English. It is also important to realize that adults are not too old to learn a foreign or second language. Research indicates that adolescents and adults are much better at learning languages than children in spite of the Critical Age Hypothesis (CAH). To what degree an adult learner can acquire a native like accent may not be such an issue as becoming a successful user of English, but with an accent that reflects the learner's own L1.

However, how adult learners look at spoken language and its characteristics is very much dependent on their conscious experiences in using the language. For such adults, so much of their education has probably been via the organized, printed forms of the language (sometimes having a quite different script from English) with the prescriptive judgments about proper sentence forms, criticisms of run-on sentences, redundancy, as well as the goal of neatly arranged paragraphs. We take in much of our language experience through what we read, all of which are the result of a long process of planning, writing, editing, and re-writing, all highly organized (Berendt, 2009). In addition to this is the issue of the semiliterate or non-literate adults where teachers cannot rely on written textbook exercises. They have to go right to the heart of the matter: spoken communication in English. When we talk about *written language*, this does not mean that there is one invariant type of the language associated with all forms of written discourse. But, we can refer to certain features of the language as being characteristic of the written form. In the same way, when we refer to *spoken language*, it does not imply that all forms of speech are alike, but simply that there are characteristics of the spoken mode which are similar.

To be a successful user of English involves both linguistic and communicative competence. Communicative competence includes sociolinguistic competence; that is degrees of formality and informality, appropriate lexical choice, style shifting, and politeness strategies. Strategic competence is also required such as circumlocution and approximation to compensate for the gaps in the learner's second language skills. Discourse competence, on the other hand, involves coherence, reference, and repetition among several other elements that tie the discourse together. However, in this chapter, the focus will be more on the linguistic competence as data coming from corpus linguistics studies have given us new insights into what is involved in both the lexis and grammar of spoken discourse. We can best do this by selecting paradigm cases, that is, by looking at material that exemplifies *transactional* (communicating to accomplish something, including the exchange of goods and services) and *interactional* oral communication (communicating with someone for social purposes, which include establishing and maintaining social relationships). The more relevant and realistic the material being used, the more motivated the learners are likely to be. Adults enjoy materials that relate to their personal experiences and interests, and they want to be able to apply what they are learning to the real world. This brings up the issue of the source of much of present day corpora, which has often been based on British or American English. In this chapter, the source material from the corpora reflects British English, and one would need to go to more international data bases such as the *Vienna Oxford Corpus of International English* (VOICE) to have a wider sample of English as a Lingua Franca. Since the debate is still open as to whether this descriptive corpus can be used as a pedagogical model, textbooks tend to use an exonormative native speaker model. The use of such a model is based on prestige and legitimacy of having descriptions of the language that have been codified through grammars and dictionaries.

Apart from what forms of the language are used, for adults, learning how to speak in a new language means understanding the interactive process of constructing meaning that involves producing, receiving, and processing information. Its forms and meanings will depend on the contexts in which they occur, the participants themselves, their collective experiences, the physical environment and the purposes for speaking. Although speech is often spontaneous, open-ended, and evolving, it is not always unpredictable. Language patterns tend to recur in certain discourse situations and need to be identified for the learner

(Burns and Joyce, 1997). Speaking requires learners not only knowing how to produce specific features of language such as pronunciation, vocabulary, and grammar, but also understanding when, why, and in what ways to produce appropriate language in a given situation. This is why *transactional* conversation has been the stable diet of textbooks. Whereas "interactional" language has been presented more like *scripted language* and hardly representative of the way we actually speak. The fact is that the way we speak is the critical site for the negotiation of social identities, so it is expressive of our wishes, feelings, attitudes, and judgments. Thornbury and Slade (2006) have pointed out that if you have a casual *interactional* conversation with someone, you talk with them, usually in an informal situation. Such conversation has certain features. "It is generally informal, interactive talk, which happens in real time, is spontaneous, has a largely interpersonal function, and in which participants share symmetrical rights" (Thornbury and Slade, 2006, p. 25). Having said this, so many examples of *speaking* in course materials would not have many of these features. The following is an example of how spoken texts are often presented in textbooks.

Door-to-door-salesman [possible textbook version]
    The context is that of a door-to-door salesman calling with a bag full of household goods such as dusters and dishcloths. The housewife is investigating what he has to offer before agreeing to purchase something. In this service encounter, ellipsis and deitic language is used quite extensively while the structure is chiefly organized by discourse markers.

Door-to-door-salesman [possible textbook version]

Salesman:	There are yellow dusters, dishcloths, oven gloves like this one and demist pads. Also gentlemen's socks.
Housewife:	It's a weird assortment of things.
Salesman:	Yes it is. There are hankies for men as well as for ladies. I have super scissors, which can be used for cutting food, flowers and also has a wire stripper.
Housewife:	I see.
Salesman:	We also have a first aid kit, with all sorts of things in it, in case of an accident.
Housewife:	Really?
Salesman	Not that we are looking for an accident but at least it is always there if you need such things. I have chamois leathers and different types of sponge mitts.
Housewife:	Sorry what?
Salesman:	Sponge mitts, they go on your hands when you are washing things. Then there are super chamois reduced from the marked price.
Housewife:	How much are they?

If we now present the same text as more realistic conversation, we would see that many of the features that occur in *transactional* conversation are missing in the *scripted* version given above.

Door-to-door-salesman [transcript (.) indicates pauses]

Salesman   anyway, there's yellow dusters er dishcloths um oven gloves is like them ones er there's demist pads (.) there's gentlemen's socks.

Housewife: it's a weird assortment of things in'it?

Salesman: yeah there's hankies (.) well there's men's and then there's ladies hankies as well right we got super scissors you can use these for flowers for cutting food and they've got like a wire stripper on as well.

Housewife: yeah

Salesman: um (4) then (.) also (.) this is like (.) got all sorts of different bits in (.) if you have an accident.

Housewife: yeah

Salesman   but (.) uh (.) it's not very optimistic is it if (.) I mean I suppose it's always there if you need them (.) uh (.) anyway there's chamois leathers like different types sponge mitts.

Housewife: it's a what?

Salesman   sponge mitts that goes on your hands for washing stuff and then super chamois (.) uh (uh) them are reduced from marked price them ones.

Housewife: how much are they then?

(Pridham, 2001, p. 71)

So What Characterizes Conversation?

Conversation is Spoken

Transcribing a text means that most of the prosodic features are lost (e.g., stress, intonation, tempo, articulation rate, rhythm, and voice quality). The fact that phonemes differ from one language to another means that some of the sounds common in English are quite unusual in other languages.

An example of this would be the "th" sound in *think* and *the*, which is relatively rare in the phonemic inventory of the world's languages. Distinctive features may also be a problem, for example, in Thai, people often do not distinguish between "l" and "r." Suprasegmental phonemes can change the meaning of an utterance depending on where the stress is placed. The misuse of these suprasegmentals can cause the adult second language speaker to be misunderstood and even receive poor job evaluation (Gumperz and Tannen, 1987). However, we must also take careful note of research done by Jenkins (2000) on intelligibility and accent with reference to English as a Lingua Franca.

Conversation Happens in Real Time

Notice how the textbook version follows the conventions of written language . . . a subject and predicate while real conversation even in transactions has *um* or *uh*, false starts, and back-tracking.

Salesman: but (.) uh (.) it's not very optimistic is it if (.) I mean I suppose it's always there if you need them (.) uh (.) anyway there's chamois leathers like different types sponge mitts.

Housewife: it's a what?

Transcripted speech occurs in real time. The textbook version has, probably, been through a production process of several stages of drafting, editing, and publication. The real time spontaneity of talk accounts for a number of features that distinguish it from writing.

hesitations
word repetitions
false starts
repairs
unfinished utterances
ungrammaticality [in terms of written norms]
fillers
borrowing chunks from the previous speaker's utterance
utterance launchers

                                                    (Thornbury and Slade, 2006, p. 12)

Real conversation is often made up of loosely linked clauses and phrases… maintaining a continuous flow of discourse. This can often tax the processing ability of listener, especially in adult learner contexts.

Conversation Takes Place in Shared Contexts

In the textbook version, it is difficult to establish shared contexts unless there is a theme or story running through the unit being used. In real conversation, many more pronouns are used because of the shared context, far fewer can be found in the textbook version. For example, there are 20 pronouns used in the real conversation, but only 14 in the textbook version. The frequency of deictic items: *this, that, there, then, things*, etc.

Textbook
Salesman: Not that we are looking for an accident but at least it is always there if you need such things. I have chamois leathers and different types of sponge mitts.

Transcript
Salesman: but (.) uh (.) it's not very optimistic is it if (.) I mean I suppose it's always there if you need them (.) uh (.) anyway there's chamois leathers like different types sponge mitts

Ellipsis, where what has been omitted can be reconstructed from the context.

Textbook
Salesman: We also have a first aid kit, with all sorts of things in it, in case of an accident.

Transcript
Salesman: um (4) then (.) also (.) this is like (.) got all sorts of different bits in (.) if you have an accident
Deitics, words that "point" to something (*a, the, this, that, here, there, I ,you, them*)

Textbook
Salesman: There are yellow dusters, dishcloths, oven gloves like *this* one and demist pads. Also gentlemen's socks.
Housewife: *It*'s a weird assortment of things.

Transcript
Salesman: anyway, there's yellow dusters er dishcloths um oven gloves is like *them* ones er there's demist pads (.) there's gentlemen's socks
Housewife: *it*'s a weird assortment of things in'it?

Non-Clausal Expressions That Can Stand Alone

Conversation is dialogic... jointly constructed and multi-authored. It is constructed through the taking of successive and often overlapping turns by two or more participants. Speakers respond to, build upon, and refer to the previous utterances of other speakers.

Salesman: anyway, there's yellow dusters er dishcloths um oven gloves is like them ones er there's demist pads (.) there's gentlemen's socks
Housewife: it's a weird assortment of things in'it?

Discourse Markers

Discourse markers are used in order to signal the direction the talk is heading, certain words and phrases occur frequently at the beginning of a speaker's turns: *yeah, anyway um, no, but uh*, etc.

Textbook
Salesman: There are yellow dusters, dishcloths, oven gloves like this one and demist pads. Also, gentlemen's socks.
Housewife: It's a weird assortment of things.
Salesman: Yes, it is. There are hankies for men as well as for ladies. I have super scissors which can be used for cutting food, flowers and also has a wire stripper.
Housewife: I see.

Transcript

Salesman: anyway, there's yellow dusters er dishcloths um oven gloves is like them ones er there's demist pads (.) there's gentlemen's socks.

Housewife: it's a weird assortment of things in'it?

Salesman: yeah there's hankies (.) well there's men's and then there's ladies hankies as well right we got super scissors you can use these for flowers for cutting food and they've got like a wire stripper on as well.

Housewife: yeah

Written language also has discourse markers, but not with the frequency found in interactive talk. Also, they tend to be very often what we might find in academic writing: *therefore, however, moreover*, etc.

Backchanneling and Repairs Because of Ambiguities, Which Need to Be Cleared up

Backchanneling (*um*) or showing interest (*really)* is possible because the speakers are at least audibly present.

Textbook

Housewife: It's a weird assortment of things.

Salesman: Yes, it is. There are hankies for men as well as for ladies. I have super scissors which can be used for cutting food, flowers and also has a wire stripper.

Housewife: I see.

Transcript

Housewife: it's a weird assortment of things in'it?

Salesman: yeah there's hankies (.) well there's men's and then there's ladies hankies as well right we got super scissors you can use these for flowers for cutting food and they've got like a wire stripper on as well.

Housewife: yeah

Conversation is Interpersonal

Many textbooks present oral conversation as *transactional* conversation such as a service encounter in this case a door-to-door salesman (message oriented). The speakers have practical goals to achieve, and the success of the exchange depends on the achievement of that goal.

Typical transactional exchanges might include buying a train ticket, negotiating a loan at the bank, or simply buying something at the local store. There are good arguments for having *transactional* conversations in textbooks and practicing such activities in the classroom, especially for adults. Indeed, such forms of conversation characterize classroom interaction in that information is transacted and where the rights to speak are not equally distributed. This is particularly true in a teacher dominated classroom.

Interactional conversation, on the other hand, is primarily listener oriented and in the past textbooks did not supply enough material of this form of spoken language. Spoken language is more informal and is characterized mainly by lexical choices—colloquial language, slang, and even swearing.

Interactional Language

Textbook:

[The context is that William after supper has lit his pipe and walked over to his brother's house. Tom welcomes him and they sit down and have this conversation.]

William: You're looking well, Tom. Your fall didn't do you any harm then?
Tom: None at all. I'm feeling all right. You're smoking William. I want to smoke too.
William: You're turning out all your pockets. Why?
Tom: I'm looking for my pipe. I had it last night and I put it in this pocket.
William: Well, it's not there now. There it is on the table.
Tom: Ah! Thanks, William. I always loose my pipe. But it always turns up again.

                                                                (Wilson, 1972, p.125)

It might well be argued that such examples of *conversation* are more likely to be found in older textbooks. But, even more recent textbooks seem to use *scripted* conversation to illustrate grammatical features as in the following [present perfect: *already, yet*, adjective + infinitive].

Emma: Have you finished with the computer yet?
Mike: Nearly, what's the hurry?
Emma: I've already asked you three times. I want to finish the front page. It's our last edition.
Mike: But I'm sending an e-mail to Australia.
Emma: Mike is it really necessary to spend all day on the computer?
Mike: What's the problem? Have you thought of a good headline yet?
Emma: No I thought of 'End of Festival', but that sounds silly.
Mike: How about 'Festival Finished'?

                                                    (Garton-Springer and Prowse, 1999, p. 88)

If we contrast the two examples given above with an actual transcript, we can see what a real interactive conversation would look like (again without the prosodic features). Informal conversation: (transcript of students from college chatting round the tea-table at home on a Sunday. The reference to "Bakewell" is a type of tart, popular in the United Kingdom).

S 1: Does anyone want a chocolate bar or anything
S 2: Oh yeah yes please
S 3: Yes please
S 2: [laughs]
S 3: [laughs]
S 1: You can have either a Mars Bar, Kit-Kat or erm cherry Bakewell
S 3: Oh erm it's a toss-up between [S 2 [laughs]] the cherry Bakewell and the Mars Bar isn'it?
S 1: Well shall I bring some in then cos you might want another one cos I don't want them
all, I'm gonna be
S 3: Miss paranoid about weight aren't you?

S 1: Yes but you know
S 3: you're not fat Mand
S 1: I will be if I'm not careful
S 2: Oh God

(Carter and McCarthy, 1997, p.85)

This transcript of the *students chatting round the tea-table* has a number of characteristics that might be found in "transactional" conversation.

Conversation is Expressive of Identity

It is through informal talk that people establish and maintain their affiliation with a particular group. Conversation is marked by continual expressions of likes, dislikes, and emotional states. Interactants express their attitudes about each other, about others who are not present, and about the world. There can be a lot of humor in conversations together with expressions such as:

Miss paranoid
You're not fat Mand. (short for Amanda)

Colloquial Language

S 1: Sound like *a right mother* don't I?

"right" in this context is a colloquial alternative to "real" or "proper" and has a certain perjorative connotation.

S 3: Oh erm it's *a toss-up* [difficult to choose between something]

Also, frequent in conversation is the use of appraisal language (Martin and White, 2005), especially evaluative language:

S 2: Oh those cherry Bakewells look *lovely*
S 3: They do don't they
S 1: Oh they were…*gorgeous*…did you say you would like a cup of tea?
S 2: yes
S 3: All right then

Tags

This conversation contains a number of *tags*, which create informality among the speakers. They do not necessarily demand a reply, but suggest a shared view of the situation.

isn't it?
are't you
don't they?
don't I?

Lexical Items

Here are examples of lexical items, which render different meanings:

- *or anything*   vague expression meaning in this context anything that goes with a cup of tea such as cake or cookies)

- *cos*   rather than "because"
- *Yeah*   instead of the more formal "yes"
- *Oh God ...*   swearing

Pronunciation

I'm gonna be (I am going to be)

Because spoken English allows both open syllables (C-V, or just V) and closed syllables (C-V-C, or V-C), as well as consonant clusters such as in the word *matched*, learners might omit word-final consonants, and thus eliminate the sound that conveys important linguistic information, as in this case the past tense.

In addition to the features mentioned above, participants are expected to follow what is called Grice's maxims (1975): principles for the conduct of talk without which coherent conversation would be impossible.

- Maxim of quantity: Make your contribution just as informative as required.

S 1: You can have either a Mars Bar, Kit-Kat or erm cherry Bakewell

- Maxim of quality: Make your contribution one that is true.

S 3: Oh erm it's a toss-up between [S 2 [laughs]] the cherry Bakewell and the Mars Bar isn'it?

- Maxim of relation: Make your contribution relevant.

S 3: Miss paranoid about weight aren't you?

S 1: Yes but you know

S 3: You're not fat Mand

- Maxim of manner: Avoid obscurity and ambiguity. Be brief and orderly.

S 1: Does anyone want a chocolate bar or anything?

S 2: Oh yeah yes please

S 3: Yes please

Given all the possibilities S1's utterance could have had, her listeners selected the interpretation that was the most relevant in the context (according to relevance theory, Sperber and Wilson, 1990). This assumption of relevance is fundamental to the maintenance of conversational coherence.

As we have indicated earlier, a more extensive use of real conversation in textbooks has been possible by using Corpus Linguistics because we now actually know how people speak rather than creating scripted speech. However, with such a vast resource as can be found in a corpus knowing approximately what size of vocabulary, we would expect our adult learners to be able to use becomes an important issue. Carter and McCarthy (1997), Nation (1990), and Schmitt (2000) have suggested that a round pedagogical figure of about 2000 words will safely cover the everyday core of the spoken language. Indeed, nearly half of all conversations consist of just 50 words, endlessly recycled. But, are the 50 words the same in written and spoken corpora? Written text consists of almost entirely function words [*the, with, but, are, when,* etc.]. Spoken text include some content words [*know, well, got, think, right*].

A closer look at the data from corpus linguistics reveals that these words are elements of discourse markers [*you know, I think, well* . . .]. Other common discourse markers include [*and, yeah, but, oh, so,* and *yes*]. However, it would be virtually impossible to sustain a coherent conversation using just these words. Nevertheless, a common core of frequently occurring words might provide the learner with a critical mass [a core lexicon] on which they can build their vocabulary. About 30 per cent of words in conversation occur in a recurrent lexical chunking. Wray (2000) points out that the storage and deployment of lexical chunks (*I mean to say, frankly speaking, I take your point but . . .*) facilitate production in that they save valuable processing time that might, otherwise, be spent on generating utterances from scratch. Many of these are idiomatic (*so long, on the other hand, out of the blue*). Others do not follow orthodox grammatical constructions (*long time no see, the sooner the better*, etc.).

Classroom Implications

As we have indicated at the beginning of this chapter, assessing the characteristics of adult students would include what knowledge is shared, point of reference, status and power relations of the participants, interest levels, and maybe differences in perspectives of particular subjects. Strategies have to be applied, which will enhance comprehensibility, such as emphasizing key words, rephrasing, and so on. Much of this would mean, on the teacher's part, using body language and gestures, paying attention to the success of the interaction, adjusting the vocabulary, and rate of speech to maximize the students' involvement.

If we accept the evidence accumulated through corpus studies, a critical mass of high frequency words around 2000 would be needed to equip them for maintaining a conversation. This spoken lexicon would need to include a high proportion of modality terms and deictic expressions, as well as vocabulary using basic nominal, verbal, adjectival and adverbial forms. Adult learners would also need a range of common lexical items used to express emotions and attitudes (appraisal lexis). Conversational fluency can be enhanced by use of a range of fillers, repetition devices, vague terms, and routine lexical phrases. In order to negotiate the flow of talk and to signal involvement, a basic repertoire of discourse markers is essential. The technique of hedging, such as vague language, can be important in interpersonal interaction as can a memorized bank of fixed phrases, including social formulae and "conversational routines" assist the smooth flow of conversation.

Apart from the lexis, too often in our classroom, there are common misconceptions about the grammar of spoken language: It is assumed either that spoken language is simply written grammar realized as speech or that spoken grammar is less complex, even degenerate form of its written counterpart. The recognition of the distinctive and systematic nature of spoken grammar has been brought to our attention in such works as *Longman Grammar of Spoken and Written English (*Biber, Johansson, Leech, Conrad, and Finegan, 1999) and the *Cambridge Grammar of Spoken and Written English* (Carter and McCarthy, 2006). This does not mean that we need to teach separate grammars; they share the same grammar of English, but we should not assume that if a grammar has been constructed for written texts, it is equally valid for spoken texts. What is true is that some forms seem to occur more often in spoken than in written and vice versa, and some forms are used differently with different shades of meaning.

Conversation may seem simplistic in terms of grammar both because of its informal structure and the constraints of real time production. Halliday (1985) argues that the structure of speech is highly complex mainly because the context of spoken language is always in a state of flux. Complexity is achieved not by embedding clauses (finite and non-finite) within a sentence, but through the successive accumulation of individual clauses. The logical connections between the clauses are indicated using discourse markers *(but, because, unless, in which case, so…)*

What studies in corpus linguistics have shown is that we often employ a process called *heads and tails*. The *head* slot typically consists of a noun phrase, which serves as a discourse marker to identify key information such as the topic and establish a common frame of reference for what follows.

S 3: *Miss paranoid* about weight aren't you?

"Tails" is more retrospective in its use, serving to extend, reinforce, clarify, or comment on what the speaker is saying.

S 1: I'm always spilling coffee, *I am*

(see Carter and McCarthy, 2006, p. 539).

Also, because spoken language is jointly constructed, it is often *ungrammatical*, which may be non-standard forms, but are tolerated by native speakers. This suggests that to demand 100 per cent accuracy in speaking activities in the classroom may not be realistic as in the following example:

S I: We can relate to chocolate…I think they're the little ones actually so you can have *one of them*, and *one of them* if you like.

Here, we see *them* being used in informal conversation instead of *those*. However, when *them* is used as an alternative to *those* such as the following, this usage is regarded as a non-standard dialect form.

Them people across the road always make a lot of noise.

Also, conversation would be unsustainable without the use of questions. A coherent conversation that consisted of nothing, but statements would be difficult to imagine. Adjacency pairs are a kind of question and answer exchange.

S 1: *Does anyone want a chocolate bar or anything?*

S 2: *Oh yeah yes please*

S 3: *Yes please*

As far as what *tense* and *aspect* to focus on, the present tense is the most common tense in casual conversation, and this reflects the speaker focus on the present and actual, as in this example: Context . . . again *Students chatting round the tea-table.*

S 3: I *like* Sunday nights for some reason, I *don't know* why

S 2: [laughs] cos you *come* home

S 3: I *come* home

S 1: and *pig out*

S 2: Yeah yeah

S 3: Sunday*'s* a really nice day I *think*

S 2: It certainly *is*

S 3: It*'s* a really nice relaxing day

Progressive aspect is found in past narrative to provide a narrative frame for the key events in the narrative. In the following extract, M (mother) is talking to D (Daughter) about a party that was to be arranged, but some are unable to attend due to previous commitments.

M: And erm we thought we'd have someone to dinner and have a party you know a dinner party over this coming weekend but they're not going to be here so.
D: well that would be boring.
M: Don't…Not quite sure when they thought we were going to do it but there we are.
D: But she's saying that erm loads of people that they're meant to be staying with can't remember [laughs]. Apparently erm someone's moving well to a new job and someone else has got relatives coming to stay. So they can't

(Carter and McCarthy, 1997, pp. 71-72)

Modality, on the other hand, is best understood by taking into account the interpersonal features of the context. The way the speakers indicate their attitudes and judgments with regard to what is being said: *such a thing probably happens; should happen, might have happened.* Modals whether in the verbs or adjuncts are very common in conversation precisely because of the interpersonal function. *Can, will,* and *would* are extremely common in conversation as are semi-modals *have to, used to, going to, may, shall,* and *must* (to mark logical necessity) are relatively infrequent. Semi-modals like *tend to* occur much more in spoken data than *ought to*. This may be to avoid bald and direct statements and may appear too assertive in conversation. Finally, what do adult learners *need* to know as far as grammar is concerned?

A *list* may look something like the following: some basic conjunctions (*and, but, so*) in order to string together sequences of clauses (finite and non-finite); the use of deictic devices (*here/there, now/then, this/that* etc.); a command of simple verb tense forms both present and past; familiarity with the use of aspect both to fame and background information in narrative, as in *it was raining . . . I'd been working*; knowledge of the most frequent modals (*can, will, would, have to, going to, used to*); the ability to formulate questions, especially *yes/no and wh*-questions; being able to use head- and tail-slot fillers-principally as discourse markers and one or two all-purposes "chunks" as *he said ... and then I said ...*

CONCLUSION

Clearly, the *need to know* given above is a very short list and bears little relation to the elaborate grammar of standard ELT materials. However, it is difficult to avoid the conclusion that a significant proportion of what corpus linguistics has identified as core grammar and lexis is reducible to formulaic language of a lexical rather than strictly grammatical nature. A repertoire of *sentence starters, discourse markers, backchanneling devices* and so on, may provide the learner with a more effective starting point into conversation than many traditional syllabuses.

Nunan (1987) pointed out that studies of classroom interaction were characterized as being teacher-learner interaction, but essentially consisting of largely *Initiation, Response, Feedback* (IRF) sequences. The speaker's rights are unevenly distributed, with the teacher asking the majority of questions, initiating topics, nominating speakers, and evaluating feedback. It is motivated by the need to achieve a pre-selected pedagogical goal. Too often, the goal was the transmission of subject-matter knowledge from teacher to learner. Syllabus specifications and examinations often control this transmission. Van Lier (2001, p. 96) observed that "Students opportunities to exercise initiatives . . . or to develop a sense of control and self-regulation are extremely restricted in the IRF format."

In a more *interaction* approach to oral communication, there is no specification as directly controlled by a syllabus or examination, but is directed more by the *turns* that each one in the interaction takes. Conversation is often more symmetrical where the speakers' rights are more evenly distributed so that the talk is collaborative, with speakers free to take turns and to introduce topics of their own choice.

Talk, typically, follows a *chat-chunk* development rather than being a sequence of IRF exchanges. In conversation, if something goes wrong, such as a breakdown of communication, speakers usually take the initiative for repairing their own utterances. In the classroom, it is typically the teacher who initiates the repair. This means that classroom talk is very often not anchored within the experiential world (the here and now), particularly of adult learners, and it does not set up expectancies of what is going to happen next. In real conversation, turns are tightly interwoven, each one firmly anchored to the preceding one and raising options for the next one (Thornbury and Slade, 2006).

Here are some suggestions for promoting speaking among adults:

- Select tasks that allow the students to speak extensively in pairs or groups. This can be done by *transactional* dialogs conducted for the purpose of information exchange such as interviews, role plays, or debates. *Interpersonal* dialogs can be used to maintain as we have indicated earlier, social relationships through such activities as personal interviews or casual conversation in role plays.
- Encourage students to focus on the speaking process not just the product by promoting techniques that generate interactive communication through extended *monologs* such as short speeches and oral reports where other participants have to ask questions as follow up.

Adult learners must make themselves understood by the people they are speaking with, and this is not an easy task. For less-than-proficient speakers, managing the multiple components of language that must work together as they speak is very demanding indeed. As language teachers, our understanding of what is involved in speaking continues to evolve with the development of corpora. Speaking is the key to communication for adults much as it is for young children. By considering what good speakers do, what speaking tasks can be used in the adult classroom, and what specific needs adult learners report, teachers can help learners improve their speaking, and thus, be able to participate in their new speech community.

REFERENCES

Berendt, E. A. (2009). *For communication and learning: Research in spoken and applied discourse*. Bangkok: Assumption University Press.

Biber, D., Johansson, S., Leech, G., Conrad, S., and Finegan, E. (1999). *Grammar of spoken and written English*. Harlow, UK: Longman.

Burns, A, and Joyce, H. (1997). Focus on speaking. Sydney: National Center for English Language Teaching and Research.

Carter, R., and McCarthy, M. (1997). *Exploring spoken English*. Cambridge: Cambridge University Press.

Carter, R., and McCarthy, M. (2006). *The Cambridge grammar of English*. Cambridge: Cambridge University Press.

Garton-Springer, J., and Prowse, P. (1999). *Shine*. Oxford: Macmillan Heinemann.

Grice, H. P. (1975). Logic and conversation. In P. Cole and J. L. Morgan (eds.), *Syntax and Semantics 3: Speech act*s (pp. 41-58). New York: Academic Press.

Gumperz, J. J., and Tannen, D. (1987). Individual and social differences in language use. In W. Wang and C. Fillamore (eds.), *Individual differences in language ability and language behaviour* (pp. 305-325). New York: Academic Press.

Halliday, M. A. K. (1985). *Spoken and written language*. Geelong, Victoria: Deakin University Press. [Republished 1989 by Oxford University Press]

Jenkins, J. (2000). *The phonology of English as an international language*. Oxford: Oxford University Press.

Martin, J. R., and White, P. R. R. (2005). *The language of evaluation: Appraisal in English*. London: Palgrave.

Nation, I. S. P. (1990). *Teaching and learning vocabulary*. New York: Newbury House.

Nunan, D. (1987). Communicative language teaching: Making it work. *ELT Journal*, 41, 136-145.

Pridham, F. (2001). *The language of conversation*. New York: Routledge.

Schmitt, N. (2000). *Vocabulary and language teaching*. Cambridge: Cambridge University Press.

Sperber, D., and Wilson, D. (1990). *Relevance*. Oxford: Oxford University Press.

Thornbury, S., and Slade, D. (2006). *Conversation: From description to pedagogy*. Cambridge: Cambridge University Press.

Wilson, J. (1972). *Look at English*. Glasgow, UK: Collins.

Wray, A. (2000). Formulaic sequences in second language teaching: Principles and practice. *Applied Linguistics*, 21, 463-89.

van Lier, L. (2001). Constraints and resources in classroom talk: Issues of equality and symmetry. In C. Candlin and N. Mercer, (eds.), *English language teaching in its social contexts: A reader* (pp 90-107.). London: Routledge.

Vienna-Oxford International Corpus of English. [Link: www.univie.ac.at/voice/].

In: Innovation and Creativity in ELT Methodology
Editors: H. P. Widodo and A. Cirocki

ISBN: 978-1-62948-146-3
© 2013 Nova Science Publishers, Inc.

Chapter 5

METACOGNITIVE STRATEGY TRAINING IN ESP READING

Osman Zakaria Barnawi

Yanbu Industrial College, Saudi Arabia

ABSTRACT

This chapter recasts how language teachers can train learners with metacognitive strategies for ESP reading. This training helps the learners raise or enhance textual and rhetorical awareness of ESP texts in which they are interested and in turn become aware of how they can raise awareness of text ownership. Specifically, this chapter discusses theoretical and empirical accounts of metacognitive strategy training in ESP reading. What follows, it describes step-by-step procedures for implementing such training inside and outside the classroom. I argue that such training takes time, process, and effort and should be well-managed so that a teacher can help students become independent and fluent readers.

INTRODUCTION

ESP has long been introduced to English language teaching (ELT) in which there has been a growing need for equipping learners specializing in specific science disciplines (e.g., science, business, and technology) with English (Widodo and Pusporini, 2010). It is no wonder that this has led to the emergence of numerous in-print and online texts, such as those in English for science and business in colleges and universities around the globe (Dudley-Evans, 2001; Flowerdew and Peacock, 2001; Fortanet-Gomez and Raisanen, 2009). This notion suggests that being able to read scientific research articles and textbooks becomes a pre-requisite skill to succeed in college and university courses. However, for many English as a foreign language (EFL) undergraduate students, reading and understanding textbooks related to their chosen disciplines is still considered as gruelling experiences (Benson, 1991). That is, many business and science undergraduate students still lack the ability to read related discipline texts more efficiently in order to extract meaning from such texts. This inability may be due to a reading habit that students adopted from their reading experience in senior high schools in which they read text in a word-for-word fashion. In addition, teachers never taught the students how to make use of particular reading strategies for grasping certain ESP texts. Consequently, most of those students experience difficulties understanding their reading materials since their metacognitive knowledge or capability is not tapped, so their awareness of using particular reading strategies is lacking.

Drawing from the above-mentioned concern, there is a need for equipping learners with metacognitive strategies for ESP reading in which this training serves as a means of scaffolding the learners to bridge the gap between their previous learning experiences (e.g., senior high schools) and reading tasks at undergraduate level. This metacognitive strategy training can be based on three interrelated tasks: (1) pre-reading task, (2) while-reading task, and (3) post-reading task. These tasks are aimed at helping students become more aware of themselves as strategic and efficient readers so that they can plan and monitor their comprehension while reading. Before discussing how the notion of metacognitive strategy training can be used in ESP reading instruction, this chapter addresses theoretical and empirical accounts of reading strategies in the field of ESP as well as metacognitive strategy training in ESP reading in a pedagogical stance.

AN OVERVIEW OF READING STRATEGIES IN THE FIELD OF ESP

Researchers and theorists (e.g., Abebersold and Field, 1997; Carson and Leki, 1993; Chamot, 1987) have defined the concept of reading strategies differently. The most widely accepted definition, however, is that reading strategies are specific problem oriented techniques that can be either conscious, unconscious, or automatic. What is more, reading strategies that an individual reader uses to approach certain texts depend largely on the nature of the text, the reader's purpose, and the context of situation (Grabe, 1991; Jiménez, Garcia, and Pearson, 1996). A reader usually uses different strategies ranging from "simple fix-up strategies such as simply re-reading difficult segments and guessing the meaning of an unknown word from the context to more comprehensive strategies such as summarizing and relating what is being read to the readers' background knowledge" (Moghadam, 2009, p.2). This notion suggests that in a college ESP program, for example, good readers are always aware of the above- mentioned reading strategies when reading scientific research articles or textbooks. They know how to visualize reading tasks and how they make sense of what they read and what they do when they do not understand (Block, 1992). Indeed, lack of consciousness of such various strategies and mental processes by readers in a college ESP program may cause some difficulties understanding the required reading materials; as a result, they cannot grasp the gist of the text.

Different studies have shed lights on the reading strategies used by good readers as well as poor readers to extract meaning from texts. Jimenez, Garcia, and Pearson (1996), for example, point out that one of the main characteristics of poor readers is that they approach all types of reading materials in the same manner. Likewise, Daoud (1991) examined the reading processes of Arab and French native speakers with respect to research articles in their chosen major of studies. In his study, Daoud sheds lights on (a) the readers' lack of ability to conceive the nature of ESP discourse and (b) their failure to recognize the rhetorical organization of scientific research texts. In order to explore the reading habits of these EFL students, i.e., Arab and French native speakers, Daoud utilized verbal reports as well as three general observations. He concluded that the students' reading habits was attributed to their inability to read scientific texts meaningfully, that is to say, to read at reasonable rate and with good comprehension.

Undisputedly, having a strong ability to comprehend various scientific research articles from both rhetorical and stylistic levels is the core of success in undergraduate programs. Nonetheless, the above studies seem to pay little attention to meta-text (author's purpose, audience, and context) as well as metacognitive strategies of reading. Reading strategies are the cognitive and metacognitive actions that individuals either consciously decide to use or use automatically when attempting to access a written text (Macaro, 2003).

METACOGNITIVE STRATEGY TRAINING IN ESP READING INSTRUCTION

Undeniably, ESP programs of which goal is to develop EFL learners' reading skills would not only focus on mechanical skills like words and sentences structures, but such programs also deal with tapping into the learners' mental abilities in the reading process. This notion implies that reading comprehension is not just understanding words, sentences, or even texts, but it involves a complicated integration of the reader's prior knowledge, language skills, and their metacognitive strategies (Hammadou, 1991) as well. Therefore, it is not surprising to see that metacognition is considered by most educators to be a crucial element for many cognitive learning tasks. According to Flavell (1976, p. 232), metacognition indicates "one's knowledge concerning one's own cognitive processes and products or anything related to them." Such cognitive process includes "the active monitoring and consequent regulation and orchestration of these processes in relation to the cognitive objects or data on which they bear, usually in the service of some concrete goal or objective" (p. 232). As O'Malley and Chamot (1990) have pointed out, metacognitive strategies have two core features: (1) knowledge about learning called metacognitive knowledge and (2) control over learning known as metacognitive strategies. Thus, as pinpointed by Hyde and Bizar (1989), metacognitive processes "are those processes in which the individual carefully considers thoughts in problem solving situations through the strategies of self planning, self monitoring, self regulating, self questioning, and self reflecting" (p.51).

Thus, metacognitive readers (i.e., successful readers) are supposed to have the appropriate skills that help them realize when something does not make sense and they take appropriate action to do something about it. Therefore, in this chapter, metacognitive strategies are referred to as the activities that EFL readers do to plan, control, monitor, and evaluate their own comprehension of scientific research articles and textbooks they are reading in ESP programs. EFL learners in undergraduate programs are often required to read various scientific research articles and textbooks. As researchers such as Eskey (1986), Li and Munby (1996), and Shih (1992) argued for most second language readers, the major problem in academic reading would simply be having an ability to efficiently read and comprehend scientific research articles and textbooks in their chosen disciplines. Certain studies have emphasized the importance of reading strategy training that could lead to the level of the metacognitive awareness of students in EFL contexts (e.g., Carrell, 1996; Dhieb-Henia, 2003; Jimenez, Garcia, and Pearson, 1996). In a review of strategy training studies, Carrell (1996) has pointed out metacognitive knowledge used in various empirical studies. This includes declarative knowledge, procedural knowledge, and conditional knowledge. Declarative knowledge is referred to the knowledge about oneself as a learner and about factors that affect his or her performance (i.e., what he or she is learning). Procedural knowledge has to do with knowledge of useful strategies for learning, memory, and reading (i.e., how learners go about learning skills). Conditional knowledge pertains to knowing why and when to utilize certain strategies (Jacobs and Paris, 1987). In this regard, metacognitive awareness is a key to fluent and competent reading. Simply stated, as Devine (1993) nicely elaborates, metacognitive strategy is not simply a way of utilizing productive strategies, but of doing so metacognitively or with solid awareness. This awareness entails knowledge of strategies such as planning—selecting the right strategies and setting goals; monitoring comprehension—regulating the learning process; and self assessment of skill needed—controlling learning and making the necessary adjustments to strategies. Effective readers always have the skills to plan, monitor, and adjust their strategies based on the nature of the text, their purpose of reading, and the context of situation. However, such a notion does not necessarily mean that poor readers lack the cognitive ability or strategy in EFL reading, but their reading skills are not well tapped. Several empirical studies (e.g., Carrell, 1996; Dhieb-Henia, 2003; Hudson, 1991) have demonstrated that readers could be trained to utilize a range of reading strategies, to gain metacognitive awareness, and to monitor comprehension. Most researchers (e.g., Garner 1994, Li and Munby, 1996; ONeill, 1992) have argued that certain strategic reading behaviors (e.g., note taking and summarizing) would help develop metacognitive knowledge and awareness among EFL readers. Generally speaking, EFL students usually approach their academic tasks, such as reading according to their academic and cultural background, their individual learning styles, and the nature of the tasks assigned. These students utilize different types of reading strategies effectively or sometimes ineffectively according to how well they understood the reading materials. This implies that metacognitive strategy training helps EFL readers develop the skills of reading effectively and meaningfully. Thus, the awareness of planning, monitoring, and making necessary adjustment to reading strategies when reading scientific research articles and textbooks is the key to becoming fluent and effective readers in ESP programs. Alongside this notion, this chapter attempts to provide how metacognitive strategy training can be incorporated into an ESP program in three reading stages: pre-reading, while-reading, and post-reading. It is important to note that such a strategy can be applied to intensive reading and extensive reading inside and outside the classroom, depending on the ultimate goal of reading instruction.

IMPLEMENTING METACOGNITIVE STRATEGY INSTRUCTION IN COLLEGE ESP READING

Pre-Reading Task

In the pre-reading stage of metacognitive strategy instruction, a teacher can implement orientating and planning tasks. In an orientating task, it aims to activate student background knowledge or prior knowledge so that the teacher can determine the demand of the reading task and set up reading goals. Suppose a teacher teaches "English for Information and Technology (IT)" in which the focus of a topic is on "software," he or she can ask survey questions to IT students, as listed below.

Orientating Task: Survey Questions

- What kind of software do you always use for antivirus?
- What kind of system software are you using for your laptop or desktop?
- What kinds of articles on "software" (e.g., system, programming, or application) written in English do you always read?
- Why do you always read such articles?
- What linguistic difficulty do you often experience?
- How do you usually solve this problem?
- What content information difficulty do you always encounter?
- How do you always resolve this difficulty?

This orienting task is geared to activate student prior knowledge. To make this task more interactive, a teacher can get students to take turns asking and answering the orientating task questions in dyads.

Once the students are done with this task, a teacher can have them proceed to the planning task. She or he can guide the students to self question and answer the following points:

Planning Task: Self Questioning

- What kind of text on "software" will I have to read?
- Why will I need to read the text?
- What text type of the text (e.g., descriptive, factual recount, explanation, or information report) will I read?
- Where and how will I find such a text?
- Will I learn something new from reading the text?
- Will I be able to tackle these problems: understanding content information and linguistic complexity while reading the text?
- Will I do a set of slow reading or quick reading?
- Will I read the entire text or main points or the gist of the text?

This planning task enables students to decide what to do in a while-reading phase. To enable the students to carry out two tasks: orientating and planning successfully, the teacher can provide how to do such tasks. In this teacher modeling, the teacher shows the students the way to answer the questioning tasks for orientating and planning.

It is worth noting here that at the pre-reading stage, some students might be familiar with some reading strategies that the teacher has shown; this is what researchers called it declarative knowledge—knowing what something is (Garner, 1994; Li and Munby, 1996;

O'Neill, 1992). Nevertheless, knowing certain knowledge does not necessarily mean knowing how to use that knowledge meaningfully.

Thus, teacher's modeling in the pre-reading phase is intended to help students become more aware of their skills or knowledge as well as to promote students' positive attitudes towards reading content knowledge or information related texts in that not all students are familiar with metacognitive strategy in ESP reading. More importantly, this pre-reading task helps students become reading planners who are aware of what to read, why to read, and how to read.

While-Reading Task

A while-reading task is geared to develop students' procedural knowledge—knowing how to do something or putting the knowledge into action. In this task, a teacher should ask his or her students to start reading the chosen text based on their topics of interest on "software."

In this phase, a set of readings can be done either in the classroom if class hours permit or outside the classroom due time constraints. If the latter is the case, a teacher needs to provide a reading journal so that the students can monitor how much they did a set of reading on the chosen text. In this stage, students are told to do the following task: executing and monitoring.

Executing Task: Implementing Reading Strategies and Skills

✓ Reading the chosen text
✓ Apply these basic reading strategies: previewing, scanning, and skimming
✓ Recognize these reading skills:

- Identifying main facts/details
- Identifying minor facts/details
- Identifying references
- Relating cause-effect
- Identifying sequences of ideas
- Inferring meanings from contextual clues
- Identifying structural devices
- Identifying organizational patterns of texts
- Identifying purpose of a text
- Identifying attitude or tone of an author
- Identifying source of the text

Monitoring Task: Self Awareness of Reading Strategy and Complexity

o recognize reading strategies for comprehending the text
o identify what strategies worked and what did not work
o recognize an alternative strategy for understanding the text

- o notice linguistic complexity (e.g., unfamiliar words, phrases, or topic-specific terminologies)
- o notice content information complexity
- o deliberately confirm the meaning of the text

To observe what the students have done, a teacher should prepare a reading journal or diary so that she or he can keep track of student reading record. The content of the journal can be adopted from executing and monitoring task questions. This journal or diary can be used as database or foundation for whether the students could transform declarative knowledge into procedural and conditional knowledge and reflect on what they have known and planned, self monitored, and self evaluated.

Post-Reading Task

This task aims at ensuring coverage and understanding of the text that the students read. At this stage, two post-reading tasks: evaluating and elaborating that a teacher can assign to the students.

Evaluating Task: Self Awareness of Reading Process and Outcome

- o review and interpret what has been read
- o take note of success and failure
- o take note of useful findings
- o verify that reading goals have been achieved
- o reflect on what needs to learn more regarding reading strategies?
- o envision what to do further?

Elaborating Task: Self Awareness of Text Ownership

- • list and define key technical words, phrase, and concepts
- • summarize each portion of the selection
- • summarize the entire selection
- • arrive at conclusions about the content of the selection
- • paraphrase what has been read
- • summarize what has been read
- • connect, compare, and contrast the information from the selection
- • with other information
- • draw inferences from the information in the selection

Such tasks can be done step by step as the students go through class periods in the entire semester. Thus, to help strengthen students' awareness of what makes their language learning successful, a teacher needs to demonstrate in class: (1) how to set the purpose of reading, (2) plan for reading, (3) identify and solve problems at lexical, phrasal, textual, rhetorical, and organizational levels, (4) self monitor for problems in reading, and (5) self evaluate how well the overall goals have been attained. These steps can be figured below.

CONCLUSION

By incorporating metacognitive strategies for reading texts into ESP instruction, an ESP teacher will be able to help students become independent learners, monitor their own comprehension, and adjust their reading strategies according to what they read, reading goal, and nature of a text. It is important to note that the development of reading strategy and awareness is a very important element of the reading process. To achieve this end, an extensive reading approach can be included in metacognitive strategy training because students can freely choose their own texts based on their reading goals, needs, level of reading proficiency, and academic needs. Indeed, such training needs a good learning management and takes time, process, and effort in a way that students can become strategic and fluent readers. By allowing students varied opportunities for that kind of training, they will be able to get used to using metacognitive strategies for reading different ESP texts, thereby helping the students succeed in undergraduate programs where most required texts are written in English.

REFERENCES

Abebersold, J., and Field, M. (1997). *From reader to reading teacher*. New York: Cambridge University Press.

Benson, M. J. (1991). University ESL reading: A content analysis. *English for Specific Purposes, 10*, 75-88.

Block, E. (1992). See how they read: Comprehension monitoring of L1 and L2 readers. *TESOL Quarterly, 26*, 319-343.

Carrell, P. L. (1996). *L2 reading strategy training: What is the role of metacognition?* Paper presented at the 30th TESOL Annual Convention, Chicago, IL, 26-30 March.

Carson, J., and Leki, I. (1993). *Reading in the composition classroom*. Boston, MA: Heinle and Heinle.

Chamot, U. A. (1987). The learning strategies of ESL students. In J. Rubin and A. Wenden (Eds.), *Learner strategies in language learning* (pp.71-83). London: Prentice Hall International.

Daoud, M. (1991). *The processing of EST discourse: Arabic and French speakers' recognition of rhetorical relationships in engineering texts*. Unpublished PhD thesis, University of California, Los Angeles.

Devine, J. (1993). The role of metacognition in second language reading and writing. In G. Joan and L. I. Carson (Eds.), *Reading in the composition classroom, second language perspective* (pp. 105-130). Boston, MA: Heinle and Heinle.

Dhieb-Henia, N. (2003). Evaluating the effectiveness of metacognitive strategy training for reading research articles in an ESP context. *English for Specific Purposes, 22*, 387-417.

Dudley-Evans, T. A. (2001). *English for specific purposes: The Cambridge guide to TESOL*. Cambridge: Cambridge University Press.

Eskey, D. E. (1986). Theoretical foundations. In F. Dubin, D. E. Esky, and W. Grabe (Eds.), *Teaching second language reading for academic purposes* (pp. 3-23). Reading, MA: Addison-Wesley.

Flavell, J. H. (1992). Metacognition and cognitive monitoring: A new area of cognitive-development inquiry. In T. O. Nelson (Ed.), *Metacognition: Core readings* (pp.3-8). Boston, MA: Allyn and Bacon.

Flowerdew, J., and Peacock, M. (2001). *Research perspectives on English for academic purposes*. Cambridge: Cambridge University Press.

Fortanet-Gomez, I., and Raisanen, C. A. (2009). ESP in higher European education: Teaching language and content. *English for Specific Purposes, 28*, 211-213.

Garner, R. (1994). Metacognition and executive control. R. B. Ruddell and M. R. Ruddell (Eds.), *Theoretical models and processes of reading* (pp. 715-732). Newark, DE: International Reading Association.

Grabe, W. (1991). Current developments in second language reading research. *TESOL Quarterly, 25*, 375-406.

Hammadou, J. (1991). Interrelationship among prior knowledge, inference and language proficiency in foreign language reading. *The Modern Language Journal, 75*, 23-37.

Hudson, T (1991). A Context comprehension approach and technology to reading English for science. *TESOL Quarterly, 25*, 77-104.

Hyde, A., and Bizar, M. (1989). *Thinking in context*. White Plains, NY: Longman.

Jacobs, J. E., and Paris, S. G. (1987). Children's metacognition about reading: Issues in definition, measurement and instruction. *Educational Psychologist, 22*, 255-278.

Jiménez, R. T., Garcia, G. E., and Pearson, P. D. (1996). The reading strategies of bilingual Latina/o students who are successful English readers: Opportunities and obstacles. *Reading Research Quarterly, 31*, 90-112.

Li, S., and Munby, H. (1996). Metacognitive strategies in second language academic reading: A qualitative investigation. *English for Specific Purposes, 15*, 199-216.

Macaro, E. (2003). *Teaching and learning a second language*: *A guide to current research and its applications*. London: Continuum.

Moghadam, M. K. (2009). *The effect of strategies-based instruction on student's reading comprehension of ESP texts*. Retrieved January 2, 2011, from www.itvgil.ac.ir

O'Malley, J., and Chamot, A. (1990). *Learning strategies in second language acquisition*. Cambridge: Cambridge University Press.

O'Neill, S. P. (1992). Metacognitive strategies and reading achievement among developmental students in an Urban community college. *Reading Horizons, 32*, 316-330.

Shih, M. (1992). Beyond comprehension exercises in the ESL academic reading class. *TESOL Quarterly, 26*, 289-318.

Widodo, H. P., and Pusporini, R. (2010). Materials design: English for specific purposes (ESP). In H. P. Widodo and L. Savova (Eds.), *The Lincom guide to materials design in ELT* (pp. 147-160). Muenchen, Germany: Lincom Europa.

In: Innovation and Creativity in ELT Methodology
Editors: H. P. Widodo and A. Cirocki

ISBN: 978-1-62948-146-3
© 2013 Nova Science Publishers, Inc.

Chapter 6

EXTENSIVE READING IN ENGLISH LANGUAGE TEACHING

Rob Waring

Notre Dame Seishin University, Japan

ABSTRACT

This chapter introduces the idea of Extensive Reading and why it is necessary. The chapter begins by setting out the case, from a vocabulary perspective, why learners cannot avoid Extensive Reading. The frequency of word occurrence and the number of times a word needs to be met shows all learners should be exposed to massive amounts of text. However, typical course books do not cover the required volume of text needed for long-term retention; therefore, complementary input is necessary. The chapter shows how to set up an extensive reading program, and suggests ways to manage the program and get it running effectively.

INTRODUCTION

There was a time, not long ago when most EFL practitioners had not heard of Extensive Reading (ER) or its sister Extensive Listening (EL). Now, this is not the case. In the past two decades, hundreds of research papers and books have been published. Thousands of graded reading materials are now available, and there are numerous websites, courses, symposia, and discussions all promoting Extensive Reading. So, what happened?

Historically in EFL, language teachers were seen as product providers – their job was to teach – and by doing so give information about the vocabulary, the grammar and other systems that make up a language. However, this atomistic approach to EFL instruction did not allow learners to build up their own sense of how the language works as a whole because each element was taught and learned in discrete and mostly abstract ways. In other words, the learners of the "EFL-as-product" era knew a lot *about* English (its vocabulary and grammar, for example), but could hardly communicate using it.

In the 1980's and 1990's, there came the realization that language study should include fluency and be based on communication on top of the "break-the-language-into-pieces-and-teach-the-bits" approach that had been so common until then. This was an improvement, but it meant learners were still largely not expressing themselves, nor necessarily working in their own way. It was still to some extent a dictatorial system directed by the teacher.

In the past two decades, our field has discovered that rather than see a class as a group. It is beneficial to allow learners to explore their own language development and work towards their own goals through discovery, transformation, and creative manipulation of their second language at their own pace. The current boom in Extensive Reading is a by-product and a natural outcome of this vision.

EXTENSIVE READING (ER)

When learners are reading extensively, they are primarily focused on the message of the text and what it is saying. By contrast, *intensive reading* focuses on developing language knowledge and discrete reading skills presented as "language work" to "study" in a reading text. Typical intensive reading passages can be found in course books and "reading skills" texts. The texts are typically short – less than one page of text – and function not only to introduce the unit's theme, but also to present and teach its vocabulary and language points. The result of this is that the texts are often difficult, and the reading is typically slow and often requires dictionary use.

The main aims of extensive reading, by contrast, are to build the learners' fluency, reading speed, and general comprehension of reading texts as well as practicing the skill of reading itself. Typically, learners will be reading a text with a very high percentage of the words already known, so they can read fluently and smoothly with high levels of comprehension. In other words, for this to happen, the learners should READ:

*R*ead quickly and…
*En*joyably with…
*A*dequate comprehension so they…
Do not need a dictionary.

If the learners are reading slowly because unknown language slows them down, it means they have stopped reading for communication (i.e., understanding the content), but have to focus on the language items (words and grammar, for example). In other words, they are "study reading" – not READing. Just as one cannot drive quickly over speed bumps in the road, learners cannot build reading speed or fluency if the text is too difficult. Reading to study language items when learners read intensively is a useful activity. However, there is a time for study, and time for practice just like there is time for driving school and a time for enjoying a drive along the coast on a sunny day. Extensive Reading is the practice time where learners read a lot of easy-to-read texts.

One of the well-known benefits of reading a lot is the effect it has on vocabulary development. The more words a learner meets and the more frequently they are met, the greater the likelihood long-term acquisition will take place. The question is though, how well can learners learn from reading extensively? Estimates of the uptake (learning rate) of vocabulary from reading extensively vary considerably. For example, Dupuy and Krashen (1993) state that 25% of their target words were learned, and in other studies, the figures range from 20% (Horst, Cobb, and Meara, 1998), to 6.1% (Pitts, White, and Krashen, 1989), and to 5.8% (Day, Omura, and Hiramatsu, 1991). More recent estimates put the uptake rate of 25% and 4% (Waring and Takaki, 2003), depending on the type of test used to measure gains. However, it is clear that learners need to meet words numerous times for them to be retained for the long term. Waring and Takaki (2003), for example, suggest that an average word be met more than 25 times for it to be known well enough to understand it and not slow down comprehension when reading. Other research also showed that some words met over a hundred times are still not known. An important point here is that most of the above uptake rates are based on measurements taken immediately after reading or learning. However, when the subjects are given delay tests some weeks or months later, their retention drops precipitously, suggesting their vocabulary knowledge gained while reading was fragile. These data together suggest that learners must read (and listen to) massive amounts of text to not only retain what they know, but to develop it too. This would apply to grammar, phrases, and collocations as much as it does to individual words (Waring, 2009).

The next thing to determine is whether learners are meeting the required volume of language in their course books to ensure that they not only meet words sufficient times, but also retain them for the long-term. Thus, the next questions are: "how much language do learners meet only in their course work?" and "is it sufficient for long-term vocabulary acquisition?" An analysis of a typical 4-skills course book in Waring (2009) showed that 60% of the English words in the 5-level Beginner-to-Intermediate series is made up of function words (e.g., *in*, *of*, *the*, and *under*) and high frequency delexical verbs (e.g., *be*, *go*, *do*, and *have*), which are fairly representative of the language as a whole (Nation, 2001). Waring's analysis shows that 82.88% (Table 1) of the running words in the series are words, which occur more than 51 times, but these actually only account for 400 of the total of 4358 types (different spellings) in the 5 level series. Moreover, 79.21% of the words are from the first 1000 most frequent words in English. This means a smallish vocabulary accounted for the vast majority of the volume of words in a series. 795 types occurred more than 20 times, but accounted for only 18.25% of the total types met in the books. 43.08% of the types were singletons (single occurrence words) and doublets, which are very unlikely to be learned due to their infrequency of occurrence.

Table 1. The percentage of the total number of running words by recurrence rate by frequency band level in sequences (from Waring, 2009, p. 104)

Frequency band	51+	21-50	20-10	9-5	4-3	2-1	Total
1-1000	79.21%	4.49%	1.28%	0.47%	0.12%	0.06%	85.63%
1001-2000	1.91%	1.75%	1.03%	0.62%	0.19%	0.16%	5.67%
2001-3000	0.53%	0.25%	0.48%	0.33%	0.12%	0.12%	1.83%
3001 +	1.22%	1.16%	1.32%	1.21%	0.74%	1.21%	6.87%
Total	82.88%	7.65%	4.11%	2.64%	1.18%	1.54%	100%

The above suggests that if learners want to master many words in their language classes, they will need to meet them repeatedly, but a typical course book series does not give them enough exposure to learn them deeply enough for long-term retention. The obvious conclusion, therefore, is to require learners to read and listen to massive amounts of text *in addition to* their coursework—such as that provided by reading or listening to graded readers.

GRADED READERS

Graded readers are books written at various levels of difficulty from beginner to advanced and are the typical, but not only, materials used for Extensive Reading. A "beginner level" graded reader contains only "beginner" level vocabulary (as few as only 75 different word forms in the entire book) and grammar found in the earliest stages of a course book series as well as having a simple story plot to make the reading easier and manageable at this level. A higher level book will step up the difficulty by adding more advanced grammar and vocabulary, and so on up the levels to the highest level books, which may contain several thousand different words and complex grammar. In this way, beginning level learners would read beginning level books, while intermediates would read materials written at their level too. By choosing a book at the right reading level, the learners can read the book reasonably quickly as they will not be meeting much unknown language, which allows them to build reading speed and fluency. This has the enabling effect of allowing them to read more, which allows them to deepen their knowledge of the language through repetitively meeting words and grammar they met in their course book. Thus, graded readers should be seen as complementary to course books, not as a competition for them.

Graded readers are a valuable resource for learners who can select from a very wide range of age-appropriate materials at all levels, and for all interests. There are currently about 1,500 different titles available in all genres both fact and fiction, and a brief look at any of the major EFL/ESL publisher's catalog will show a list of dozens if not hundreds of graded readers. The vast majority of these come with audio recordings to allow learners to read while listening or just listen if they prefer. This allows learners to choose to just read, read-while listen, or listen only to these books to practice in the way they feel most comfortable.

SETTING UP AN ER PROGRAM

Recently, there has been a growing awareness of the need for learners to have access to comprehensible reading material at or about their language level so that they can develop reading fluency, practice the reading and listening skills, and deepen partially vocabulary and grammar learning. This realization has led many teachers to set up Extensive Reading (ER) programs. Some of these programs have been small and modest – often just one class with a library of a few dozen books. Others are more ambitious and widespread involving whole schools, universities, and even whole school districts with thousands of books and dedicated libraries. Many of these programs are very successful and well run. But sadly, among these programs, there are many that have not lasted, and many programs have faltered. This is not usually from a lack of interest or enthusiasm for ER, but due to inadequate planning, poor execution, or insufficient resources.

This section will provide a roadmap for implementing, maintaining, and running an extensive reading program. First, let us consider what the program will look like when it is up and running. When the program is fully functional, it will:

- be an integral part of the school's curriculum;
- raise the learners' reading ability and general English levels and have knock-on effects on their writing skills, spelling, grammar, and speaking;
- motivate the learners to read and learn from their reading;
- have goals that set out how much reading should be done and by when;
- have a reading library from which learners can select their own texts;
- have systems in place for cataloging, labeling, checking out, recording, and returning the reading materials;
- have a variety of materials to read, not only graded readers, but other simplified materials as well;
- show teachers, parents, and the administration that you take ER seriously;
- have targets of both learner and program attainment that clearly show the success of the program; and
- be bigger and more resilient than one teacher and have sufficient support that it will continue indefinitely.

Preparation of the ER Program

But, how does one get there? Probably the most important piece of advice is to "think big, act small" (Hill, 1997). This means building management and pedagogical systems, which can be expanded or contracted with minimal pain as the program evolves. If a successful program is to prosper, it has to have vision and the will to survive potential threats to its existence.

Among these threats are increases in lost or mislaid materials, insufficient resources to maintain a library, teaching and financial resources being moved to other projects, and a general lessening in enthusiasm after the highs of the "big start." Therefore, the program should be well-planned, but should have built-in flexibility and adaptability for future changes.

The very first step is to find ways that the program will fit within the goals, aims, and objectives of the school; otherwise, the ER program may fail from lack of direction or purpose. Moreover, it needs to not only be part of a larger reading program, but also part of the larger language learning program within the institution because reading extensively should co-exist with "normal course work" as we have seen. There also needs to be instruction and practice in intensive reading and the development of reading strategies and skills, for example. Thus, the key to a successful reading program is striking a good balance of course work and extensive reading. Too much intensive reading leads to not enough work on developing fluency.

Too much extensive reading can lead to a learner not noticing certain language, and too much work only on reading skills will not practice the skill of reading. Not enough work on vocabulary leads to learners who cannot develop their reading fast enough. The balance of these elements for learners at different ability levels must be determined before the programs can take shape.

The next step is to ensure that *everyone* is involved not only in the planning and in the setting up, but also in decisions that are made as a group. If the staff or learners do not feel they have a stake in the program, their lack of commitment may lead to frustration and anger if things do not go well.

It may even result in resentment if it is felt that something is being pushed upon them – especially something that they do not understand, nor care about. This implies a lot of careful groundwork and planning to ensure that everyone involved understands the reasons for the program and its aims, goals, and objectives. This includes the learners and possibly their parents. Experience from countless ER programs shows that the more the learners are involved in the funding, setting up, and running of the library, the higher the chances are that the program will flourish.

After there has been a decision to go ahead, there will need to be funding for reading materials. If the program is using graded readers, there will need to be enough funds not just to buy the initial stock, but to ensure there is follow-up funding for improving the stock and to replace damaged and lost items as well. Most schools and school districts will have a budget for books, but if this is not available, money can be requested from sponsors, parents, or the learners themselves, or raised at school events or by sponsoring learners in a reading marathon, and so on.

There is no need to wait to start ER until the library has hundreds of titles. Initially, the program can start with a bag of books which the teacher takes to class for the learners to read. Learners can share these books. They do not need to buy a new book each time they finish one. The school would have to provide one book per learner (or even one between two if books are shared), and these can be rotated each week at a designated return date. Eventually, the ER program will need three to four books per learner to ensure sufficient variety, range of levels, and interest.

The effective library management of graded readers and other fluency based reading materials needs a lot of forethought and planning specific to each institution or class. Some schools and colleges are lucky enough to have their library keep the books. However, many libraries are too under-resourced to deal with an additional load of books to check-out, check-in, and restock. To get around the resource issue, some schools request the learners to work in the school library to take turns to administer the book lending.

In the absence of support from the school library, teachers will need to set up book management systems, which should be simple and transparent to anyone who picks up a book. The first thing to do is to make a grading scheme so that materials can be graded by difficulty (and age appropriacy). The Extensive Reading Foundation's Grading Scale (see Figure 1), is one commonly used way to level books. Teachers put different colors labels on each book depending on their level. For example, the yellow level might refer to books below 300 headwords, green books may be between 300 and 450. It is not a good idea to code them by the publisher's levels of *elementary*, *intermediate*, and *advanced* because these vary tremendously between publishers.

	Beginner			Elementary			Intermediate			Upper Intermediate			Advanced		
	Alphabet	Early	Mid	High	Early	Mid	High	Early	Mid	High	Early	Mid	High	Early	Mid	High
Headword[1] count	1 — 50	51 — 100	101 — 200	201 — 300	301 — 400	401 — 600	601 — 800	801 — 1000	1001 — 1250	1251 — 1500	1501 — 1800	1801 — 2100	2101 — 2400	2401 — 3000	3001 — 3600	3601 — 4500

Figure 1. The extensive reading foundation's graded reader scale.

Many foreign and second language ER programs use a 6 to 8 level scheme going from the easiest materials to the more difficult. The books and materials can, then, be kept in boxes or on different shelves and should have color tape on the spine for ease of identification.

If the program has too few levels, the gap between levels can be too large and off-putting for learners who need a steady sense of progress and accomplishment. In addition, each book should be numbered and if so desired, coded by its level and book number. Book numbers are necessary to account for multiple copies of titles. For example, a book may be coded *G4070* (G = Green level, 4 = biographies, and 070 is the book number). Other coding schemes can be used to identify class sets of readers, or readers for a particular class or set of classes, or even short term loan books. Whatever the code, it should be clearly visible on the cover and very transparent to everyone, including the learners. There is probably no need to put them in author or book number order, —just drop them in the appropriately color coded box.

The program will need a book borrowing system. It is not a good idea to use an "honor system," as colleagues from around the world report high instances of "lost" or "forgotten" books, so a system needs to be set up. For a single class, this can be as simple as a check-out sheet with the learner's name and book number listed by week (see Figure 2). When books are returned, they are crossed off. Alternatively, a different sheet can be made for each learner that includes the book title, the book number, and the borrowing and return dates (see Figure 3). It is also much easier if all the learners borrow and return books; at the same time, the library can be managed effectively. For example, they could put the returning books in the "drop box" at the beginning of class (or after the time allocated for discussing their reading with others is over). In a quiet moment, the teacher (or the learners in rotation) check off which books have been returned and those which have not. Books should only be returned to the borrowing stock once the books have been crossed off. Teachers will probably want to know which books each learner has read, how many pages, and at which difficulty levels so that they can monitor (or assess) their reading.

Name	April 1	April 8	April 15	April 22	...
Akiyo Nagai	~~G5345~~	~~G2453~~	G3232		
Bert Nuefelt	~~Y1785~~	~~Y2121~~	Y2778		
Shu Wei	P2352	~~P2099~~	G6435		
Carlos Sanchez	~~543~~	~~547~~	444		

Figure 2. A checkout sheet for a single class.

Name *Akiyo Nagai*			**Learner number ...** *032012*	
Title	**Book number**	**Borrowed**	**Returned**	**Comments**
Alice in Wonderland	G5345	April 13	April 16	I really enjoyed this book because....
The green eye	Y1785	April 16		

Figure 3. A check-out sheet for a single learner.

There are many ways to do this, but this is commonly done by requiring learners to write (or give an oral) short report on each book in a notebook, or on a specially prepared questionnaire (examples of these are on the websites described below). However, there are dozens of other ways to assess their reading, such as making posters, drawing a picture of a scene, talking about the characters and the plot, reaction reports, and tests as well if preferred. Alternatively, teachers can use an online system such as that at *www.moodlereader.org* to track their learners' progress.

INTRODUCING THE ER PROGRAM

Once the preparation has been done, teachers will need to introduce the ER program to the learners. However, it should be noted that poorly planned and executed introductions to an ER program is one of the leading reasons for its failure. Many teachers get enthused by ER and tend to force it upon their learners trying to "sell" it and its benefits instead of bringing it slowly and gradually as well as in a well-planned way. Learners tend to be busy, and any idea, no matter how wonderful, will be resisted by learners if they are not doing the reading willingly. Just introducing the reading and making learners take the books home from day one is likely to lead to opposition especially if the work is considered "extra" or because the learners do not know why they are doing it and how it benefits them. The key points for a successful introduction are to start out with easy materials for the whole class and gradually introduce the reading over several weeks. It is best not to introduce the library of books to the learners before they understand what ER is and why it is important. The following is a typical introduction to reading graded materials. The teacher should have multiple copies – one for each learner – of an "introduction book" (one that is very easy for the class) to use to introduce this kind of reading. The teacher shows the book cover to the learners, and the learners guess what it is about and do other pre-reading (non-language based) activities. They read (or read and listen to) the story together as a class for the first say chapter or two – but no more than about 5-8 minutes. The teacher stops them (they close their books), and the learners recall what has already happened and predict what will happen next. The teacher takes back the books and returns them in the following class after the learners have been reminded of their predictions. Then, the next chapters of the book are covered in the same way that the books are taken away and returned. This continues in the same way until the story is finished over several classes. The teacher, then, sets up a discussion about the book focusing on the content, the learners' reactions to it, and their favorite moment or character.

The teacher should *not* test them on the content of the book. By testing their understanding, it gives the message that *all* reading must and will be tested, which goes against the spirit of ER, which is to help learners read for themselves without pressure so that they can build a life-long love of reading in English.

Once the learners have read a book as a class, it is wise to repeat this with two or three more titles so that they get the idea of this type of reading. To ensure a successful launch, it is essential, therefore, that the first book they read together is very easy for most learners so that they will be able to READ it easily. The suitability of the book can be ascertained beforehand by asking a representative lower ability level learner within the class in a private moment whether the book under consideration can be READ easily or not. Some teachers may worry that the learners will not understand the book.

However, if it is established that the book will be easy to read *before* they read it, there is no need to test their comprehension anyway. The point of using easy materials that they can READ quickly with high levels of comprehension is to make learners notice the difference between the intensive reading in their course books and the easy reading of these story books. Once the class has read two or three graded readers as a class as described above, the teacher can introduce the library from which the learners will choose their own individual reading books.

When the teacher introduces the library of graded readers, she or he needs to explain to the learners why Extensive Reading is important and convey this to learners as often they cannot see the benefits of this reading and just see it as yet more homework. Not introducing the library well is the leading cause of failure of ER programs. The learners need to understand that their course book provides them with the new language, but Extensive Reading helps them build their reading speed and automaticity in reading of *already met language* in a pleasurable way.

As we saw above, if they do not read or listen extensively, they cannot build reading speed and gain all the benefits that come from it. Figure 4 can be very helpful for explaining the difference between intensive and extensive reading to learners (based on Welsh, 1997). It is also important for the learners to know how many times they need to meet words to learn them and what that means for the volume of reading they need to do.

Intensive Reading		Extensive Reading
Analysis of the language	WHY?	Fluency, skill forming
Usually difficult	DIFFICULTY?	Very easy
All learners study the same material	WHAT MATERIAL?	All learners read different things (something interesting to them)
Little	AMOUNT?	A book a week
Teacher selects	SELECTION?	Learner selects
In class	WHERE?	Mostly at home and in class
Checked by specific questions	COMPREHENSION?	Checked by reports / summaries

Figure 4. A table for explaining the difference between intensive and extensive reading to learners.

Nishizawa, Yoshioka, and Fukuda (2010) found that Japanese EFL engineering learners of English needed to read 300,000 words to get to the threshold where they were able to read fluently without translation and reach the point at which they felt the true enjoyment of reading in English.

They also found that programs that required less than 100,000 words of reading per semester had little or no effect on the learners' long-term affinity with ER. Learners who read over 1,000,000 words made significant gains (over 200 points) on their TOEIC scores and significantly outscored their age-peers in other disciplines including learners who had studied abroad for ten or more months. Teachers should bear these findings in mind when deciding how much reading needs to be done.

Finding Their Own Reading Level

Once the learners understand the difference between Intensive and Extensive Reading, it is the time to show the library of books they will read from. However, before they select a title to read, they should be made aware that the books are written at varying levels of difficulty, and each learner will need to find his or her own "reading level." One easy way to do this is to spread out the books (color coded as described above) on a table in level order, left to right, and let the learners choose a title they like. They, then, should read a page of a book.

If the material is too difficult (i.e., their reading speed is under 80 words per minute, and if there are more than 1 or 2 unknown words per page, and if they do not have high levels of comprehension), they should choose a book at an easier level. If they feel it is okay, they could try another book at that level to be sure. If they feel a given level is easy, they can then go up levels until they still feel comfortable. If the next level down is also difficult, they should go down again until they find the "right" level.

Once they know their "level," they select a book they want to read at that level and go back to their seat and read it silently until everyone has finished finding a book. Some teachers ask learners to take a vocabulary or reading placement test as an alternative, but there is not always a good correlation between their fluent reading ability and their vocabulary level, so this should be used with caution.

Whichever way is chosen, the learners will need help in finding their comfort level and will need advice about finding suitable material. Therefore, it is important for there to be a sustained silent reading time for 10-15 minutes once every few classes when the learners read their book. At this time, the teacher should go around the class monitoring that they are reading at the right level by talking to each learner individually asking if their book is easy and if they understand it.

If they are not enjoying the book, or it is too difficult, the teacher should recommend them to stop and read something else and maybe come back to it later. To make sure the learners understand what to do and know they are making appropriate choices of both materials and their level, there should be some silent reading time so that teachers can check. Once the teacher is sure, the learners have selected their first book appropriately, the learners can either take this book home to finish or bring it to the next class to continue reading. It is also important that teachers read a large number of the titles in the library so that they can help them to select appropriately. In addition to the above, the learners also need to know:

- the goals of the Extensive Reading program;
- when they have to return books;
- how much they need to read either by number of books or page targets (research suggests a "book a week at their own level" is sufficient);
- how many books they can borrow;
- how their reading will be evaluated (if at all);
- when they have access to the library; and
- whether they have to do follow up exercises or write reports.

CONCLUSION

In contrast to the past, many teachers have now heard of Extensive Reading, but there are still too few teachers that require it for their learners. Extensive Reading is still most often seen as "additional" or "supplemental" to a main program, which can be omitted if time does not allow. This chapter argues that it should be a core part of every language program's curriculum, and all language programs should have an extensive reading component to deepen and enrich the language the learners meet in their coursework. This chapter, also, presents ideas for setting up and running an Extensive Reading program so that this necessary listening and reading may be done.

REFERENCES

Day, R., Omura C., and Hiramatsu, M. (1991). Incidental EFL vocabulary learning and reading. *Reading in a Foreign Language, 7*, 541-551.

Dupuy, B., and Krashen, S. (1993). Incidental vocabulary acquisition in French as a foreign language. *Applied Language Learning, 4*, 55-63.

Hill, D. (1997). Setting up an extensive reading programme: Practical tips. *The Language Teacher, 21*, 17-20.

Horst, M., Cobb T., and Meara, P. (1998). Beyond a clockwork orange: Acquiring second language vocabulary through reading. *Reading in a Foreign Language, 11*, 207-223.

Nation, P. (2001). *Teaching vocabulary in another language*. Cambridge: Cambridge University Press.

Nishizawa, H., Yoshioka, T., and Fukuda, M. (2010). The impact of a four-year extensive reading program. *JALT 2009 proceedings*. JALT: Tokyo.

Pitts, M., White, H., and Krashen, S. (1989). Acquiring second language vocabulary through reading: A replication of the Clockwork Orange study using second language acquirers. *Reading in a Foreign Language. 5*, 271-275.

Waring, R. (2009). The inescapable case for extensive reading. In A. Cirocki (Ed.), *Extensive reading in English language teaching* (pp. 93-112). Muenchen, Germany: Lincom Europa.

Waring, R., and Takaki, M. (2003). At what rate do learners learn and retain new vocabulary from reading a graded reader? *Reading in a Foreign Language, 15*, 130-163.

Welch, R. (1997). Introducing extensive reading. *The Language Teacher, 21*, 51-53.

USEFUL RESOURCES

- List of current graded readers by level: www.robwaring.org/er/scale/ERF_levels.htm
- Rob Waring's ER website: www.robwaring.org/er/
- The Extensive Reading Discussion list groups.yahoo.com/group/ExtensiveReading/
- The Extensive reading website: www.extensivereading.net
- The Extensive Reading Foundation: www.erfoundation.org
- The Extensive Reading Foundation Graded Reader Scale: www.erfoundation.org/erf/node/44

In: Innovation and Creativity in ELT Methodology
Editors: H. P. Widodo and A. Cirocki

ISBN: 978-1-62948-146-3
© 2013 Nova Science Publishers, Inc.

Chapter 7

CREATIVE WRITING WITHIN A REGIONAL CREATIVE WRITING GROUP

Jayakaran Mukundan
Universiti Putra Malaysia, Malaysia

ABSTRACT

This chapter discusses how a loosely organized hence un-established regional group of teachers meets each year to do creative writing both poetry and stories. The group has been together since 2003 and has succeeded in writing stories and poems in ten anthologies; nine of which were published by Pearson-Longman Malaysia. The Regional Creative Writing Group has successfully helped teachers realize their writing potential and probably enabled them to become more confident in teaching writing.

The development of writing skills has expanded in these teachers, but the more important gain is in their awareness of the importance of professional development in their lives.

INTRODUCTION

Writing is not the easiest skill for teachers to teach. One of the reasons is that teachers, especially foreign or second language teachers of English are reluctant writers. When language teachers themselves are reluctant writers, one can imagine the consequences of this on learners.

The questions are "Can these teachers be coerced into writing?" When will this matter occur in classrooms if they are coerced; will they be pro-active and get their learners hooked on writing as well? And, even if there is an attempt to get these teachers to write, what will the approach be?

This chapter will discuss one attempt at getting teachers in the Asian region to write. It will provide an in-depth discussion on how it first started, what the aims of the project were, and the effects of this on the teachers who participated.

THE BACKGROUND TO THE FORMATION OF THE REGIONAL CREATIVE WRITING GROUP – THE INITIAL MEETING IN BANGKOK

It all started in 2003 when a small gathering of teachers within the South East Asian region gathered at the Assumption University, Bangkok, Thailand in Creative Writing Workshops conducted by Alan Maley. The group was small with about twenty teachers. The workshops were well-planned. Prior to the gathering in Bangkok, the participants were asked to write a story and poem in which at the workshops, these poems became fertile avenues for peer revision routines. Apart from peer revision, the participants were also provided input, which basically introduced form poem patterns and other techniques of invention, which depended on scaffolding or support.

The word "invention" became a keyword at this first attempt at getting teachers to write. In fact, it was the emergence of inventive approaches to poetry that kept this group together. As many of the teacher-writers were from countries like Thailand, Myanmar, Vietnam, Cambodia, Lao PDR, and Indonesia (where English is a foreign language), one common characteristic of the group was that they needed support – and this support took the form of input, which was provided by the key facilitator, Alan Maley. As a writer of teacher resource books (mostly on poetry and the teaching of it), he provided the initial scaffolding for them to initiate writing, and then start inventing on their own. The end result of the first workshop was phenomenal. Every member of the group was a contributor, and most members of the group passed in work (both poems and short stories), which exceeded the minimum that was expected of them.

TEACHERS SUPPORTING TEACHERS: THE REGIONAL CREATIVE WRITING GROUP MOVES

After the Bangkok workshops, the group met in Melaka, Malaysia (2004); Fuzhou, PR China (2005); Hanoi, Vietnam (2006); Salatiga, Indonesia (2007); Kathmandu, Nepal (2008), Ho Chi Minh City, Vietnam (2009); and Jakarta, Indonesia (2009). One of the reasons that the group was successful in having the workshops at least once a year is that the writers themselves were committed to both their individual pursuits in becoming better writers and that the group aim was to consolidate and strengthen the group. Some writers volunteered to organize the event in their home countries, and this led to the workshops being held in different parts of Asia.

The rationale for the activities of the group can be summarized as follows:

- The belief in the value of creative writing in English both for teachers and eventually their students;
- The belief in teachers that they should be writers, and they can be writers;
- The belief that these materials will provide useful input for promoting reading and other activities in English; and
- The belief in the value of professional and personal development.

THE CHALLENGES FACED BY THE GROUP IN THE BEGINNING YEARS

While the idea of starting the group was noble, there remained challenges that had to be given immediate attention. The first challenge was in the composition of the group itself. Teacher-writers came from diverse backgrounds, and typically they comprised people from ESL (English as a second language) and EFL (English as a foreign language) countries. Therein lay the problem. There were teachers who had near-native proficiency in the English language, and these were teachers, mostly from places where English was regarded ESL (e.g., Singapore, Nepal, Hong Kong, and Malaysia). Then, there were teachers from foreign language contexts who had opportunities to pursue postgraduate degrees in English speaking countries like the UK, Australia, and USA and were proficient in the use of the English language. There were, however, a reasonably large number of teachers with low proficiency levels; their writing was in most ways affected by poor language use.

There were problems trying to get across the core objective of the group to those members who were already fluent in the language, which was to get them to accept the fact that if the group was to serve the region, there had to be sacrifices made, and those who were not fluent in the language had to be assimilated into the group and provided more attention. Some members of the group who were near-native speakers, initially, complained that they were disadvantaged because they were coaching the weaker ones rather than finding critical peers during the revision process. This soon became a thing of the past as the group continued to function, and dissenter to the group view sometimes left the group, but came back after a while and adopted the notion of regional goals rather than individual (perhaps selfish) ones.

THE MAGIC OF THE CREATIVE WRITING GROUP: WHAT CONTRIBUTED TO THE MAGIC?

This Creative Writing Group was somewhat like a loose gathering of teachers without any formal or rigid structure and system for operation. The participants pay their airfares only as all other expenses are covered by the host country. The facilitators (Alan Maley and I) had control over the schedule for the 3-day program. This enabled the facilitators to place more emphasis on input, especially when the group conducted its activities in countries where English was a foreign language, and teachers themselves had problems with writing. Even then, the group has managed to get the participants to write and publish their products. Prior to the meeting, the participants were asked to write at least 2 poems (one form and one free poem) and 2 stories (one a 600-word story and the other a story of between 1500-2000 words). These products are usually to be sent at least a month before the 3-day meeting. A typical three-day workshop for teachers generally constitutes the following:

Day 1. Poetry: Input by facilitators – scaffolding techniques (3 word poems, acrostics, stem poems, etc.). The emphasis at first is on form poems – teachers become comfortable with these, and then they start writing free poems a bit later. Teacher-writers very easily learn from patterns and become comfortable. For example, teachers are asked to write 3-word poems featuring animals in noun/verb/adverb formation, and they quite easily produce poems like these:

Bees	Ducks
Buzz	Dive
Busily	Deep

Poems can also be taught to beginner poets by way of use of "stems." These stems provide the scaffolding required for inexperienced writers. One way is to provide stems to sense poems, which allow the writers to explore the five senses through themes:

When I think of a ...
I can see...
I can smell...
I can feel...
I can taste...

Day 1. It ends with peer review sessions, and teachers work in pairs and review poems written and handed in before the 3-day meeting.

Day 2. Travel writing – an excursion is planned where the participants are taken to some unique place – usually a monastery or an ancient historical site where they write from close observation. The writing usually starts as soon as they board a bus and this, according to the facilitators, is amazing. As soon as the bus starts moving, note pads are out, and the participants start jotting notes in them. Photography is encouraged, and when writers find good themes, they often incorporate texts or poetry with visual capture. On the return journey, writers read poetry they have started working (work in progress) on the bus, and this takes place right up to arrival at their accommodation (usually a budget hotel or university guest house).

Day 3. It includes report of observations during the travel writing phase, reading of poetry, and perhaps experimentation with variations of Japanese poems like the *Haibun*. Then, peer review of stories begins. Teachers work in pairs and review each others' stories. The day ends with round-up of the entire 3-day event and discussion of future possibilities.

Usually after the 3-day event, the teacher participants volunteer to do papers or workshops in a local 2-day seminar/conference organized by the entire group for local teachers.

Usually about 250-300 teachers attend. The members of the group, usually, provide input on idea generation in creative writing. After the 3-day event (and the 2-day conference), the participants leave for their home countries. They are given deadlines for submission of their final drafts.

The next stage will be for the facilitators (Alan Maley and I) to make the products ready for submission to the editors in Pearson-Longman. Usually, all the work submitted is accepted and published after a lengthy review process.

THE ACHIEVEMENTS OF THE REGIONAL CREATIVE WRITING GROUP

There is no need for a formal evaluation of the group and its activities, and this chapter does not attempt to do that either. In this section, critical discussions take place on the founding rationale and how the group fares in this.

The Belief in the Value of Creative Writing in English both for Teachers and eventually Their Students

The group members were convinced of the value of creative writing, and this was clear in the papers produced by individual teachers from the group, which were published in two volumes: *Creative Writing in EFL/ESL Classrooms* (Tin, 2004) and *Creative Writing in EFL/ESL Classrooms II* (Mukundan, 2006). Many of these teachers started developing their own philosophies on creative writing, and this was evident in the many papers written by members on what they think creative writing is. Doa thi Kim Khanh and Nguyen thi Hoai An, group members from Vietnam attempt to define creativity as a process of combining contrastive elements: common and uncommon ideas, imagination and courage, and private voice and public voice (Khanh and An, 2004). They believe that many of their learners, especially from their Vietnamese context will be safe in their writing than take risks and in saying so that they state very clearly in their article that "teachers need to experience creativity before teaching it" (p. 9). This is a clear indication of the success of the Regional Creative Writing Group in making teachers aware of the value of Creative Writing to them, not just their learners. The value of creative writing to teachers can also be measured, especially if it is measured from a pre- to post-experience. Writers who never missed a single workshop (there was one workshop almost every year), had at least fourteen poems and seven short stories published in anthologies. This was evidence that the main value of creative writing within the Regional Creative Group is that it has changed the perception of teachers that their own writing stops after college or university and much as they believe that expository essays of college and university days cannot have a significant presence in situations where they work (as teachers); it can be in the form of invention in creative writing, which ends in publishing. With the exception of the facilitator (Alan Maley), none of the others had reported writing any poetry in the past. Now, all of them have published poems in anthologies (see, for example, Maley and Mukundan, 2005, 2008, 2009; Maley, Mukundan, and Rai, 2009). Some teachers have even started their students on creative writing and published their work (Lin, 2006).

The Belief in Teachers that They Should Be Writers and They Can Be Writers

This rationale was fully realized, but more than achieving this is the awareness of what constitutes writing in the new perspective that ought to be subscribed by teachers. The emergence of portfolio based writing and evaluation (Burnham, 1996) has changed the way some writing teachers who adopted it viewed writing – they now feel that writing can have a bigger utilitarian value – what one writes one does so for the purpose of publishing. The creative writers in the Regional Creative Writing Group can, now, see the philosophies behind approaches such as portfolio writing and evaluation from a personal viewpoint as writers. They now know that when they write, they are doing so for the purpose of publishing (they are informed of the group's association with Pearson-Longman Malaysia who has agreed to publish the work of the teachers). These teachers also soon become aware of the need for discipline and endurance if their work is to be published. Discipline is of utmost importance as works not regarded as ready for publication will be rejected either by the facilitators (Alan being the main editor at this stage) or the Pearson editorial team (which can be very ruthless and uncompromising). Endurance can lead the writer to keep working on rejected pieces until success is achieved. This Regional Creative Writing Group is probably one of the few in the world that has enabled teachers who have never published their work to continuously write and publish year after year. Ever since the start of the workshops, there have been ten anthologies of teacher-writers' work published; nine of which have been published by Pearson-Longman Malaysia:

Asian Stories for Young Readers: Volume 1 (Maley and Mukundan, 2005)
Asian Stories for Young Readers: Volume 2 (Maley and Mukundan, 2005)
Asian Poems for Young Readers: Volume 3 (Maley and Mukundan, 2005)
Asian Short Stories for Young Readers: Volume 4 (Maley, 2007)
Asian Poems for Young Readers: Volume 5 (Maley, 2007)
Asian Short Stories for Young Readers: Volume 6 (Maley and Mukundan, 2008)
Asian Poems for Young Readers: Volume 7 (Maley and Mukundan, 2008)
Asian Short Stories for Young Readers: Volume 8 (Maley and Mukundan, 2009)
Asian Poems for Young Readers: Volume 9 (Maley and Mukundan, 2009)

There is also a volume published by a Nepali publisher, Bhundipuran Prakashan:

Life in Words and Words in Life: Poems and Stories for Asian students
(Maley, Mukundan, and Rai, 2009)

The impressive ten volumes show the impact of the group in transforming teachers into teacher-writers. As individuals, teachers have achieved almost one hundred percent acceptance from the publisher. Teachers who attend every workshop get, at least, one story and two poems published each year. Hoai An, a teacher writer from Vietnam, for instance, published at least one story for every workshop she has attended:

For the Future (Volume 1)
Nam (Volume 2)
The Canine Rescuer (Volume 4)
Warmth for a Small Soul (Volume 6)

She also had poems published in all the poetry anthologies. The impact of the group and its activities has probably in many ways changed the way she has viewed writing. She probably views going to these workshops as an opportunity for further publication and further growth as a teacher-writer.

The Belief That These Materials Will Provide Useful Input for Promoting Reading and Other Activities in English

Some people believe that teachers intuitively know what their learners need and want. This is quite true in the case of the teachers and their work in the Regional Creative Writing Group. The teachers in the group were not provided conditions before they embarked on their writing. Despite this, they managed to write for their audience (their students). This would make their products become useful input for promoting reading within their own teaching situations. Mukundan and Aziz (2008) did content analysis studies of stories written by teachers in the group in Volumes 1 and 2 and found that most of the stories were in the fairly easy range (70-80) on the Flesch Reading Ease Formula and pitched at learners in Asian countries who would be in the early years of secondary schooling.

Mukundan and Aziz (2008) also analyzed the stories in Volumes 1-4 to see if aspects of Lifetime Developmental Tasks (Havighurst, 1972) were considered by the teachers. Lifetime Developmental Tasks are those in which young adults should involve themselves if they are to become balanced individuals cognitively, morally, and affectively, and able to assimilate into adult life in ways that are expected by society. Again, although writing is intuitive without explicit awareness of developmental tasks, these teachers produced stories, which at least considered one of the following tasks outlined by Havighurst:

- achieving new and more mature relations with age mates;
- achieving proper masculine or feminine social role;
- adapting to physical changes and using body effectively;
- achieving emotional independence from parents and other adults;
- preparing for marriage and family;
- preparing for an economic career;
- acquiring a personal ideology or value system; and
- achieving social responsibility.

Most of the tasks have, at least, three developmental tasks featured while some have even up to six out of the eight tasks incorporated. A remarkable thing happens, it seems, when teachers write for their audiences. They seem to have an intuitive sense of themes that are necessary and that will appeal and even engage learners.

The Belief in the Value of Professional and Personal Development

To what extent these teacher-writers will benefit from involvement in the group in terms of professional and personal development can only be fully illustrated if long-term studies are conducted, which enable researchers to map indications of cognitive and affective growth and all other aspects of it. Despite the lack of research on the effects the group have on the professional and personal development of teachers, the following assumptions can be made:

1. Personal growth, especially from the perspective of growth as writers will take a steep climb up the levels of competency. Most of the teacher-writers will have

accumulated mileage in terms of revision and editing sessions with peers and facilitators, something that will never happen in their work situations where they will, in most cases, be only involved in grading student compositions.

2. Professional development of teachers, which is sometimes not very common in developing countries due to budget constraints, can have negative effects on teachers. The Regional Creative Writing Group, however, gets teachers' self-esteem high, makes them become more confident and brings about awareness that there are opportunities to continuously upgrade their professional skills.

IMPLICATIONS OF THE ACTIVITIES OF THE CREATIVE WRITING GROUP ON INDIVIDUALS

Writing teachers must be writers, and this has been the belief held by most teachers involved in the Regional Creative Writing Group. Many of the teachers involved in the group from the beginning consider writing to be year round activity. They also have begun to accept the notion of their roles being closer to that of the roles of professional writers in society – that they may be teachers, but they write for real audiences, have good opportunities to publish their work, are aware of the possibilities of rejection and frustration, and are constantly made aware of the realities in writing of this nature, which is governed by deadlines and discipline.

The teachers, many of whom were only exposed to poetry, which was tested in public examinations like the General Certificate of Examination (GCE) O, or A levels had developed phobias for poetry. These teachers were forced to study Tennyson, Yeats, Wordsworth, and many other poets who they thought were difficult.

I am one of those who were also resistant to poetry for the same reason. The notion of poetry as "play" as encouraged by this group soon changed the writer's view of poetry, and this slow immersion into creative poetry via play soon paid dividends. There was a lot more poetry produced by these teachers.

Even, the aspect of discipline soon registered in their minds – especially when they played with *haiku*. Many realized that it was so easy to write a bad haiku even when the syllable counts were right.

The teachers also developed as story writers. Many started off as not having a clue about what makes stories. Some realized this the hard way. They wrote descriptive essays rather than stories.

The facilitators were mindful of this and provided a lot of models in the beginning. This developed in these teachers the notion that stories are not commentaries. Soon a few teachers developed an eye for establishing conflict and conflict resolution – something missing in their writing previously.

Most of the teachers also realized the vast amount of background experiences they could tap on for their stories. I was one of those when I incorporated ideas from my early childhood living with my immigrant Indian parents in a rubber plantation run by the English. This tapping in on background knowledge enabled me to write many stories and poems on that theme.

IMPLICATIONS OF THE ACTIVITIES OF THE CREATIVE WRITING GROUP ON THE TEACHING PROFESSION

The teaching profession will, definitely, gain from projects such as this. First, this project is in no way connected to mainstream activities in professional development that teachers are usually associated with. This is a very specialized and unique form of professional development that motivates teachers intrinsically (because they know of the transformations going through them and are aware of it) and extrinsically (they are aware of the rewards that come with publishing).

The experiences gained by the teachers within the group will also make them good on their jobs. As writers, they will become more aware of the problems faced by their student-writers. This project might also encourage them to start their own creative writing workshops for their students (this has already been done by some teachers within the group.)

IMPLICATIONS OF THE INFLUENCES OF THE CREATIVE WRITING GROUP ON THE TEACHING OF CREATIVE WRITING IN SCHOOLS

There will be far-reaching consequences of this project on teachers, especially in the way they conduct themselves when they are teaching creative writing in classrooms. Some of the possible changes that can take place in classrooms include the following:

1. Changes in the way teachers conduct themselves – many teachers who previously were authoritative in their approach to teaching writing will feel the niceness of the new approaches they have experienced within the Creative Writing Group, responsive in nature. Writers are encouraged to ask, and facilitators respond to them in a friendly manner.
2. Teachers in the group have realized that "timed writing" is never encouraged within the group. No writer is subjected to handing in work immediately after a session. There are deadlines, but these take into consideration the needs of the writers. The writers are always consulted before deadlines are set.
3. Teachers will learn from the group that peer collaboration is very much an important part of the writing routines. Peer-review sessions may feature more in their classrooms.
4. Teachers will feel empowered from the success they have had in getting their writing published. This may induce teachers to exploit aspects of extrinsic motivation of learners within their own settings. Although getting commercial publishers to publish students' work may not be possible, there may be attempts made by teachers to send students' work to the local publisher who can do a budget production. Some teachers may also realize that publishing from the larger sense of the word can also incorporate such things as wall mounts of successful writing.
5. Teachers will have a wider perspective of what creative writing encompasses. Their new experiences within the group will inform them that creative writing is a wide area where poetry and prose can come in a large variety of forms. Teachers after experiencing this within the group will have more ideas, and this will lead them into

exposing poetry form humble stem poem formation to sophisticated *haiku* and *haibun* and free poems. The short story will take different meaning with the introduction of mini saga and flash fiction into classrooms.

6. Teachers will understand how important it is for learners to write after close observation. They may, then, get learners to spend more time outside classrooms so that they can explore through close observation aspects of the environment they want to write about.

7. Teachers may as a result of influences of this group encourage their learners to start their own creative writing groups.

CONCLUSION

There have been attempts to formally establish this group. So far, this has not happened. And while it still stands as a loose grouping of teacher-writers from the region, it has, nevertheless, been a champion for creative writing among teachers. There is no other similar group operating like this anywhere in the world. Perhaps, the magic of the success of the group is due to its "looseness." Unlike formal organizations where people sometimes fight for positions, this Creative Writing Group has no such problems. There are no elected office bearers, only facilitators who are in that position because of their experience. Writers can either remain or leave the group. Some writers may choose to leave the group for a while and then return after a few years. This has, indirectly, had an effect on the writers – they know that any future involvement in the activities of the group will depend entirely on their own levels of enthusiasm.

REFERENCES

Burnham. C. (1996). Portfolio evaluation: Room to breathe and grow. In B. Leeds (Ed.), *Writing in a second language: Insights from first and second language teaching and research* (pp.190-199). New York: Longman.

Havighurst, R. (1972). *Developmental tasks and education*. New York: David McKay.

Khanh, D. T. K., and An, N. T. H. (2004). Creativity and creative writing. In T. B. Tin (Ed.), *Creative writing in EFL/ESL classrooms* (pp.1-9). Serdang, Malaysia: UPM Press.

Lin, L. (2006). Using creative writing as a pre-class activity in the ESL classroom. In J. Mukundan (Ed.), *Creative writing in EFL/ESL classrooms II* (pp.8-19). Petaling Jaya, Malaysia: Pearson-Longman.

Maley, A. (Ed.) (2007). *Asian short stories for young readers: Volume 4*. Petaling Jaya, Malaysia: Pearson-Longman.

Maley, A. (Ed.). (2007). *Asian poems for young readers: Volume 5*. Petaling Jaya, Malaysia: Pearson-Longman.

Maley, A., and Mukundan, J. (Eds.). (2005). *Asian stories for young readers: Volume 1*. Petaling Jaya, Malaysia: Pearson-Longman.

Maley, A., and Mukundan, J. (Eds.). (2005). *Asian stories for young readers: Volume 2*. Petaling Jaya, Malaysia: Pearson-Longman.

Maley, A., and Mukundan, J. (Eds.). (2005). *Asian poems for young readers: Volume 3.* Petaling Jaya, Malaysia: Pearson-Longman.

Maley, A., and Mukundan, J. (Eds.). (2008). *Asian short stories for young readers: Volume 6.* Petaling Jaya, Malaysia: Pearson-Longman.

Maley, A., and Mukundan, J. (Eds.). (2008). *Asian poems for young readers: Volume 7.* Petaling Jaya, Malaysia: Pearson-Longman.

Maley, A., and Mukundan, J. (Eds.) (2009). *Asian short stories for young readers: Volume 8.* Petaling Jaya, Malaysia: Pearson-Longman.

Maley, A., and Mukundan, J. (Eds.). (2009). *Asian poems for young readers: Volume 9.* Petaling Jaya, Malaysia: Pearson-Longman.

Maley, A., Mukundan, J., and Rai, V.S. (Eds.). (2009). *Life in words and words in life: Poems and stories for Asian students.* Kathmandu, Nepal: Bhundipuran Prakashan.

Mukundan, J. (Ed.). (2006). *Creative writing in EFL/ESL classrooms II.* Petaling Jaya, Malaysia: Pearson-Longman.

Mukundan, J., and Aziz, A. (2008). *The development of young adult readers: An Asia-Pacific experiment.* Unpublished Research Report.

Tin, T. B. (Ed.). (2004). *Creative writing in EFL/ESL classrooms.* Serdang, Malaysia: UPM Press.

In: Innovation and Creativity in ELT Methodology
Editors: H. P. Widodo and A. Cirocki

ISBN: 978-1-62948-146-3
© 2013 Nova Science Publishers, Inc.

Chapter 8

TEACHING ACADEMIC LITERACY: RAISING GENRE AWARENESS IN A GRADUATE SCHOOL OF EDUCATION

Mary Jane Curry and Hee-Jeong Oh

University of Rochester, US

ABSTRACT

Learning academic literacy in English requires understanding and gaining practice with a considerable range of writing genres, which vary across geographical and disciplinary contexts. In this chapter, we present an approach to teaching about the genres in circulation in a U.S. graduate school of education, exemplified by extracts from doctoral student writing. We describe some of the teaching activities we use in writing workshops with graduate students, focusing, in particular, on reflective genres that were new to students. We end by suggesting some ways that students (and their teachers) located outside of Anglophone contexts might be able to expand their awareness of the range of genres in circulation in the contexts which they anticipate joining.

INTRODUCTION

Between 1999 and 2007, the number of internationally mobile students increased by 53% to around 2.8 million (UNESCO, 2009). While three of the top five destinations are Anglophone—the United States, the United Kingdom, and Australia—increasingly, universities situated outside of Anglophone contexts are offering English medium programs (Brock-Utne, 2007). Many multilingual students will, therefore, need to use English to write academic papers or essays, examinations, theses, and dissertations. However, the discursive requirements of higher education vary considerably across transnational contexts and across disciplines. In this chapter, we, thus, explore how to prepare multilingual students for the range of English academic literacy practices they will find in new contexts.

We begin by situating ourselves theoretically, and then briefly present three approaches to teaching English academic writing or literacies. Next, we propose a genre approach to helping students learn foundational aspects of academic writing: rhetorical purpose, text structure, audience, and register. At the same time, we situate this approach in an academic literacies perspective (Lea and Street, 2006), which enables the problematizing of academic literacies, that is, consideration of the social contexts and power dimensions of academic literacies, and the ways in which students' identities are engaged in literacies within particular contexts. Without a critical dimension, genre approaches risk transmitting what can appear as static models of writing that are decoupled from their social contexts (Morgan, 2009). And although much research and advice about academic writing is concerned with improving the mechanics and surface level features of student writing, here we focus on genres as a "way in" for students to understand and critique the practices and values of academic communities. Because the number of genres in circulation across contexts is infinite, we do not pretend to address all genres. Instead, we exemplify our approach by: (1) reporting on writing workshops that Curry developed at the Warner School and (2) providing writing samples from four multilingual doctoral students in education that illustrate the genres of critical commentary, reflections or journal entries, and portfolio narratives (a particular kind of reflection).

We choose these genres because they stand in contrast to more common essayist or expository genres, and they were unfamiliar to these students before coming to the Warner School. The experiences of these doctoral students highlight that while most multilingual graduate students enter our programs highly proficient in English, students vary in previous experience with English medium academic literacies. We conclude by considering how teachers across contexts might adapt this approach.

THEORETICAL FRAMEWORK

Over the past few decades, the "social turn" in writing studies has changed conceptions of writing from a solitary activity based on individual cognition and linguistic competence to the view that writing entails participating in the practices emerging from specific sociopolitical contexts (Barton and Hamilton, 1998; Lillis and Curry, 2010). In contrast to approaches that aim to teach writing by focusing on discrete "skills" (Curry, 2003), the "academic literacies" perspective signals that writing and reading are social practices embedded within the intersections of language, culture, identity, and power relations (Lea and Street, 2006)—and it avoids viewing students through a deficit lens (Lillis and Scott, 2007). The plural form "literacies" indicates the centrality of the multiple modes and communicative activities that go beyond the notion of literacy as text (Lillis and Scott, 2007).

Pedagogically, the field has shifted from a product focused prescriptivism to a more open exploration of the forms, purposes, and power dynamics inherent in academic writing (Curry, 2004). For multilingual students, these power dynamics include the global status of English— whether it has, indeed, become an "academic *lingua franca*" (Pakir, 2009) and its role in student mobility.

For teachers, while shifting to teaching literacy practices or genres may be challenging, it may also help students engage more deeply with the kinds of academic texts they will write in new locations, particular disciplines, or other purposes, and it creates spaces in which students can consider the interplay of language, education, power, and identity.

THREE APPROACHES TO TEACHING ACADEMIC WRITING

Much research has been conducted, and advice has been presented on how to teach writing; this overview, therefore, sketches out only some of the existing approaches and perspectives. Approaches to teaching academic writing can be broadly categorized as focusing on 1) text, 2) process, and 3) social practice (for extended discussion, see Casanave, 2004; Coffin, Curry, Goodman, Hewings, Lillis, and Swan, 2003). Text focused approaches, traditionally, concentrate on rhetorical structure, argument, language, and mechanics (punctuation, spelling, and grammar), often from a perspective that considers these aspects of writing as discrete skills that can be learned outside of particular contexts (Curry, 2003; but see Swales and Feak, 2004, for a text focused approach based on particular disciplines). More recently, genre approaches, while also text focused, are grounded in the understanding that writing takes place in social contexts for specific purposes and audiences (Widodo, 2006). As Dudley-Evans notes, "genre analysis provides a way of introducing and discussing the expectations of the academic community in general and the discourse community that the students aspire to join" (1995, p. 6). Characterizing genre approaches is not simple; Hyon (1996) maps out "three traditions" of genre emerging from differing academic disciplines and geo-historical locations: systemic functional linguistics, English for academic purposes (EAP), and rhetoric or composition studies. Some approaches also pay attention to the skills underpinning traditional text focused approaches as parts of broader understandings of purposes and audiences (see Hyland, 2004).

In process approaches, writing comprises an iterative cycle that entails stages of pre-writing (with strategies for writers to identify prior knowledge, build knowledge, and develop ideas), drafting (multiple times), and revising text in response to feedback from peers and experts (see Coffin, Curry, Goodman, Hewings, Lillis, and Swann, 2003). Although the process approach has been criticized for a heavy focus on personal expression, its component steps are useful in demystifying writing and reducing students' anxiety. Along with Badger and White (2000), we see the process and genre approaches as complementary rather than conflicting. That is, a (critical) genre approach can develop students' awareness of text types and the contexts in which they are written; at the same time, a process approach can help students to instantiate genres.

Finally, social practice approaches—including academic literacies, as discussed above—while including aspects of the foregoing approaches, centrally emphasize the situated and social nature of academic communication (Barton and Hamilton, 1998) and adopt an "ideological stance [which is] explicitly *transformative* rather than *normative*" (Lillis and Scott, 2007, p. 12). This perspective rests on the understanding that language and literacy involve power dynamics; for example, academic discourse functions as a gatekeeper to and within higher education (Curry, 2001).

Approaches that share this transformative commitment include critical EAP (e.g., Benesch, 2001; Canagarajah, 2002)—which also highlights how student identities are constructed in relation to social practices, specific communities, and power dynamics—and critical literacy, which aims to engage students in social activism (Morrell, 2008).

TEACHING THE GENRES OF EDUCATION

We, now, turn to present our approach. First, a starting point for academic writing is reading, specifically, deconstructing texts (Hirvela, 2004). Students tend to enter graduate programs highly proficient at reading for content; they can identify the main message or research findings in an article or book.

Our first writing workshop centers on the deconstruction of sample texts to help students move from reading primarily for content to becoming able to: (1) identify how an author locates the text in the academic (sub)field by discussing and referencing previous work; (2) construct an argument; (3) use theory and evidence; and (4) make use of other aspects of research articles (see *Teaching Activity 1).*

The second workshop helps students identify and analyze the genres common in the graduate school of education. (We present these early workshops as the foundation of this genre based approach; subsequent workshops cover the writing of critiques, literature reviews, and extended texts such as theses, dissertations, and conference abstracts or proposals.)

Teaching Activity 1. Analyzing Academic Texts

In the "Critically Reading Academic Texts" workshop, we provide techniques for reading for argument, structure, rhetorical moves, use of evidence, and understanding how language accomplishes these textual dimensions.

First, students are given the handout reproduced in Table 1, which prompts them to read for a purpose and to engage with the text at the level of structure rather than word by word. After whole-group discussion of the points on the handout, students work individually to apply this technique to the introduction and subheadings of a published research article. Then, in small groups, students apply the technique to three sections of the body of the text and the conclusion, and finally summarize these sections for the entire group.

After deconstructing the published article, workshop participants discuss how this approach can help scholars or students select the most relevant articles from the vast quantity of academic literature.

Next, they work with the guiding questions presented in Table 2, which aim to help them develop nuanced understandings and intuitions about academic texts, the authority that authors claim, and ways that readers engage with text.

Students begin by identifying obvious sources of information; often someone also suggests more sophisticated approaches. For example, to answer question one, a reader might check the author's institutional affiliation and, if included, a biographical sketch that indicates an author's position or rank.

A more experienced reader will also check the references to see if the author has self cited and/or includes co-authors familiar to the reader, as self references establish an author's reputation in a field and contribute to the text's authoritative ethos.

Table 1. An approach to reading academic texts (handout)

Step 1. Skim the following parts of the article.

- Publication information: author, contact information, year, title, source (e.g., journal, book, or encyclopedia);
- Abstract: may state broader or narrower contexts, purpose, methods, and conclusions (perhaps challenging existing views or proposing something new);
- Headings/subheadings: a road map to the structure of the text;
- References: establish credibility; identify influences on author's thinking and those with whom he or she is in conversation;
- Introduction: may change shape from broad to narrow; may situate research in larger social context; may state research questions or purpose; may give rationale or explanation for research; may state "gap" in research (Swales, 1990); may introduce claims and evidence;
- Conclusion: may reiterate research question or purpose, claims and evidence; may suggest directions for future research; and
- Main text/body: states and elaborates on claims and evidence.

Step 2. When you finish reading, think about what stays in your mind. What questions arise?

Step 3. Read the entire text closely—if possible, and if you have determined that it is worthwhile to do so—and try to answer your questions.

Table 2. Guiding questions for academic reading

1. Who is the author of the text?
2. What kind of authority does she or he have? How do you know?
3. What can you tell about the author's opinions, positions, etc.?
4. Identify any words or phrases that indicate the author's subjectivity.
5. Who appears to be the audience or "ideal reader" for this text? How can you tell?
6. What is the purpose of the text? What are its goals? What is its argument or message?
7. What is excluded, or not discussed in the text? Is this exclusion stated explicitly? If not, why do you think something might be excluded?
8. What questions do you have after reading the texts? What, if any, arguments or agreements do you have with the author?

Teaching Activity II. Developing Genre Awareness

In the second workshop, "Genres of Academic Writing," we use Chapter 1 of Roe and den Ouden (2003), which presents examples from genres including real estate advertisements, poems, wedding invitations, personal advertisements, and catalog copy. Identifying these diverse genres enables participants to articulate their intuitive understandings of genres operating in our daily lives. Workshop participants, then, brainstorm the range of academic genres they have written so far in graduate school or have heard about but not yet attempted, as listed in three categories in Table 3, analytic, reflective, and professional—although in some cases the professional genres are incorporated into course assignments.

Table 3. Academic genres at the warner school

Analytic	Reflective	Professional/Public
annotated bibliography book review comprehensive examination (for doctoral students) critical commentary (summary/ critique/analysis) doctoral dissertation/thesis email ethnography literature review master's essay presentation (in classes) summary and synthesis term/research paper transcription (of audio or video tapes) video analysis	autoethnography blog posts personal narrative (for master's teaching certificate and doctoral portfolio) reflection/journal entry	abstract (conference, paper, article) journal article (for publication) poster presentation proposal (e.g., research, conference, grant) report speech/talk

Teaching Activity III. Analyzing Genres

We use the categories presented in Table 4 as a heuristic to help participants explore these genres and the interpretive contexts for these texts. (In the following section, we provide extracts from sample student texts.)

The category of "purpose" focuses students' attention on reasons for writing a text—both immediate, such as a course assignment, and implicit, as in the instructor's reasons for assigning a particular genre. The category of "audience," while often indexing an instructor, may include secondary audiences such as peers or entirely different audiences such as the faculty evaluators of portfolios submitted by master's students (for teaching certification) and doctoral students (after one year of full-time study).

The "argument or claims" category is perhaps the most familiar as it covers a text's knowledge and propositional content. In the category of "register/style," we aim to highlight language use in terms of (in)formality, hedging, pronominal usage, lexis, and disciplinary terminology—all aspects that help characterize particular genres (see Coffin et al., 2003). Agreeing with Chapman that "any consideration of form should be descriptive rather than prescriptive" (1999, p. 484), we hold an open ended discussion of how these texts function in academic communication, including the power dynamics involved in writing for professors as one kind of audience. In addition to exploring the categories in Table 4, participants discuss the paper's format, the use of footnotes or endnotes, reference style, and other features.

Table 4. Heuristic for analyzing academic genres

Type of text (sample genres)	Purpose	Audience	Argument/claims	Register/style
Critical commentary/ response paper	Identify key points in an argument and discuss their significance Highlight strengths and weaknesses in the argument or extend it.	Instructor Peers Members of online discussion forum or blog, e.g., in a particular class	Signal the writer's perspective Deconstruct the underlying assumptions of the argument Raise issues and problems Evaluate, critique, and make suggestions	- Formal - Synthetic - Analytic - Critical
Reflection/ journal entry	Discuss issues and arguments from a text or an experience Explore issues deeply in relation to personal opinions	- Instructor - Peers - Oneself	Explore one's ideas and initial thoughts about a text Develop one's ideas critically Reflect, aiming for deep insight and careful consideration Observe one's process of thinking and critique Represent one's ideas, thoughts, values, and commitments	- Informal - Summary - Commentary - Opinion
Portfolio narrative "includes curriculum vitae, program of study, narrative statement, and two papers that have been submitted for, and evaluated in, Warner School courses, including all comments written by the instructor, and the grade for the paper."*	Provide a personal assessment of the strengths and weaknesses of one's work thus far. Present an organized summary of one's academic achievement and potential. Reflect on one's experiences, attitudes, and feeling; revise present goals; make plans for the future.	Committee (three faculty members from across departments) Advisor - Oneself	"Show promise to develop a breadth of knowledge about a specific research focus. Provide evidence to identify coherence between interest, program of study, motives, and scholarly work produced thus far. Reflect on your intellectual trajectory and scholarly direction and focus on your plans to achieve your research goals."*	Hybrid of formal and personal (e.g., use of first person)

http://www.rochester.edu/warner/programs/portfolio

Reflective genres such as journal entries, reflections, autoethnographies, and the personal narratives for portfolios frequently generate much discussion as they may be new to students, especially transnational students (see Crème, 2003). Discussing the features of these genres throws into relief the categories of purpose and argument as well as conventions of academic writing such as avoiding the first person. In presenting the following authentic examples of writing by multilingual doctoral students at the Warner School, we aim to illustrate the application of the analytic categories in the heuristic in Table 4 as well as to demonstrate the nature of the education genres we have chosen. However, because the implicit context is academic, we do not elaborate on the audience beyond the notes included in Table 4.

Sample Genre 1. Analyzing the Critical Commentary

The purpose of the critical commentary genre is to identify the main points of one or more course readings and to critique these reading(s), which requires establishing a theoretical position from which to evaluate the texts. In Example 1, Nan, a Chinese Ph.D. student in the Teaching and Curriculum program introduces a commentary she wrote for a seminar, Language and Literacy across Cultures and Contexts:

Example 1:

... In this critical commentary, I will discuss literacy practices from the following two aspects: (1) the interaction of literacy and ethnic networks and (2) the dependence relationships of individuals on the "gatekeepers" of literacy, people who control access to literacy (Lillis and Curry, 2006). Again this paper will synthesize and analyze these two themes using examples from the readings for this course and other articles I have read to illustrate them.

Here, Nan states her purpose by establishing the theoretical grounds that she draws on to engage with the readings—ethnic networks and literacy gatekeepers—evidencing a sophisticated understanding of the academic engagement required at the doctoral level. In Example 2, a commentary written for the course Policy Analysis in Education, Leman, a Turkish student in the Educational Policy and Theory program, provides her purpose:

Example 2:

... This paper attempts to delve into this bleeding problem of the "achievement gap" and explore how the problem has been addressed by educational policy, which population(s) has been targeted, and what barriers and/or weaknesses have come along the way, in the light of the related readings we have read so far in ED439.

Leman also opens by identifying the focus of her paper, but in very broad brush strokes ("achievement gap"), and then signals the specific areas her analysis will cover (policy, population, barriers). Unlike Nan, who introduces readings from outside the course syllabus, Leman limits her references to the course readings (sometimes a requirement of assignments in this genre). The second analytic category, *argument*, is central to the critical commentary genre because critiquing the readings requires students to argue for a particular position or understanding of text. In Example 3, for instance, Nan contrasts the experiences of participants in one research study with findings from other literature:

Example 3:

... However, compared with the experience of Chou and Pao Youa (Weinstein-Shr, 1993), different densities of networks within ethnic groups function differently in education for Chinese immigrant students to America and Canada (Li, 2003; Zhou and Kin, 2006).

Nan's claim that varying network densities have different consequences for different groups is supported by her knowledge of the research literature beyond the course syllabus. Her commentary, therefore, embodies the social practice of doctoral level research in which students are expected to develop expertise in a subfield, which in turn enables them to take a critical stance on course readings. Third, applying the analytic category of *register* or *style* to the genre of critical commentary, we see that students use a formal academic register, as construed by lexical choices, sentence complexity, and in-text quotations and citations. Example 4 from Hee Jeong, a PhD student from Korea in the Department of Teaching and Curriculum, demonstrates these features:

Example 4:

... Morrell (2008) states that "philosophy is meant for real people to deal with real problems of everyday life" (p. 207) and that we should be "doing philosophy" (p. 207). A good example of this doing philosophy in terms of critical literacy was in the early 1970s in Korea. There was a great Citizen's Movement opposing the military dictatorship of the government and, surprisingly, the majority of the people demonstrating on the streets were high school students...

In sum, the critical commentary genre is perhaps most closely related to traditional essays or papers in which students are required to argue a thesis and supply evidence from research sources, primary data, or literature; while the genre offers space for students to insert the personal voice, the first person seems less crucial to the genre than it is in reflections.

Sample Genre 2. Analyzing the Reflection or Journal Entry

The main *purpose* of the reflection or journal entry genre is for graduate students to consider particular issues deeply and become familiar with arguments made in the literature about these issues—while filtering arguments and issues through their own thoughts and experiences. In writing this genre, students present the results of reflection as a type of hybrid—although reflections require the presentation of "personal" opinion, this opinion emerges as a product of the interplay between academic literature and personal experience (e.g., as a student, teacher, or some other capacity related to education). The reflection or journal entry, thus, demonstrates that the student has not only read and considered particular readings, but also related them to personal experience. Example 5 from Leman's reflection illustrates this hybridity:

Example 5

... this paper aims to reflect a bit of [my] experience to let readers acquire a view of "ability grouping" and "tracking" in Turkey from a student standpoint. To familiarize ourselves with the educational system in Turkey, first, I feel there is a need to supply a piece of information.

While it may appear that in this genre *argument* is not a salient analytic category, in fact "opinion" functions here as a type of argument. In this case, opinion is not equivalent to personal opinions about general topics; rather, reflections or journal entries represent a type of academic analysis that draws much more explicitly on personal grounds of evidence than do critical commentaries, as in Example 6.

Example 6

My being a racehorse started while I was at the 5th grade. At the end of the 4th grade, our primary school teacher convinced the parents of her few successful students to send their children to "after-school programs" so that there would be a much higher possibility of going to better secondary schools. . . . I can barely remember how I felt about being in a high-track class then, but looking back now, I can see a child lost in tests struggling to meet everyone's expectations. (Leman)

Here, Leman uses personal experience—analyzed through the metaphor of being a "racehorse"—to critically explore the issue of educational tracking in Turkey.

The *register* or *style* of the reflection or journal entry is much less formal when compared with the critical commentary, as in, for example, Leman's phrase above, "I feel there is a need to." The use of the first person pronoun is not only accepted, but also expected as a key means of establishing the author's subjective stance. Casual diction is also evident in Leman's choice of verbs, such as *to be, to remember,* and *to look back,* as compared with academic verbs such as *to argue, to suggest,* and *to examine.*

Sample Genre 3. Analyzing the Portfolio Narrative

The *purpose* of the portfolio narrative is to reflect on one's intellectual development over a time period or during an educational experience. It has a temporal trajectory from the past to the future both retrospective and prospective as in Example 7 from Hee Jeong's doctoral portfolio narrative:

Example 7

... Although I loved teaching English and researching issues on the English language, I always felt the need to enhance my teaching skills based on a more theoretical and methodological approach to English language teaching and learning. In addition, I wanted to

expand my understanding of education out of the Korean context and hold a broader perspective.

In Example 7, Hee Jeong supplies the reasons she entered a PhD program. In Example 8, she signals her development during her first year of study, which also provides a rationale for the two papers she is presenting to the Portfolio Committee that evaluates her progress:

Example 8

The great knowledge and broad understanding in education from the courses lead me to reconsider English education in Korea ...therefore, the two papers I selected for my portfolio reflect my academic development and exhibit my current scholarly interests, especially in the context of Korea.

In the portfolio narrative genre, student writers make explicit *arguments* about their progress toward the PhD while the narrative and the two course papers they have selected as portfolio artifacts implicitly argue for the quality of the student's work. Example 9 comes from the narrative of Kankana, a PhD student from India in the Human Development program.

Example 9

Two things inspired me to shift from mainstream economics to an interdisciplinary graduate study program. My first source of inspiration was learning about the concept of capability formation. ...My second source of inspiration was my experience working as a researcher in an educational program for women in a rural village in India...

The *register* or *style* of the portfolio narrative genre is another hybrid, both personal and neutral as it moves from personal information to an academic positioning of the writer. In Example 10, Leman mixes informal and formal diction in discussing the personal experience related to her academic interests:

Example 10

During my second semester, I took the ED 457 Autism Spectrum Disorders class . . . so that I could have a closer view and, by this, better understanding of disability studies. Since my little brother was diagnosed with autism at the age of three, the classes not only extremely motivated me but also let me build upon my experience...

Generally, students move from using informal language when describing personal experience (as above) to using a more formal register when introducing argument or claims about their scholarly trajectory, particularly by using specialized terms of the field. Example 11 provides the conclusion to Kankana's narrative:

Example 11

The knowledge and skills that I have acquired thus far have enabled me to focus and understand that I am primarily interested in women's learning in informal settings, especially women between the ages of 18-40 and from low socio-economic backgrounds . . . I am now interested in looking further into the social entrepreneurial characteristics exhibited by this population in various community projects...

Here, the prospective nature of the doctoral portfolio narrative is evident and the argument and register or style categories overlap to support the writer's aim to persuade the committee to pass her portfolio.

In addition to raising awareness of the conventions of genres, we also need to ask critical questions about these conventions. Workshop participants, typically, raise questions about why the conventions of academic writing often privilege, for example, the third person voice. Discussions usually touch on how, at least in education, positivist epistemologies have left a legacy of pseudo objectivity in academic writing. That is, academic writing conventions have traditionally downplayed the author's subjectivity in favor of an "objective" stance; this ideology is embodied in the avoidance of the first person "I."

CONCLUSION

In this chapter, we have aimed to show that multilingual students need to become aware that the range of genres that comprise "academic writing" may be much broader than traditional textbooks and assessments often imply (as Table 3 indicates). However, it is not enough for students to learn only to deconstruct texts whether closely analyzing a particular research article or exploring more broadly—they must also "reconstruct" particular genres (Chapman, 1999, p. 488). Indeed, students must write these specific genres—not unrelated genres or exercises. We cannot assume that students can easily transfer skills or experiences with limited types of writing to the genres required in new contexts. In this process, many students appreciate the opportunity to see sample texts written by other students—ideally, a range of authentic texts written for similar purposes.

Because writing teachers may not have access to the kind of institutional knowledge—or knowledge of specific genres—that we have been discussing, the question of the transferability of this approach arises. First, how can teachers and students begin to identify the range of genres in circulation in other contexts? Given the ubiquity of the Internet, multilingual students might be able to undertake a research project in which they ask friends or former schoolmates who are now in Anglophone contexts to answer a questionnaire about the kinds of English-medium academic writing they are doing—and if possible, to send examples of their texts for analysis. Second, where else might authentic student texts be available? We posted queries on two list-serves to find publicly available samples of authentic English-medium student academic writing. Our results are listed in Appendix; these texts could be useful as material for deconstruction and reconstruction by multilingual students.

ACKNOWLEDGMENTS

We are grateful to Kankana Mukhopadhyay, Leman Kaniturk Kose, and Nan Zhang for permission to use their texts in this chapter.

REFERENCES

Badger, R., and White, G. (2000). A process genre approach to teaching writing. *ELT Journal, 54*, 153-160.

Barton, D., and Hamilton, M. (1998). *Local literacies: Reading and writing in one community.* London: Routledge.

Benesch, S. (2001). *Critical English for academic purposes: Theory, politics, and practice.* Mahwah, NJ: Lawrence Erlbaum.

Brock-Utne, B. (2007). Language of instruction and research in higher education in Europe: Highlights from the current debate in Norway and Sweden. *International Review of Education, 53,* 367-388.

Canagarajah, A. S. (2002). *Critical academic writing and multilingual students.* Ann Arbor, MI: University of Michigan Press.

Casanave, C. (2004). *Controversies in second language writing: Dilemmas and decisions in research and instruction.* Ann Arbor, MI: University of Michigan Press.

Chapman, M. (1999). Situated, social, active: Rewriting genre in the elementary classroom. *Written Communication, 16,* 469-490.

Coffin, C., Curry, M. J., Goodman, S., Hewings, A., Lillis, T. M., and Swann, J. (2003). *Teaching academic writing: A toolkit for higher education.* London: Routledge.

Crème, P. (2003). Why can't we allow students to be more creative? *Teaching in Higher Education, 8,* 273-277.

Curry, M. J. (2001). Preparing to be privatized: The hidden curriculum of a community college ESL writing class. In E. Margolis (Ed.), *The hidden curriculum in higher education* (pp. 175-192). New York: Routledge.

Curry, M. J. (2003). Skills, access, and "basic writing": A community college case study from the United States. *Studies in the Education of Adults, 35*(1), 5-18.

Curry, M. J. (2004). UCLA Community College Review: Academic literacy for English language learners. *Community College Review, 32*(2), 51-68.

Dudley-Evans, T. (1995). Genre models for the teaching of academic writing to second language speakers: Advantages and disadvantages. In T. Miller (Ed.), *Functional approaches to written text.* Retrieved April 17, 2010, from http:/ eca.state.gov/ education/ engteaching/ pubs/BR/ functionalsec4_11.htm

Hirvela, A. (2004). *Connecting reading and writing in second language writing instruction.* Ann Arbor, MI: University of Michigan Press.

Hyland, K. (2004). *Genre and second language writing.* Ann Arbor, MI: University of Michigan Press.

Hyon, S. (1996). Genre in three traditions: Implications for ESL. *TESOL Quarterly, 30,* 693-722.

Lea, M., and Street, B. (2006). The 'academic literacies' model: Theory and applications. *Theory Into Practice, 45*, 368-377.

Lillis, T. M., and Curry, M. J. (2006). Reframing notions of competence in scholarly writing: From individual to networked activity. *Revista Canaria de Estudios Ingleses, 53*, 63-78.

Lillis, T. M., and Curry, M. J. (2010). *Academic writing in a global context: The politics and practices of English-medium publishing.* London: Routledge.

Lillis, T. M., and Scott, M. (2007). Defining academic literacies research: Issues of epistemology, ideology and strategy. *Journal of Applied Linguistics*, *4*(1), 5-32.

Morgan, B. (2009). Fostering transformative practitioners for critical EAP: Possibilities and challenges. *Journal of English for Academic Purposes, 8,* 86-99.

Morrell, E. (2008). *Critical literacy and urban youth: Pedagogies of access, dissent, and liberation.* New York: Routledge.

Pakir, A. (2009). English as a lingua franca: Analyzing research frameworks in international English, world Englishes, and ELF. *World Englishes, 28*, 224-235.

Roe, S., and den Ouden, P. (2003). *Designs for disciplines: An introduction to academic writing.* Toronto: Canadian Scholars' Press.

Swales, J. (1990). *Genre analysis: English in academic and research settings.* Cambridge: Cambridge University Press.

Swales, J., and Feak, C. (2004). *Academic writing for graduate students* (2nd ed.). Ann Arbor, MI: University of Michigan Press.

UNESCO. (2009). *Global education digest.* Retrieved April 17, 2010, from www.uis.unesco.org./publications/GED2009

Widodo, H. P. (2006). Designing a genre-based lesson plan for an academic writing course. *English Teaching: Practice and Critique, 5*(3), 173-199.

SOURCES OF STUDENT WRITING

Books

Bass, R. (1999). Border texts: Cultural readings for contemporary writers. Boston, MA: Houghton Mifflin.

Biggam, J. (2008). Succeeding with your master's dissertation. Milton Keynes, UK: Open University Press.

Divakaruni, C. (1997). We, too, sing America: A reader for writers. New York: McGraw-Hill Humanities.

Harste, J., Burke, C., and Short, K. (1995). Creating classrooms for authors and inquirers. Portsmouth, NH: Heinemann.

Penfield, E. (1998). Short takes: Model essays for composition. New York: Longman.

Sladky, P. (1994). The Great American Bologna Festival and other student essays. New York: St. Martin's Press.

Sommers, J., and Lewiecki-Wilson, C. (1999). From community to college: Reading and writing across diverse contexts. New York: Bedford/St. Martins.

Websites (as of April 2010)

http://www.teacherjoe.us/Comps.html: A collection of essays from students in China, compiled by Joe Deveto

www.learningdevelopment.plymouth.ac.uk: The Writing for Assignments E-library (WrAssE)

In: Innovation and Creativity in ELT Methodology
Editors: H. P. Widodo and A. Cirocki

ISBN: 978-1-62948-146-3
© 2013 Nova Science Publishers, Inc.

Chapter 9

TEACHING ENGLISH PRONUNCIATION FOR ADULT LEARNERS: EIGHT REASONS NOT TO TEACH PRONUNCIATION (AND WHY THEY ARE ALL WRONG)

Lynda Yates and Beth Zielinski
Macquarie University, Australia

ABSTRACT

Although pronunciation is a crucial part of a learner's communicative competence, we have heard teachers give many reasons as to why they do not teach it in their classrooms. In this chapter, we draw on research from a number of different theoretical perspectives to counter some of the more common of these and provide teachers with the confidence and expertise they need to give pronunciation the attention that it deserves as an essential part of the curriculum. We explore different aspects of learning and teaching pronunciation, consider different goals for adult learners, and provide insights into why they might find this part of learning English particularly challenging. In this chapter, we offer a systematic approach to teaching pronunciation together with practical ideas of how teachers can accommodate a range of learner needs and integrate pronunciation teaching and learning into their regular daily activities in the English language classroom.

INTRODUCTION

Whether they are communicating with native speakers or using English as a Lingua Franca, it is absolutely vital that learners' speech is intelligible. If people cannot understand what they are saying, it does not matter how well their grammar or how extensive their vocabulary is. And yet, pronunciation rarely gets the attention it deserves in class, and is all too often tackled only as an afterthought or even an "extra" remedial class for learners with problems. Many teachers seem to lack confidence in their abilities to understand the issues and are confused about how to teach pronunciation systematically. In this chapter, we address head-on some of the reasons we have heard teachers give for not teaching pronunciation and counter them with insights from research and our own experience to offer some practical advice on how to make the teaching of pronunciation both effective and fun.

In its broadest sense, and the way we will use it in this chapter, pronunciation refers to the way someone sounds when they speak and the impact this has on their intelligibility. It, therefore, refers to all aspects of the way we make and put together sounds in connected speech, including stress, intonation, rhythm, sounds, and the way they blend. These are our major focus here, but are not the only aspect of a speaking performance that can interfere with intelligibility; other aspects of delivery such as fluency, hesitation, confidence, body language, and interpersonal pragmatics are also important (for detailed information on the features of different varieties of English, see Celce-Murcia, Brinton, and Goodwin [2010] for *American English*; Underhill [2005] for *British English*; Walker [2010] for *English as a Lingua Franca*).

As will be evident when you read this chapter, we will draw on research into learning and teaching pronunciation from a number of different theoretical perspectives. Learning to speak a language intelligibly involves a range of cognitive and mechanical skills and is also influenced by sociocultural factors and conceptions of self. Moreover, the way we teach pronunciation should take into account a wide variety of learner factors and learning contexts (see suggestions for further reading).

WE DO NOT NEED TO TEACH PRONUNCIATION BECAUSE IT IS NOT IMPORTANT AND STUDENTS JUST PICK IT UP BY THEMSELVES ANYWAY: REASON # 1

Are You Kidding!

Learners whose pronunciation interferes with their intelligibility will find it very difficult to communicate effectively in English even if they are very competent in other areas (e.g., vocabulary and grammar).

Even sympathetic interlocutors will eventually get tired and give up, and the learners themselves are likely to become embarrassed and become more and more reluctant to speak. Thus, in a vicious cycle, learners who need practice communicating in spoken English find that they are less and less able or willing to do so. So, it is absolutely vital that teachers pay attention to pronunciation in their classes, and far from being an optional extra, pronunciation needs to be an integral part of the process of learning English. Research tells us that students think it is vital, too, whatever their other language learning needs are (Derwing, 2003; Derwing and Rossiter, 2002).

Adult Learners and the Influence of Their First Language

Adults usually find that their first language (L1), or sometimes the language of their previous studies, is a major influence on their pronunciation in English. Typically, they do not "pick up" pronunciation by just being exposed to English in general English classrooms. This is because as they were learning their first language, they also learned ways of thinking about and categorizing important features in language, and so they will tend to "hear" and make sense of any new language they learn using the same categories. Because the categories they established in their first language act as a kind of filter through which they hear or understand the sounds and patterns in language, they may find it very difficult to make sense of the sound system in English, and they often transfer their understanding of how a sound is produced from their first language to the new language – English. Adults, therefore, often have to "unlearn" some habits, assumptions, and expectations that work in their first language, but not in English.

This can be a particular challenge where sounds and patterns found in English are not found in their first language (as in word stress patterns for Vietnamese speakers, for example), or where sounds considered to be two different sounds in English are considered to be the *same* sound in their first language. This is the case for the sounds "s" and "sh," for example, which are separate sounds that can make (quite important!) differences in meaning in English, but sound *the same* to many speakers from Indonesia, so the differences between them can be difficult to hear and make. One way of thinking about this is that we all have *L1 ears*, that is, the assumptions and categories we have developed about language through learning our L1 colors the way we perceive what is going on in other languages that we learn later.

Adult learners, therefore, need to learn which features of pronunciation make a difference to meaning in English and which do not, as well as how to use them in connected speech. This involves a whole new way of thinking about features of pronunciation and how they fit together.

Adult learners will, therefore, need plenty of time to listen to English and reflect on how the pieces fit together and how this might be different from the assumptions they might make based on their experience with their L1. They often find it challenging to understand the differences between the way they pronounce English and the models they hear around them. We cannot just assume that they can listen and repeat what they hear without any support!

Some Practical Tips for Dealing with "L1 Ears"

Teachers can use a range of use techniques that tap into a range of different senses to help learners conceptualize and use the different features of English pronunciation. For example, when making a learner aware of the stress pattern of a word as well as saying the word out loud, a teacher can also demonstrate *visually* which syllable is stressed in a number of different ways, including:

- stretching a rubber band as she or he says the stressed syllable, but not for the others;
- opening both hands (with palms facing the learner) as she or he says the stressed syllable and closing them for the others; and
- drawing a large circle under the stressed syllable in the written form of the word.

A teacher could also tap into the learner's sense of movement to reinforce the stress pattern kinaesthetically as *they* practice saying the word by getting them to:

- stretch a rubber band or open both hands as they say the stressed syllable, but not for the others;
- stand up as they say the stressed syllable and sit down for the others; and
- point to the stressed syllable in the written form of the word (marked in some way, e.g., underlined, written in uppercase letters or with a large circle underneath).

Further examples of different ways to reinforce some other pronunciation features can be found in Yates and Zielinski (2009) and Celce-Murcia, Brinton, and Goodwin (2010).

I Do Not Speak English "Well" Enough to Teach Pronunciation (I Am a Non-Native Speaker/I Come from Australia/Alaska /Scotland/ Singapore): REASON # 2

We Can All Teach Pronunciation

If you can speak English and are a teacher of English, you should teach pronunciation. Teachers do not need to worry about having a different accent - we all have an accent of some kind, and most learners will never sound like native speakers and do not necessarily want to. In any case, teachers can use recordings of a wide variety of different speakers when teaching pronunciation. This not only makes it easier to focus on aspects of pronunciation, but the students are exposed to a wide variety of speakers, which will help them to prepare for the real world.

What Should Be Our Goals and Models for Teaching?

Having an accent *per se* will not necessarily make someone difficult to understand. An accent only becomes a problem if it is so strong that people cannot understand what you are saying or when the people you are talking to are not familiar with that particular accent. We have a British English and an Australian accent, and both of us have had occasional difficulty being understood by native speakers of American English, just because they are used to hearing a different variety. Which variety a teacher aims for in class will depend on who the students are and why they are learning English. While international students or immigrants settling in the USA may find a North American English model more appropriate, learners in Britain or Australia will find it helpful to be able to speak and understand British and Australian models.

However, in our global environment, students are best equipped if they can, at least, understand a range of different varieties of English, including so-called "new Englishes" spoken in post-colonial contexts such as India, Singapore, and Africa.

Also, in many contexts, interactions in English usually take place between speakers from different language backgrounds who speak English with a variety of different accents. The goals for pronunciation teaching in these contexts are likely to be different again (see Walker, 2010).

TEACHING PRONUNCIATION SIMPLY DOES NOT WORK: REASON # 3

Research Shows That Pronunciation Certainly Can Be Taught Effectively

There is certainly research evidence that explicit pronunciation instruction does lead to improvement whether the focus is on the production of sounds (Couper, 2006, 2009), stress in words (Park, 2000 as cited in Couper, 2009), or features of connected speech such as intonation, rhythm, and stress patterns in phrases and sentences (Derwing, Munro, and Wiebe, 1998).

What Works?

As with the teaching of any new skill, it is important that pronunciation is taught in a systematic way that allows learners to progress through a sequence of stages or levels of practice as they learn to understand and master features of pronunciation. This allows them to practice at a level they are able to manage, and to move from controlled, structured practice to freer practice in a range of different contexts. The following sequence offers a systematic way to approach pronunciation teaching:

1. Listening and awareness: These activities allow learners to become more aware of a target feature (for example, a new sound) through focused listening, reflection, and discussion. In this way, they develop an awareness of the features and how it might be different from features they are familiar with in their first language.
2. Control: Control based activity or task can give opportunities to practice saying the target feature in limited contexts, so learners can gain control over the mechanical aspects of pronunciation.
3. Practice: This provides opportunities to practice using the target feature in different structured contexts that increase in difficulty as they improve.
4. Extension: Extension focused activities allow opportunities to put new knowledge and skills into operation in less structured contexts inside and outside the classroom.

At each of these stages, it is very important that learners are given feedback on their attempts, so they understand whether they are pronouncing the target feature accurately or if not, how they might need to change their pronunciation to achieve better results. In Appendix 1, we provide examples of how practice at each of these stages can be incorporated into a general classroom activity.

Progress Might Be Gradual

For adult learners, progress might be gradual and can seem to be very slow. It may take a while for learners to move from becoming aware of a pronunciation feature they need to change to being able to put this knowledge into practice; or they might be able to use a feature accurately only in very structured and controlled contexts, but find it difficult to use in spontaneous speaking contexts. It might, therefore, seem as if they are not improving, or that they forget everything they have learned when they leave the classroom! However, this is not necessarily the case. As discussed below, learning pronunciation requires progress through a number of different stages, and this takes time. Just because they have not reached the endpoint, it does not mean they have not improved. The important thing is to develop awareness among learners of the road they are travelling and a culture of supportive attention to pronunciation in the classroom.

TEACHING PRONUNCIATION MEANS REPETITIVE DRILLS, WHICH ARE BORING AND DO NOT FIT WITH THE WAY I THINK ENGLISH SHOULD BE TAUGHT: REASON # 4

Teachers Can Integrate Repetition Naturally into the Overall Aims of a Lesson in Ways That Are Meaningful and Fun

Activities that incorporate repetition do not need to interfere with more communicative based classroom activities, and can be incorporated as a necessary part of a classroom task completion (see Trofimovich and Gatbonton, 2006). In this way, they can enhance rather than detract from the overall aim of a lesson. For example, if the aim is to learn how to complete a form requiring personal details, a teacher can incorporate a pronunciation task related to this by having the learners ask the other class members one by one for a particular type of information and then present the information they have gathered to the class. This task requires them to ask the same or similar questions to all members of the class and so presents an ideal opportunity for the teacher to introduce some focused listening, awareness raising, and practice. Similarly, structured pronunciation activities like this can be used as a part of a lesson on understanding a newspaper article, writing a report, and making phone calls to request information. They can target a number of different pronunciation features, such as stress patterns in short questions, intonation patterns in different types of questions, the pronunciation of specific key words, or consonants and vowels.

For example, as outlined by Yates and Zielinski (2009), in a lesson on giving personal information, voiceless "th" (as in thankyou) is made the focus of both listening and practice in structured connected speech. Once the learners have listened to models and known the words they are going to say, the mini dialog below is practiced as a kind of drill across the class and then leads onto some sort of extended practice or form filling activity. Learner A asks Learner B the question, *When's your birthday?* and B must answer saying only the date, not the month. Then, Learner A prompts *What month?* as in the dialog below:

A. When's your birthday?
B. The 13th
C. What month?
D. May

An important way of incorporating repetition without detracting from the overall aim of a lesson is to shift the focus back and forth between the communication based activity and the specific pronunciation features being targeted. By "zooming in" from the communication based activity to a specific pronunciation feature when the need arises, and then back out to provide opportunities to practice it in context, pronunciation becomes an integral and essential part of the lesson, and the learners can appreciate the importance of the pronunciation feature to communication (see Isaacs, 2009).

PRONUNCIATION SHOULD BE TAUGHT IN A SPECIALIST COURSE NOT IN A GENERAL ENGLISH CLASS: REASON # 5

Specialist Classes Versus Incorporating Pronunciation into General Classroom Activities

While a separate pronunciation class may be very helpful for learners who have developed unhelpful pronunciation habits and need some targeted attention to help them "unlearn" them or others who need extended individual attention, pronunciation is an integral part of language and should be taught in a way that integrates it thoroughly into all aspects of language learning. Learners cannot say a word of English without pronouncing it. Specialist classes can be great for some learners, but the real challenge is to improve learners' pronunciation while they are using English in classroom activities and in real communication outside. To do this, teachers need to consistently include pronunciation as an essential part of the curriculum. Incorporating pronunciation into general classroom activities allows for targeted features of pronunciation to be practiced in a range of meaningful contexts, and for learners to become aware of how they sound to others and where their pronunciation might need to change if they want to be easier to understand. Attention to pronunciation can become part of teachers' classroom routines so that for example, they would not even think of teaching a new word without modeling the pronunciation and getting learners to say it first, and would never consider writing it on the board without marking its stress pattern.

A Pronunciation Goal for Everything We Teach

One way of consistently including pronunciation in our lessons is to always have a pronunciation goal in mind, no matter what we are teaching. This allows us to approach pronunciation teaching in a systematic way (as outlined earlier under Reason # 3) and to focus on the particular feature of pronunciation we have as our goal in everything we teach. In the example provided earlier (under Reason # 4), we saw how a lesson on how to complete a form requiring personal details, which is usually a reading and writing task, could also be used to provide an opportunity to practice a particular feature of pronunciation. As teachers, we need to be creative and always think about how we might use general classroom activities to achieve pronunciation goals alongside other language goals.

Of course, pronunciation will frequently not be the primary aim of a lesson, but teachers should always be aware of the pronunciation opportunities and consequences of whatever the primary focus is. So, if the focus is how to give a narrative, which involves using the past tense, a teacher needs to also be aware that the word final clusters that result from adding past endings will pose a challenge for learners who have difficulty with either word final consonants or clusters or both. Activities that will help learners focus on particular features of pronunciation and practice them in a supportive, meaningful way can be prepared with any lesson. For example, if the major aim of a particular lesson is report writing, a teacher can pay attention to word endings or to stress patterns in words, or to different feature that might be a pronunciation goal for a particular group of learners. Some examples of how this might be done can be seen in Appendix 1. Further examples can also be found in Celce-Murcia, Brinton, and Goodwin (2010).

You Cannot Teach Pronunciation to Beginners. They Cannot Understand the Theory: REASON # 6

Where Possible, Pronunciation Must Be Tackled from the Very Beginning

Attention to pronunciation should be proactive and starts from day one of learning a language. Beginners need pronunciation just as much as advanced learners do, and starting early helps them tackle pronunciation issues throughout their learning. Pronunciation skills are best taught and learned experientially rather than theoretically, that is, the important thing is that learners are able to *do* pronunciation rather than know the theory of it, and so learners as any level can learn good pronunciation, just as they will learn accurate grammar or vocabulary. So, when learners encounter a new word or practice a dialog, pronunciation awareness, and practice should be part of the activity from the very first lesson.

Although learning about the theory of pronunciation is not the aim of teaching pronunciation, it can be very helpful for teachers to develop a way of talking about the different features of pronunciation that learners can understand and relate to. To enable learners to talk about pronunciation and to understand the teacher's feedback on their attempts, it is very helpful for them to be introduced to some simple words and concepts related to pronunciation right from the beginning (e.g., stress, weak form, vowel, consonant, beginning/middle/end of word). However, if teachers talk about pronunciation in this way, it is of the utmost importance that they ensure that their learners understand what the terms actually mean. Otherwise, they will make them confused rather than help them understand.

Adults Find It Embarrassing and Difficult and I Feel Uncomfortable Correcting Them All the Time: REASON # 7

It is Even More Embarrassing to Speak and Not to Be Understood

Because teaching pronunciation is not about "fixing errors", but should be thought of as "teaching how to speak," it should be no more embarrassing to teach pronunciation than any other aspect of language. If teachers make sure learners have good, clear models and the time to become aware of what English sounds like, they will feel supported and motivated to *have a go* at good pronunciation.

Giving Feedback to Adults

Learners really benefit from developing their understanding of where and when their pronunciation is intelligible and when it is not, so it is really important that their teacher provides feedback on their attempts and helps them understand how they might need to change their pronunciation to improve their intelligibility. There are many sensitive and productive ways of providing feedback, so it does not seem like the learners are being corrected all the time. It is often more beneficial as well as more pleasant to indicate to the learners that they have not got something quite right; the teacher guides them to make improvements themselves rather than correct them directly. If a teacher simply corrects students, they do not have to think very hard to understand what went wrong and how to improve the next time, but if the teacher cues the students to the fact that there is something not quite right, they will need to reflect a little more carefully on what they have been doing and find their own solution.

There are times in a lesson when feedback can be immediate, but it can also be delayed if the focus of a lesson is on something else at the time. In any case, to be effective feedback is best targeted to specific goals at specific stages of learning (see Reason # 3 above) rather than random features that learners may not yet be familiar with.

When giving feedback, it is also useful to have a way of talking about the different features of pronunciation (see Reason # 6 above). It can also help develop hand signals or some other gesture, or expression can be useful cues, and it is useful to have a repertoire of different signals that a teacher can use to guide learners towards a realization of what it is that they need to change. For example, a punch in the air can indicate a difficulty with stress, or a hand waved up and down can mark an intonation difficulty. A teacher can invent his or her own cues; the class will soon learn what the teacher means. For more approaches to correcting and giving feedback see Underhill (2005, pp. 132-144) and Yates and Zielinski (2009, pp. 85-86).

YOU CANNOT TEACH PRONUNCIATION IN A MIXED BACKGROUND CLASS BECAUSE THEY ALL NEED SOMETHING DIFFERENT: REASON # 8

Some Pronunciation Goals Are Common to Learners from Many Language Backgrounds

While it is certainly true that learners from different language backgrounds will have different needs and priorities for pronunciation, some of these will be common to all or many learners in a class.

For example, many learners whatever their backgrounds find using stress and intonation in English quite challenging. This makes these good areas for attention in mixed background classes because the topic should be relevant and motivating to a wide range of students, and yet the particular issues that they may have will differ.

For instance, some may be tempted because of their L1 to stress every syllable in a word equally, while others may transfer from their L1 the tendency to put the word stress in a particular position.

Another example of pronunciation feature that is difficult for learners from a variety of L1 backgrounds is the pronunciation of consonants at the ends of words. Learners from different L1 backgrounds might have different issues with consonants at the ends of words, but the overall goal of pronouncing the ends of words accurately would be relevant to many.

A teacher can easily listen and take notes on the pronunciation needs of individual learners to determine what the common goals might be for the learners in their class. One way of keeping a record of pronunciation needs to establish both individual and class goals, is to use a pronunciation chart as demonstrated in Yates and Zielinski (2009).

Having Learners from a Mix of L1 Backgrounds Can Actually Be Helpful When Teaching Pronunciation

As mentioned above, there are some pronunciation features that learners from a variety of L1 backgrounds need to work on. There are other features, however, that some learners find difficult, but others do not. This diversity in a classroom can be a blessing rather than a curse when teaching pronunciation. It can be very useful to put people from different L1 backgrounds to work in pairs since one might be strong in an area in which they can help their partner and vice versa; they can monitor each other's attempts; and each can be the "expert" at some aspect of pronunciation, which can be a boost to confidence. Mixed L1 classes also have the advantage of giving the learners exposure to different accents, and an awareness of how different features of pronunciation affect intelligibility for learners from different L1 backgrounds.

In a mixed L1 class, pronunciation homework is a great idea for individualizing pronunciation practice. Once a teacher becomes aware of something that a learner really needs to practice, homework can be set that targets that particular feature at the appropriate level of practice (see Reason # 3).

CONCLUSION

As we have demonstrated, there are many good reasons for teaching pronunciation and no good excuses for avoiding it. It is great fun and greatly appreciated by learners – and it is not hard to do.

If as teachers, we do not pay attention to pronunciation, we are sending the message that it does not matter how learners say things, and that is really not helpful for when they try out their English in the world outside the classroom.

If we do not help them with their pronunciation, who will? If we do not give them feedback and support, who will? With a strong commitment and a little preparation, any lesson can be turned into an opportunity for a focus on pronunciation that will strengthen our learners' awareness of how to use English intelligibly and increase their communicative confidence.

REFERENCES

Celce-Murcia, M., Brinton, D. M., and Goodwin, J. M. (2010). *Teaching pronunciation: A course book and reference guide* (2nd ed.). New York: Cambridge University Press.

Couper, G. (2006). The short and long-term effects of pronunciation instruction. *Prospect, 21* (1), 46-66.

Couper, G. (2009). *Teaching and learning L2 pronunciation: Understanding the effectiveness of socially constructed metalanguage and critical listening in terms of a cognitive phonology framework.* Unpublished PhD thesis, University of New England, Armadale, NSW, Australia.

Derwing, T. M. (2003). What do ESL students say about their accents? *The Canadian Modern Language Review, 59,* 547-566.

Derwing, T., Munro, M., and Wiebe, G. (1998). Evidence in favour of a broad framework for pronunciation instruction. *Language Learning, 48,* 393-410.

Derwing, T. M., and Rossiter, M. (2002). ESL learners' perceptions of their pronunciation needs and strategies. *System, 30,* 155-166.

Isaacs, T. (2009). Integrating form and meaning in L2 pronunciation instruction. *TESL Canada Journal, 27*(1), 1-12.

Park, J. (2000). *The effects of forms and meaning-focussed instruction on ESL learners' phonological acquisition.* Unpublished PhD Thesis, the University of Pennsylvania, PA.

Trofimovich, P., and Gatbonton, E. (2006). Repetition and focus on form in processing L2 Spanish words: Implications for pronunciation instruction. *The Modern Language Journal, 90,* 519-535.

Underhill, A. (2005). *Sound foundations: Learning and teaching pronunciation* (2nd. ed.) Oxford: Macmillan.

Walker, R. (2010). *Teaching the pronunciation of English as a lingua franca.* Oxford: Oxford University Press.

Yates, L., and Zielinski, B. (2009). *Give it a go. Teaching pronunciation to adults.* North Ryde, NSW: AMEP Research Centre, Macquarie University. Online version available at: http://www.ameprc.mq.edu.au/resources/classroom_resources/give_it_a_go

Some Additional Suggestions for Further Reading

Boyer, S. (2002). Understanding English pronunciation: An integrated practice course. Glenbrook, NSW: Boyer Educational Resources.

Gilbert, J. B. (2005). Clear speech: Pronunciation and listening comprehension in North American English (3rd ed.). New York: Cambridge University Press.

Gilbert, J. B. (2008). Teaching pronunciation: Using the prosody pyramid. Cambridge, New York: Cambridge University Press. Online version available at: http://www.cambridge.org/other_files/downloads/esl/booklets/Gilbert-Teaching-Pronunciation.pdf

Grant, L. (2007). Well said intro: Pronunciation for clear communication. Boston, MA: Thomson Heinle.

Hancock, M. (2003). English pronunciation in use. Cambridge: Cambridge University Press.

Hansen Edwards, J. G., and Zampini, M. L. (Eds.). (2008). Phonology and second language acquisition. Amsterdam: John Benjamins.

Harmer J. (2007). *How to teach English* (2nd ed.). London: Pearson Education.

Hewings, M. (2004). Pronunciation practice activities: A resource book for teaching English pronunciation. Cambridge: Cambridge University Press.

Nation, I. S. P., and Newton, J. (2009). Teaching ESL/EFL listening and speaking. New York: Routledge.

Nunan, D. (Ed.). (2003). *Practical English language teaching*. New York: McGraw-Hill/Contemporary.

Pennington, M. C. (1998). The teachability of phonology in adulthood: A re-examination. *International Review of Applied Linguistics in Language Teaching, 36,* 323-341.

In: Innovation and Creativity in ELT Methodology
Editors: H. P. Widodo and A. Cirocki

ISBN: 978-1-62948-146-3
© 2013 Nova Science Publishers, Inc.

Chapter 10

LEARNING VOCABULARY IN ACTIVITIES

Stuart Webb

Victoria University of Wellington, New Zealand

ABSTRACT

This chapter examines vocabulary learning activities and aims to shed light on what teachers need to consider when designing, selecting, and modifying activities. It looks at questions like: Which words should be learned in activities? To what degree are words likely to be learned in activities? Does the activity make efficient use of learning time? Which features of activities contribute to learning? How effective is an activity likely to be? A list of criteria for examining activities is described, and two activities are evaluated and then modified to increase their potential for vocabulary learning.

INTRODUCTION

There are many different vocabulary learning activities. Many focus attention on linking form and meaning; some aim at learning the forms of words; and others focus attention on how words are used. The range of activities allows teachers the choice of using a variety of techniques to teach vocabulary. Teachers need to evaluate activities and select the ones that are appropriate for their learning context. They should select activities according to the following criteria:

1. the vocabulary to be learned;
2. the aspect or aspects of vocabulary knowledge that may be learned;
3. task time; and
4. the relative effectiveness of the activity.

The following sections will look at each of these factors. The discussion is oriented towards using activities with adult learners. However, many of the points are also relevant with younger learners.

WHICH WORDS ARE LIKELY TO BE LEARNED THROUGH COMPLETING THE ACTIVITY AND WHAT IS THE VALUE OF THESE WORDS TO THE LEARNERS?

The most important feature of a vocabulary learning activity is the vocabulary learning goal. One way to evaluate the vocabulary learning goal would be to count how many words are likely to be learned through completing the activity. This is significant because as teachers, we want our students to learn as many words as possible. However, the number of words learned can be a function of how long the activity takes as well as the degree to which the words are learned. What is more important than how many words are learned is which words are learned. There is little meaning in completing an activity if the target words have little value to the learners. Different words have different values to learners. For example, the words *believe*, *complete*, and *near* are of greater value to learners than *clarify*, *eliminate*, and *intermediate*, and all of those words are of greater value than *attain*, *emigrate*, and *potent*. In the previous sentence, the first three words are high frequency words; the second set of three words is academic words; and the final set of three words is lower frequency words. Word frequency and the needs of the learners are the best indicators of the relative value of words.

There are approximately 2000 high frequency word families. The high frequency words will be encountered and used most often in language, so these words have the greatest value to learners and should be taught. Language learners in an English as a second language (ESL) context will encounter high frequency words in spoken and written discourse, inside and outside the classroom, in dialog with native speakers, in television programs and movies, and on the radio every day. Lower frequency words will be encountered or needed for speaking and writing less often. For example, the most frequent 1000 word families make up 75.5% of the words in newspapers and 84.3% of the words in conversation (Nation, 2001), 85.11% of the words in television programs (Webb and Rodgers, 2009a), and 86.52% of the words in movies (Webb and Rodgers, 2009b). In contrast, the most frequent 6001st to 7000th most frequent words families account for 0.28% of the words in conversation (Nation, 2006), 0.32% of the words in television programs (Webb and Rodgers, 2009a), and 0.25% of the words in movies (Webb and Rodgers, 2009b). These figures reveal that the high frequency words will be encountered and used in language often; knowing these words is central to comprehension of spoken and written discourse and is necessary to effectively communicate in speech and writing. In contrast, the lower frequency words will not be encountered or needed nearly as often, so their value is much lower to learners. While lower frequency words still have value, with limited time for vocabulary learning in the classroom lower frequency words do not merit attention in activities unless they represent a particular need for learners.

Teachers need to be aware of the relative value of words and focus on teaching the most useful words in activities. This means that teachers need to know which words are high frequency words and which words are not. This may be done intuitively, but it is not as easy as it sounds. Alderson (2007) found that there was considerable variation between judgments of the frequency of words between individuals and reported that highly educated native speaker intuitions are often not accurate.

A more reliable method of judging frequency is using lists of high frequency words derived from corpus data. The best known words lists are *West's* (1953) *General Service List* at the 1000 and 2000 levels, *Nation's* (2004) 141000-*Word Lists*, and *Coxhead's* (2000)

Academic Word List (*AWL*). Teachers and institutions may use these lists to help sequence vocabulary learning from the first 1000 words to the second 1000 words. Focusing on learning words in the lists in that order provides the greatest benefits for comprehension and use. Emphasis on learning high frequency words in activities does not mean that low frequency words should never be taught. Sometimes, there will be a need for learners to know lower frequency words; however, teachers should deal with these words quickly and provide the maximum amount of time for teaching words of greater value.

After frequency, the next criterion for selecting words is learner need. Adult learners often have specific vocabulary learning needs such as learning for academic purposes, business, and living or traveling in a second language context. The items in Coxhead's (2000) AWL are most useful for learners who already know the high frequency words and plan to study at university in an English speaking country. The AWL was derived according to the frequency and range of use of words in academic written text outside of the high frequency words. Technical word lists for specific professional situations may be lacking. Ideally, lists will be created through the frequency and range of occurrence of words in a corpus derived from topic related materials. However, if teachers have the background knowledge, they may intuitively create their own lists by analyzing the materials that the learners will be using in their profession.

If we plan the vocabulary that we teach to learners around word frequency, we need to know the extent to which our students know words at different levels of frequency. The most useful test for determining this is the Vocabulary Levels Test (VLT) (Nation, 1983, 1990; Schmitt, Schmitt, and Clapham, 2001). The VLT provides an accurate and reliable measure of the most frequent 2000, 3000, 5000, 10000, and academic vocabulary. It is not necessary to administer all sections of the test. If students have a relatively small vocabulary size, giving them just the 2000 level section of the test is sufficient. The VLT should be administered to students at the start of a course to help teachers effectively plan the words to teach during the course.

VOCABULARY KNOWLEDGE

Another factor that can be used to evaluate language learning activities is vocabulary knowledge. Nation (2001) provided the most comprehensive description of vocabulary knowledge.

He demonstrated that vocabulary knowledge could be broken down into nine different aspects of knowledge, and each of these could be broken down further into receptive and productive knowledge. This means that to learn words there needs to be some focus on developing both receptive and productive knowledge, and there also needs to be emphasis on learning the different aspects of knowledge that make up form, meaning, and use. Different vocabulary learning activities focus attention on different aspects of knowledge. This means that it is likely to take a number of encounters with a word in a number of different activities to fully learn a word.

Teachers should consider which aspects of vocabulary knowledge such as written form, form and meaning, and collocation might be learned through completing an activity. Although activities may contribute to multiple aspects of knowledge, most activities have a central focus on one aspect of form, meaning, and use. For example, the central focus of a crossword puzzle is written form. To achieve the primary learning goal, you need to correctly spell the target words. Crossword puzzles also often contribute to form and meaning when the clues are in the form of definitions or translations.

Although it is possible to modify the clues in crosswords so that they also contribute to knowledge of grammatical functions and collocation, these aspects typically receive little attention. In contrast, learning words in concordances has a central focus on collocation and grammatical functions with a smaller focus on form and meaning.

TIME ON TASK: HOW LONG DOES IT TAKE TO DO THE ACTIVITY?

The third factor that should be used in evaluation of activities is time on task because there is limited time to teach vocabulary, and some activities take longer than others. Teachers need to consider whether the knowledge gained through completing the activity justifies the amount of time taken.

In other words, does the activity contribute to worthwhile gains in vocabulary knowledge in a reasonable amount of time? For example, a demanding crossword puzzle with 20 items may take 20 minutes to finish while learning a set of 20 word cards may take half that time. If an activity takes longer, that does not mean that it should be discarded; the learning gains from the extra time may be considerable.

However, it is important to question whether longer activities result in superior learning. In the above example, we need to consider whether the extra 10 minutes necessary for the crossword will result in greater learning than what else we might achieve in that time such as learning from word cards for 10 minutes and another 10 minute activity.

The justification for longer activities may be that the greater a number of words are learned, the greater depth of vocabulary knowledge will be gained, or that words will be retained longer. If activities that take longer result in the same vocabulary learning gains as shorter activities, that time is not being used effectively.

HOW EFFECTIVE ARE ACTIVITIES?

There are two methods of evaluating the relative effectiveness of vocabulary learning activities: *Involvement Load Hypothesis* and *Technique Feature Analysis*. Laufer and Hulstijn's (2001) Involvement Load Hypothesis is the more established method.

It involves looking at the degree to which three factors (need, search, and evaluation) are present in the activity. Nation and Webb's (in press) Technique Feature Analysis is more complex, but highlights key features that contribute to the effectiveness of activities in a way that teachers may be able to relate to.

The Technique Feature Analysis involves 18 questions grouped according to psychological conditions that contribute to vocabulary learning. The answer to each question is scored as 0 or 1 with the total score indicating the relative value of that activity. The highest score possible is 18. The questions are shown below.

Criteria	Score
Motivation	
Is there a clear vocabulary learning goal?	
Does the activity motivate learning?	
Do the learners select the words?	
Noticing	
Does the activity focus attention on the target words?	
Does the activity raise awareness of new vocabulary learning?	
Does the activity involve negotiation?	
Retrieval	
Does the activity involve retrieval of the word?	
Is it productive retrieval?	
Is it recall?	
Are there multiple retrievals of each word?	
Is there spacing between retrievals?	
Generation	
Does the activity involve generative use?	
Is it productive?	
Is there a marked change that involves the use of other words?	
Retention	
Does the activity ensure successful linking of form and meaning?	
Does the activity involve instantiation?	
Does the activity involve imaging?	
Does the activity avoid interference?	
Maximum score	18

(Adapted from Nation and Webb, in press)

To become familiar with how the analysis above works, let us look at each question briefly and then look at how a number of activities score on each question.

Motivation

Is There a Clear Vocabulary Learning Goal?

Students are more likely to achieve the learning goal if they are aware of what the learning goal is. A lack of awareness may lead to misplaced focus and smaller learning gains. Activities that have a clear vocabulary learning goal such as learning with concordances, cloze activities, and word parts tables would all get 1 point under this criterion.

Does the Activity Motivate Learning?

When evaluating activities, it is important to consider the extent to which the activity might motivate learners. Although empirical studies are lacking, Dörnyei (1994) suggests that tasks and materials have the potential to motivate learning. This is clearly apparent in some vocabulary learning activities such as crosswords and riddles, which are typically done for pleasure and to a lesser degree in activities such as multiple choice questions, true/false questions, and cloze activities that present a challenge to learners. Activities such as word cards and the keyword technique that raise awareness of successful learning are also likely to motivate learning and get a point under this criterion.

Do the Learners Select the Words?

Self selection of words may have a positive influence on learning because students have indicated that these words are considered beneficial. This is also reflected in the need component of Laufer and Hultsijn's (2001) Involvement Load Hypothesis.

Noticing

Does the Activity Focus Attention on the Target Words?

There are often different ways to do activities and what teachers expect their students to do is not always what occurs. One way to increase the potential for vocabulary learning in activities is to focus attention on the target words.

Does the Activity Raise Awareness of New Vocabulary Learning?

Designing activities to focus attention on target word does not ensure that vocabulary learning will occur. Some activities may fulfill a testing function rather than a learning function. In other activities, words may be ignored, considered irrelevant, or students may feel that there is nothing new learned through completing the activity. When students focus attention on words and find something new, their processing of that information contributes to learning. New learning may result from seeing or using words in original sentences, being aware when knowledge is strengthened, and seeing an improvement in performance.

Does the Activity Involve Negotiation?

Research indicates that when learners negotiate the meanings of words encountered in a text, these words are more likely to be learned than non-negotiated items (Newton, 1995). The words that are negotiated will likely depend on their relevance to the activity. If it is not necessary to know the target words in an activity, or the words are not present in the activity, learners are less likely to negotiate their meanings. Teachers can design activities so that the target vocabulary is presented in places critical to completing the activity such as in the instructions.

Retrieval

Does the Activity Involve Retrieval of the Word?

It is well-established that successfully retrieving a word is likely to facilitate the learning of that word (Baddeley, 1990). When learners see a word in a text or hear a word in speech, they need to retrieve its meaning. Similarly, when learners need to convey information in speech or writing, they need to retrieve the L2 forms of words. It is important to note that if both the L2 word and the meaning are given together, there is no retrieval because there is nothing to retrieve.

Is It Productive Retrieval?

Retrieval may occur in two ways. First, if a L2 word is encountered in a text or heard in speech, the meaning of that word needs to be retrieved. This type of retrieval is called receptive retrieval. Second, if learners want to convey a particular meaning in L2 speech or writing, they need to retrieve the L2 word to convey that meaning. This is called productive retrieval. It is easier to see a L2 word and retrieve its L1 meaning (receptive retrieval) than to see the L1 meaning and retrieve the L2 form (productive retrieval), so productive retrieval gets a point under this criterion.

Is It Recall?

We can also differentiate between the different ways in which words are retrieved. For example, words or meanings can be recognized from a number of choices in an activity such as in multiple choice questions. When there are different choices, and learners have to recognize which one is correct, this is called recognition. If there are no choices and the learners need to retrieve the word or meaning from memory, this is called recall. Recall is more demanding than recognition, so it gets a point.

Are There Multiple Retrievals of Each Word?

If learning is enhanced, the more word is successfully retrieved. Each successful retrieval strengthens the link between L2 form and L1 meaning making it easier to retrieve the word from memory. This has been reflected in research on word cards, showing impressive learning gains in short periods through repeated retrievals (Webb, 1962) as well as in studies of incidental learning (Webb, 2007).

Is There Spacing of Retrievals?

Research has also shown that it is better to space retrievals over time rather than to mass retrievals together (Baddeley, 1990; Dempster, 1987; Hulstijn, 2001). This is called the spacing effect on learning. Interestingly, the superiority of spacing is also reflected in the superiority of repeated study sessions versus cramming (Kornell, 2009).

Generation

Does the Activity Involve Generative Use?

Generative use occurs when a word is encountered or used in a new way. Typically, generative use relates to context, but it can also be reflected at the word level when words are used with different derivations and inflections. Encountering or using a word in an original context gets a point under this criterion. Encountering or using different derivations of the word would also get a point.

Is It Productive?

Generation can be receptive or productive. Receptive generative use is when words are encountered in a new way. Productive generative use is when words are used in new ways. Productive generative use is more demanding because it requires learners to not only understand the forms and meanings of words, but also to know how to use the words to be successful.

Is There a Marked Change in the Context that Involves the Use of Other Words?

There can be different degrees of generation in activities. Research has shown that a greater degree of generation can have a positive effect on vocabulary learning (Joe, 1998). There should be an aim to having students use words in original ways. This will deepen and strengthen knowledge of words. Consider the following sentences:

Original: He analyzed the paper.
No generation: He analyzed the paper.
Minimal generation: He was analyzing the paper. He analyzed the essay.
Reasonable generation: He tried hard to analyze and figure out the paper.
High generation: The paper was confusing, and concentration and analysis were necessary.

When the degree of generation is constrained by the structure of the activity such as in role plays and rewording sentences, the degree of generation would be low. In sentence production activities the degree of generation would be high. This criterion is only used for productive generative use.

Retention

Does the Activity Ensure Successful Linking of Form and Meaning?

Many activities focus on strengthening the link between form and meaning. However, in many cases, linking form and meaning depends on successful recognition or recall of the item. If errors occur, there will be a negative effect on learning rather than a positive effect. Providing learners with both form and meaning at the start of an activity ensures a very high degree of success if learners do try to retrieve the word during later stages of the activity. Successful retrievals strengthen the link between form and meaning (Baddeley, 1990), so ensuring a high degree of success has merit.

The one disadvantage of providing both form and meaning is that learners may not try to retrieve either form or meaning when necessary but rather check the information given. If form and meaning are given, teachers should try to encourage students to familiarize themselves with the information at the beginning of the activity and then focus on retrieving the items when needed rather than checking the details.

Does the Activity Involve Instantiation?

Instantiation refers to process of remembering through association with particular contexts. The association between the word and the context helps retrieval of the word. This can occur with genuine communication where the context of the encounter with the word helps the person retrieve the word. In particular, the visual memory of the situation can have a strong effect on aiding retrieval. Instantiation may also occur with written context where the memory of the sentence in which the word was encountered helps cue recall.

Does the Activity Involve Imaging?

Imaging is the process of using visualization as a cue to recall. The best known example of imaging is the keyword technique. The keyword technique involves linking a new L2 word with a known L1 word (the keyword) that has a similar spoken form and then creating a mental image of the meanings of the two words linked together.

For example, if you were trying to learn the Japanese word *sakana* (fish), the word *soccer* might be used as the keyword. You might, then, create the image of a fish playing soccer as the mental image which helps you to remember *sakana*.

Does the Activity Avoid Interference?

Initially, learning words with related meanings together can have a negative effect on learning (Erten and Tekin, 2008; Higa, 1963). This is because learners may cross-associate the meaning of one word for another word with a related meaning. Interference is particularly strong with synonyms and opposites, but it also occurs with words from the same lexical set such as fruits, colors, and days of the week. One example of interference is when learning *left* and *right* together.

Even though the lexical set is only two items, the L2 form of *right* may get confused with the L1 meaning of *left*. Nation (2000) found that learning words in lexical sets could increase learning time by as much as 100%. Teaching materials often present new words in semantic sets making it more difficult to learn the words. To increase learning, teachers need to carefully plan vocabulary learning and avoid teaching semantically related words together.

EVALUATING TWO ACTIVITIES

Let us look at two activities using all of the above criteria to evaluate them and then modify them to increase their learning potential. The first activity involves matching words and their meanings. The learners' task is to draw a line from each word to its definition. An example is shown below.

carrot	a round red vegetable
tomato	a long orange vegetable
cucumber	a long green vegetable

The first criterion for evaluating activities is the words. In this example, learning *carrot*, *tomato*, and *cucumber* may fill a need for learners in an ESL context because they may need to deal with these words in daily interactions. The words in the definitions are all high frequency words, so the meanings should also be understood. The second criterion for evaluating an activity is vocabulary knowledge.

Here, the focus is on strengthening the link between form and meaning. The third criterion is time on task. Matching words and their meanings is a relatively quick task with a clear focus on the words. The fourth criterion is using the Technique Feature Analysis to evaluate the learning potential of the activity. This is summarized below.

Criteria	Score
Motivation	
Is there a clear vocabulary learning goal?	1
Does the activity motivate learning?	1
Do the learners select the words?	0
Noticing	
Does the activity focus attention on the target words?	1
Does the activity raise awareness of new vocabulary learning?	1
Does the activity involve negotiation?	0
Retrieval	
Does the activity involve retrieval of the word?	1
Is it productive retrieval?	0
Is it recall?	0
Are there multiple retrievals of each word?	0
Is there spacing between retrievals?	0
Generation	
Does the activity involve generative use?	0
Is it productive?	0
Is there a marked change that involves the use of other words?	0
Retention	
Does the activity ensure successful linking of form and meaning?	0
Does the activity involve instantiation?	0
Does the activity involve imaging?	0
Does the activity avoid interference?	0
Total score	5

The table shows that the activity provides 5 positive features and one negative feature (interference). The fact that it only has a score of 5 does not mean that it is not worthwhile. Because it is a relatively quick activity, it might be possible to use it together with another activity to supplement learning. However, it is still useful to consider how we can increase learning potential. The first thing that should be done is to modify the words to avoid interference. Selecting words that are less likely to be confused with each other will lead to superior learning. A better set of words that might relate to the topic would be *carrot*, *market*, and *cost*. Another way that we might increase learning potential would be to provide sentences that the words may appear in together with the definitions. This would add receptive generation as a feature of the task. The modified task would now receive a score of 7 and might look like this:

carrot	The money you need to buy something. My lunch _____ five dollars.
Market	An orange vegetable. I grow _____ in my garden.
cost	A place that you can buy things. I buy my vegetables at the _____ every week on Sunday morning.

Let us now evaluate a sentence production activity. In this activity, learners are given a number of words together with their meanings. They are asked to write each word in an original sentence. The information given to the learners might look like the following:

objective (goal or aim)

_____

prohibit (not allowed)

_____

participate (to take part in something)

Criteria	Score
Motivation	
Is there a clear vocabulary learning goal?	1
Does the activity motivate learning?	0
Do the learners select the words?	0
Noticing	
Does the activity focus attention on the target words?	1
Does the activity raise awareness of new vocabulary learning?	1
Does the activity involve negotiation?	0
Retrieval	
Does the activity involve retrieval of the word?	0
Is it productive retrieval?	0
Is it recall?	0
Are there multiple retrievals of each word?	0
Is there spacing between retrievals?	0
Generation	
Does the activity involve generative use?	1
Is it productive?	1
Is there a marked change that involves the use of other words?	1
Retention	
Does the activity ensure successful linking of form and meaning?	1
Does the activity involve instantiation?	0
Does the activity involve imaging?	0
Does the activity avoid interference?	1
Total score	8

The sentence production activity meets many criteria for effective vocabulary learning. The target words are academic vocabulary. The activity contributes to multiple aspects of vocabulary knowledge with focus on form, meaning, and use, and writing individual sentences should not require a great deal of time for learners who know the high frequency words.

One way in which it might be improved would be to add one or two examples of each word used in context. This would not add to the Technique Feature Analysis score because it already receives points for generation, but it may contribute to vocabulary knowledge. The examples may also help the learners to complete the task and save class time for further learning.

If multiple sentences were provided for each item, it would be useful to have a marked change in the way the words were used. Examples could be sampled from a concordancer. The modified activity might be presented as follows:

objective (goal or aim)
My objective is to have a high score on the test next week.
The main objective was to succeed in his business.

---

prohibit (not allowed)
Smoking is prohibited in the classroom.
The government has the power to prohibit the sale of these goods.

---

participate (to take part in something)
I always try to participate in discussions in class.
Over 100 people participated in the planning of the event.

CONCLUSION

As we have seen, preparing vocabulary learning activities involves important decisions regarding which words to teach, how vocabulary knowledge will be enhanced, whether the activity makes efficient use of learning time, and whether the activity includes features that contribute to learning. The teacher's job is to consider these factors so that activities provide the greatest learning potential. Activities may often be a useful starting point for learning words, but to develop comprehensive knowledge of vocabulary, there should be other components of a vocabulary learning program. Nation's (2001, 2008) four strands provide a useful plan for vocabulary development (see Chapter 11 for more details). Activities belong to only one of the strands, the language focused learning strand. Follow-up activities with opportunities to encounter and use words in original contexts and testing progress in vocabulary learning are also important for developing vocabulary knowledge.

REFERENCES

Alderson, J. C. (2007). Judging the frequency of English words. *Applied Linguistics*, *28*, 383-409.

Baddeley, A. (1990). *Human memory*. London: Lawrence Erlbaum.

Coxhead, A. (2000). A new academic word list. *TESOL Quarterly*, *34*, 213-238.

Dempster, F. N. (1987). Effects of variable encoding and spaced presentation on vocabulary learning. *Journal of Educational Psychology*, *79*(2), 162-170.

Dörnyei, Z. (1994). Motivation and motivating in the foreign language classroom. *The Modern Language Journal*, *78*, 273-284.

Erten, I. H., and Tekin, M. (2008). Effects on vocabulary acquisition of presenting new words in semantic sets versus semantically unrelated sets. *System, 36*, 407-422.

Higa, M. (1963). Interference effects of intralist word relationships in verbal learning. *Journal of Verbal Learning and Verbal Behavior, 2,* 170-175.

Hulstijn, J. H. (2001). Intentional and incidental second-language vocabulary learning: A reappraisal of elaboration, rehearsal and automaticity. In P. Robinson (Ed.), *Cognition and second language instruction* (pp. 258-286). Cambridge: Cambridge University Press.

Joe, A. (1998). What effects do text-based tasks promoting generation have on incidental vocabulary acquisition? *Applied Linguistics, 19,* 357-377.

Kornell, N. (2009). Optimising learning using flashcards: Spacing is more effective than cramming. *Applied Cognitive Psychology, 23,* 1297-1317.

Laufer, B., and Hulstijn, J. (2001). Incidental vocabulary acquisition in a second language: The construct of task-induced involvement. *Applied Linguistics, 22*(1), 1-26.

Nation, I. S. P. (1983). Testing and teaching vocabulary. *Guidelines, 5*(1), 12-25.

Nation, I. S. P. (1990). *Teaching and learning vocabulary.* New York: Heinle and Heinle.

Nation, I. S. P. (2000). Learning vocabulary in lexical sets: Dangers and guidelines. *TESOL Journal, 9*(2), 6-10.

Nation, I. S. P. (2001). *Learning vocabulary in another language.* Cambridge: Cambridge University Press.

Nation, I. S. P. (2004). A study of the most frequent word families in the British National Corpus. In P. Bogaards and B. Laufer (Eds.), *Vocabulary in a second language: Selection, acquisition, and testing* (pp. 3-13). Amsterdam: John Benjamins.

Nation, I. S. P. (2006). How large a vocabulary is needed for reading and listening? *The Canadian Modern Language Review, 63,* 59-82.

Nation, I. S. P. (2008). *Teaching vocabulary: Strategies and techniques.* Boston, MA: Heinle.

Nation, I. S. P., and Webb, S. (in press). *Researching and analyzing vocabulary.* Boston, MA: Heinle and Heinle.

Newton, J. (1995). Task-based interaction and incidental vocabulary learning: A case study. *Second Language Research, 11,* 159-177.

Schmitt, N., Schmitt, D., and Clapham, C. (2001). Developing and exploring the behaviour of two new versions of the Vocabulary Levels Test. *Language Testing, 18*(1), 55-88.

Webb, S. (2007). The effects of repetition on vocabulary knowledge. *Applied Linguistics, 28,* 46-65.

Webb, S., and Rodgers, M. P. H. (2009a). The lexical coverage of movies. *Applied Linguistics, 30,* 407-427.

Webb, S., and Rodgers, M. P. H. (2009b). The vocabulary demands of television programs. *Language Learning, 59,* 335-366.

Webb, W. B. (1962). The effects of prolonged learning on learning. *Journal of Verbal Learning and Verbal Behavior, 1,* 173-182.

West, M. (1953). *A general service list of English words.* London: Longman.

In: Innovation and Creativity in ELT Methodology   ISBN: 978-1-62948-146-3
Editors: H. P. Widodo and A. Cirocki   © 2013 Nova Science Publishers, Inc.

Chapter 11

TEACHING COMMUNICATIVE AND INTERACTIVE VOCABULARY FOR EFL LEARNERS

Paul Nation
Victoria University of Wellington, New Zealand

ABSTRACT

This chapter looks at the vocabulary and multiword units that learners need in an early speaking course. It also examines a range of activities across the four strands of meaning focused input, meaning focused output, language focused learning, and fluency development to show how vocabulary can be learned through communicative activities and how to prepare learners for the vocabulary demands of communication. Special attention is given to the design of vocabulary focused communicative activities and to designing a vocabulary element into typical communicative activities.

INTRODUCTION

Learning vocabulary is a means to an end, and one of the important ends that most learners of English have is to engage in conversation. This chapter looks at the kind of vocabulary that is needed for spoken use of the language, how much vocabulary is needed, how learners and teachers should deal with this vocabulary, and how vocabulary knowledge can be brought into fluent spoken use of the language.

WHAT VOCABULARY IS NEEDED FOR SPOKEN INTERACTION?

From a listening perspective, a vocabulary size of around 6000 words is needed in order to gain coverage of 98% of the running words in spoken interaction (Nation, 2006). This does not mean that a vocabulary size of 6000 words is needed to begin talking in English. West (1956, 1960) devised a minimum adequate vocabulary for speech, which was around 1200 words. This vocabulary was seen as being a starting point rather than end goal. The point is, however, that even with a small vocabulary, a considerable amount of spoken communication is possible. One of the ways of quickly becoming fluent in the language is to memorize useful phrases (Palmer, 1925). This requires careful selection of useful phrases and sentences based on the learner's immediate needs. Nation and Crabbe (1991) attempted to do this for people who want to learn a little bit of a language in order to stay a few weeks in another country. Based on interviews with people who had traveled to other countries for a short time and learned some of the local language, they devised a 120 item list of words and phrases. These included phrases like excuse me, how much does that cost? where is the toilet? thank you, and stop here.

Table 1. Spoken language phrases

Types	Instances
Apologies	pardon, sorry, excuse me, I'm sorry, I beg your pardon
Smooth-overs	don't worry, never mind
Hedges	kind of, sort of, sort of thing
Expletives	damn, gosh, hell, fuck off, good heavens, the hell, for goodness sake, good heavens above, bloody hell
Greetings	hi, hello, good evening, good morning, Happy New Year, how are you, how do you do
Initiators	anyway, however, now
Negative	no
Orders	give over, go on, shut up
Politeness markers	please
Question tags	is it, isn't it
Responses	ah, fine, good, uh, OK, quite, really, right, sure, all right, fair enough, I'm sure, I see, that's good, that's it, that's right, that's true, very good
Softeners	I mean, mind you, you know, you see, as you know, do you see
Thanks	thanks, thank you
Well	well
Exemplifiers	say
Positive	yeah, yes, yup

Table 2. The most frequent multiword units in spoken language

You know	very much
I think (that)	(no.) pound
a bit	talking about (sth)
(always, never) used to {INF}	(about) (no.) percent (of sth), in sth, on (sth), for (sth)
as well	I suppose (that)
a lot of {N}	at the moment
(no.) pounds	a little bit
thank you	looking at (sth)
(no.) years	this morning
in fact	(not) any more

The survival vocabulary has now been translated into several languages, and is a part of the vocabulary resource book available free from Paul Nation's website (see this link http://www.victoria.ac.nz/lals/staff/paul-nation/nation.aspx). The survival vocabulary can be learned in between one and two hours spread over several days, and for a small investment of learning effort gives a very large return in communicative use. One of the ways in which teachers can help learners gain early fluency in the language is to get learners to memorize useful phrases that they can use in their daily life even if this use is only within the classroom.

There is now a growing amount of research looking at the multiword units that are important in conversation. Table 1. is adapted from Stenstrom (1990, p. 144) and is derived from the London-Lund Corpus. Shin and Nation (2008) looked at the most frequent multiword units in spoken language. In contrast with the written language, the highest frequency spoken multiword units are very frequent indeed, and this has led many to claim that a large proportion of spoken language, particularly informal spoken language, consists of formulaic sequences. That is, bits of language that are stored as complete units, and are, thus, readily accessible and allow the speaker to deal with the pressure of time when producing spoken language.

Table 2. contains the twenty most frequent items from the Shin and Nation's study. McCarthy and Carter (1997, 2003) have noted the ways in which the vocabulary of spoken language differs from that of written language with interactional words like *well, know, think, right* occurring very frequently.

HOW CAN LEARNERS INCREASE THEIR SPOKEN VOCABULARY KNOWLEDGE?

It is important to take a broad view of the opportunities for learning in any language teaching situation. Thus, when looking at the ways in which spoken vocabulary can be increased, it is very useful to consider how input, output, and deliberate learning can all contribute to this growth.

One way of doing this is to make use of the four strands (Nation, 2007). Basically, a well-balanced language course consists of four strands with each given an equal amount of time in a course. These strands represent different opportunities for learning and consist of the strands of meaning focused input, meaning focused output, language focused learning, and fluency development.

The strand of meaning focused input involves learning through listening and reading. It provides learners with the opportunity to learn vocabulary incidentally, gradually increasing their breadth and depth of knowledge of particular words. Because listening is a very important part of any spoken interactive activity, the meaning focused input strand is particularly important when preparing learners for spoken interaction. The activities in the strand include listening to stories that are read aloud and taking part in communication activities and extensive reading. It is important that meaning focused input does not contain large numbers of unknown words, and that most of those that do occur are supported by helpful context. About one quarter of the time in a course should be spent gaining meaning focused input.

The strand of meaning focused output involves the learners producing language in speaking and writing. Often, learners are reluctant to use vocabulary that they feel uncertain about, and some meaning focused output activities, typically, build on meaning focused input, and previous deliberate learning. It is possible for learners to increase their vocabulary through speaking (Joe, Nation, and Newton, 1996). This involves using speaking activities that rely on written input of some kind, typically in the form of a task sheet. Such activities include ranking activities, role play activities, retelling activities, and problem solving activities. If the task sheet contains a small amount of useful vocabulary that is only partially known or unknown to many of the learners, and if this vocabulary is essential to the following spoken activity, a speaking activity can provide good opportunities for vocabulary learning (Joe, 1995; Newton, 1995). About one quarter of the time in a course should be spent for learners on producing meaning focused output.

The strand of language focused learning involves the deliberate study of language features. This could involve the study of pronunciation, the learning of word building devices, the deliberate learning of vocabulary, the development of vocabulary learning strategies, the study of grammar, and the study of discourse. One of the most important deliberate learning techniques for vocabulary is the use of word cards. These are small cards, which have a foreign language word or phrase on one side and the first language translation on the other.

The learners build up their own sets of cards and carry them around so that they can spend time going through them whenever there is a chance to do so. There is a very long history of research on this kind of learning, and it shows that large amounts of vocabulary learning are possible within a short time, that such learning results in knowledge that is not quickly forgotten (Nation, 2001, pp. 296-316), and that the knowledge gained from this learning is the kind of knowledge needed for normal language use (Elgort, 2007).

Such deliberate learning has often been out of fashion with teachers, but there is very strong research evidence to support such learning, and it is highly effective. One of the most useful jobs that a vocabulary teacher can do is to train and encourage learners in using word cards (Nation, 2008, pp. 104-114). Word cards are also a very useful means of learning multiword units (Steinel, Hulstijn, and Steinel, 2007). About one quarter of the time in a course should be spent on the deliberate study of language features.

The fourth strand is the strand of fluency development, and this is a particularly important strand for interaction. The fluency development strand does not involve the learning of new language features, but involves becoming fluent in using what is already known. That is, making the best use of what has already been learned. There can be specific vocabulary fluency development activities in a course. For example, it is very important to be able to process numbers fluently.

So, when someone tells you the price of something in a shop, you should be able to understand these numbers without having to translate them or to spend time retrieving their meaning. This fluency practice is best done with learners working in pairs with one learner acting as the teacher, but it can be done with the whole class as a teacher led activity.

The first step is a listen and point activity. In this description, a teacher can use numbers as the focus of fluency development, and assume that the teacher is working with just one learner. The learner has the numbers from 1 to 10 on a sheet in front of him.

| 1 | 2 | 3 | 4 | 5 | 6 | 7 | 8 | 9 | 10 |

The teacher says a number, for example "five", and the learner points to 5. If the learners are working in pairs, it may be necessary for the learner who is the teacher to have a list of the numbers written in their full form i.e. "one, two, three, four . . .". The teacher keeps saying numbers gradually increasing the speed so that the learner is pushed to the limits of his fluency. If the learner points to the wrong number, the teacher says "No." and says the number again. If the learner hesitates, the teacher waits until the learner points. The teacher can note which numbers are less fluently recognized by the learner and give this extra practice. Several minutes should be spent on this activity with the numbers being covered in a random order many times. This practices listening fluency. This activity should be spread across several days with a few minutes spent on it each day.

The second step is for the learner to become the teacher so that speaking fluency is practiced. The third step also practices speaking fluency. The teacher points to a number, for example 5, and the learner says it. Learners should reach a high level of fluency at Step 1 before moving on to Step 2. Fluency practice on the same items should be done on several different days so that there is opportunity for spaced retrieval (Nation, 2001). This kind of fluency development activity can also be done with greetings (where learners point to the appropriate picture), time words like *yesterday, tomorrow, next week,* and *last month* (where learners point to items on a calendar), and any picturable nouns or verbs.

There are also the general spoken fluency development activities, which do not focus particularly on vocabulary, but which result in learners being able to fluently access vocabulary. These include the 4/3/2 technique where learners work in pairs with one learner speaking on a familiar topic for four minutes while the other learner listens quietly. The pairs change partners so that each speaker now has a new partner, and they deliver the same talk, but in three minutes. They change partners again, and the same speaker delivers the same talk in two minutes. The decreasing time frame encourages fluency development. After one learner in each pair has spoken three times, it becomes the turn of the other learners to deliver their talks three times. Another useful fluency development activity is prepared talks. In such talks, the learners research and perhaps write their talks before presenting them orally. In classes with adult learners, they can be encouraged to speak on their specialist work areas. The main features of fluency development techniques are that the learners work with very familiar material, that they are pushed to go faster, that they are focused on delivering or receiving a message, and that there is quantity of practice. About one quarter of the time in a well-balanced language course should be spent on fluency development practice across the four skills of listening, speaking, reading, and writing.

LINKED SKILLS ACTIVITIES FOR VOCABULARY DEVELOPMENT

A very useful type of activity that is particularly helpful for vocabulary development is what is called *linked skills*. This involves working on the same material in different skills. For example, learners may read the text, write about it, and then talk about it. So, here, we have the same material dealt with across the three skills of reading, writing, and speaking. It is not difficult to devise linked skills activities drawing on the four skills of listening, speaking, reading, and writing. The value of linked skills activities for vocabulary learning is that the early parts of the sequence allow for slow and deliberate attention to vocabulary. In the later parts of the sequence, the vocabulary can be produced more fluently. By sticking to the same topic, the vocabulary load of the tasks is greatly reduced, and there are many opportunities for repetition of the same vocabulary. In a linked skills activity, the last skill in the sequence is the one that gets the most fluency practice. This means if the eventual goal of the activity is interaction, the last skill in the activity should involve interaction. For example, in preparing for interaction, the learners could read about a particular topic, for example, the nature of happiness. They could, then, listen to the teacher talk about what they have just read. This would allow for a little bit of question and answer. The final task in the series could be a communicative activity involving small groups doing a problem solving task related to the topic of "happiness." Linked skills activities are very useful in language courses because they provide opportunities for each of the four strands to occur. The skill of the teacher lies in being able to get the learners to spend time on the same material across a range of skills.

COMMUNICATIVE ACTIVITIES WITH A VOCABULARY FOCUS

So far, we have looked mainly at activities where the learning of vocabulary is not the main focus of the activity. This is because three of the four strands (meaning focused input, meaning focused output, and fluency development) are meaning focused strands where most of the learning is incidental learning. However, it is possible to design communicative activities, which actually focus on particular words (Nation and Hamilton-Jenkins, 2000). Here are four tasks that are based on a reading text. In effect, they are a simple form of a linked skills activity with the reading supporting the following speaking task.

Task 1. Below is a list of common reasons why people become refugees. Rank them from the most common reason to the least common.

- They become refugees because there is a war in their country.
- They become refugees because there is serious flooding in their country.
- They become refugees because their religion is not accepted in their country.
- They become refugees because they are opposed to the government in their country.
- They become refugees because there is a shortage of food in their country.

Task 2. Group these jobs into those that you think require registration (like nursing) and those that do not.

| teacher | doctor | shop assistant | plumber | bus driver |
| | lawyer | computer programmer | | engineer |

Task 3. LC had to struggle to become a nurse. Rank the reasons that made it a struggle for her from the greatest (5) to the least (1).

- struggle with English as a second language
- the demands on her time (e.g., church activities)
- have two young children

- struggle with studying after having left school a long time ago
- struggle with New Zealand customs

Task 4. LC struggled through her nursing course. What was her greatest struggle?

The words that are in bold are the target words of the activity. So, in Task 1, the teacher wants the learners to gain control of the word *refugee*. The teacher will know if the task is likely to be successful, if the learners use the word *refugee*, and if their discussion of the items to rank explores the idea that lies behind people being refugees (e.g., *Can you be a refugee as a result of flooding?*)

Task 2. focuses on the word *registration*. It is a classification task, and such tasks are very useful for vocabulary learning, particularly for vocabulary in the items, which have to be classified, and in the criterion for their classification. This is because the items have to be compared with each other, and this helps with learning their meaning. It is not a good idea, however, for all of the items to be classified to be new vocabulary. Only a few of them should be new words or recently introduced words. Although the task focuses on the meaning of *registration* when the learners do the activity, they will need to use the word. While such an activity is going on, the teacher can look for examples of negotiation where learners explain the meanings of words to each other as a normal part of the communication task.

Tasks 3. and 4 focus on the word *struggle*. Task 3 is a ranking task, and Task 4 is a simple kind of problem solving task. Each of these tasks should only take a few minutes, but they provide a focused opportunity to learn a new word as well as an opportunity to practice and develop speaking skills. These tasks are very easy to make. Such tasks, typically, ask the learners to do the following things: rank items, list causes, classify items, and analyze a complex situation.

DESIGNING VOCABULARY LEARNING INTO COMMUNICATIVE TASKS

Let us now look at how commonly used communicative activities like ranking tasks, problem solving tasks, and retelling tasks can be designed so that they contribute to vocabulary learning. There are four main guidelines to follow:

1) *Quantity of written input*: Have plenty of material on the handout so that about 10-12 new words could be included.
2) *Procedures*: Include repetition in the task.
3) *Creative use*: Encourage use of words on the handout, preferably in slightly different ways from which they appear on the handout.
4) *Deliberate attention:* Get some deliberate attention to the words.

Let us now systematically apply these four guidelines to a ranking activity, such as ranking the places where you would like to go for a holiday.

- *Quantity of written input*: Have plenty of information about the background to the situation (the places to visit) and about eight to twelve items to rank.

- *Procedures*: Get learners to do the ranking individually, then in pairs, then in groups, and then as a whole class. This is called "a pyramid procedure," with the pyramid being made up of individuals, then pairs, then groups, and then the whole class. A pyramid procedure is an excellent way of getting repetition because at each level of the pyramid, the same material is looked at again.

- *Creative use*: After the ranking has been done, report back on the final ranking and the reasons for the ranking. Reporting back is a different kind of discourse from ranking. Ranking tends to be an informal activity whereas reporting back has more formal elements. This different kind of discourse may result in small changes in the way the words are used. Using words in ways which are different from the way in which they were first met helps learning because it creates more associations with the new word.

- *Deliberate attention:* After the activity, get the learners to reflect on the new vocabulary they met. This reflection adds a deliberate language focused element to the activity. Such deliberate attention greatly increases language learning.

Let us now systematically apply the same guidelines to a problem solving activity, such as deciding where to locate a community centre within a town.

- *Quantity of written input*: Provide a lot of background to the problem, plus constraints on the solutions. Such constraints could include the nearness of neighbors, transport to the centre, and the cost of land (Nation, 1991). This background will increase the quantity of written input and provide plenty of information to stimulate the discussion.

- *Procedures*: Divide the activity into three steps: describing and understanding the problem, solving the problem, and justifying the solution. Having steps in an activity increases the amount of work that learners have to do because they have to go through each step. Having steps is a kind of procedure, just like the pyramid procedure.

- *Creative use*: Role play the activity with each participant pretending to be a person who is affected by the problem and its solution. Having role play means that learners have to change the language on the written input sheet in some way. They will also have some written input, which describes their role, and this can become a source of words to learn. In the community centre role play, you could have members of the town council, people who are opposed to the community centre for various reasons, and people who strongly support the community centre. There could also be some roles for experts such as town planners and social workers.

- *Deliberate attention:* Encourage negotiation of the new vocabulary by splitting up the handout, so each learner has a different part. By giving each learner a different piece of written information, which is essential for the task and that only the learners have, they are then encouraged to play a strong part in the activity. Because they have some words on their part the handout that others do not have, they may need to explain and negotiate these words with the others.

Let us now conclude by applying the same for guidelines to a very simple retelling task, for example, retelling a story from the newspaper.

1) *Quantity of written input*: Have plenty of material to retell. The longer the newspaper report, the more there will be to retell. It is also likely that within a longer story, there will be more repetitions of the topic words.

2) *Procedures*: Tell the information to several different people. Because the same information has to be told to different people, there will be a lot of repetition of the vocabulary. An interesting way to do this is to use an activity called *Headlines*. Half of the members of the class have different stories from the newspaper that they want to retell. They write the headline for their story in large letters on a piece of paper, and they put the piece of paper in front of them so that everyone can come and see it. Half of the members of the class are listeners, and they move around looking at the headlines, and then ask the person to tell them the story behind the headline. The idea is to have a really interesting headline so that many people ask to hear the story.

3) *Creative use*: Put the newspaper report away for later retellings or use a list of notes from the report. Retell the material from a different viewpoint from the writer of the material. For example, pretend to be one of the characters in the newspaper report, and retell the report from this character's perspective.

4) *Deliberate attention:* Give the listeners some questions to ask about the vocabulary.

By applying these four simple guidelines, a vocabulary learning element can be included into typical communicative tasks.

CONCLUSION

Spoken language differs from written language, not only in its grammar, but also in its vocabulary. It is, thus, worthwhile giving attention to specific vocabulary features that are peculiar to spoken language. It is also worthwhile seeing vocabulary as including not only single words, but also multiword units. Giving attention to multiword units is a very quick way of gaining fluency in the early stages of language learning.

This chapter has suggested that a speaking course should see the four strands of meaning focused input, meaning focused output, language focused learning, and fluency development as all contributing to speaking and vocabulary development through and for speaking.

One of the major goals of this chapter has been to show how teachers can design communicative activities to reduce the vocabulary load of such activities and to help vocabulary learning. A well-designed course takes account of vocabulary knowledge and vocabulary learning in all of the activities in the course. Vocabulary is not just something to be learned separately, but needs to be also integrated into a range of language use activities.

REFERENCES

Elgort, I. (2007). *The role of intentional decontextualised learning in second language vocabulary acquisition: Evidence from primed lexical decision tasks with advanced bilinguals.* Victoria University of Wellington, Wellington, New Zealand.

Joe, A. (1995). The value of retelling activities for vocabulary learning. *Guidelines*, 17(1), 1-8.

Joe, A., Nation, P., and Newton, J. (1996). Vocabulary learning and speaking activities. *English Teaching Forum*, 34(1), 2-7.

McCarthy, M., and Carter, R. (1997). Written and spoken vocabulary. In N. Schmitt and M. McCarthy (Eds.), *Vocabulary: Description, acquisition and pedagogy* (pp. 20-39). Cambridge: Cambridge University Press.

McCarthy, M., and Carter, R. (2003). What constitutes a basic spoken vocabulary? Research Notes: Cambridge University Press. Retrieved August 5 from www.CambridgeESOL. org/researchnotes/

Nation, I. S. P. (1991). Managing group discussion: Problem-solving tasks. *Guidelines*, 13(1), 1-10.

Nation, I. S. P. (2001). *Learning vocabulary in another language.* Cambridge: Cambridge University Press.

Nation, I. S. P. (2006). *How large a vocabulary is needed for reading and listening? The Canadian Modern Language Review*, 63(1), 59-82.

Nation, I. S. P. (2007). *The four strands. Innovation in Language Learning and Teaching*, 1(1), 1-12.

Nation, I. S. P. (2008). *Teaching vocabulary: Strategies and techniques.* Boston, MA: Heinle Cengage Learning.

Nation, P., and Crabbe, D. (1991). A survival language learning syllabus for foreign travel. *System*, 19, 191-201.

Nation, P., and Hamilton-Jenkins, A. (2000). Using communicative tasks to teach vocabulary. *Guidelines*, 22(2), 15-19.

Newton, J. (1995). *Task-based interaction and incidental vocabulary learning: A case study. Second Language Research*, 11, 159-177.

Palmer, H. E. (1925). Conversation. In R. C. Smith (Ed.), *The writings of Harold E. Palmer: An overview* [1999] (pp. 185-191). Tokyo: Hon-no-Tomosha.

Shin, D., and Nation, I. S. P. (2008). Beyond single words: The most frequent collocations in spoken English. *ELT Journal*, 62, 339-348.

Steinel, M. P., Hulstijn, J. H., and Steinel, W. (2007). Second language idiom learning in a paired-associate paradigm: Effects of direction of learning, direction of testing, idiom imageability, and idiom transparency. *Studies in Second Language Acquisition*, 29, 449-484.

Stenstrom, A. (1990). Lexical items peculiar to spoken discourse. In J. Svartvik (Ed.), The London-Lund corpus of spoken English: Description and research. *Lund studies in English* 82 (pp. 137-175). Lund, Sweden: Lund University Press.

West, M. (1956). A plateau vocabulary for speech. *Language Learning*, 7(1 and 2), 1-7.

West, M. (1960). *Teaching English in difficult circumstances.* London: Longman.

In: Innovation and Creativity in ELT Methodology
Editors: H. P. Widodo and A. Cirocki

ISBN: 978-1-62948-146-3
© 2013 Nova Science Publishers, Inc.

Chapter 12

BEFRIENDING GRAMMAR IN SECOND LANGUAGE LEARNING

Jeannine Fontaine and Rachael Shade
Indiana University of Pennsylvania, US

ABSTRACT

The inclusion of grammar in language teaching has been a subject of debate as long as languages have been taught. Trends over the past century have seen dramatic shifts in attitudes, from the grammar-translation method, which viewed grammar as central, through a plethora of "communicative" approaches, which have tended to downplay, or even omit explicit grammar instruction. In this chapter, we advocate a flexible approach to this thorny issue; given the multiplicity of situations, learner types, and structures in language, we argue that no one-method-fits-all pedagogy can succeed. We also underscore the complexity of the original question; to even formulate the question fully, we would need to first grapple with the nature of implicit (as compared with explicit) learning, and with the nature of grammar itself, which may go beyond the kinds of rules that can be made available to speakers. In spite of these problems, we support the incorporation of explicit grammar instruction as a necessary part of language teaching.

INTRODUCTION

With the word's dire fate today, many would be amazed that the word *grammar* once referred to learning in general, and that it shares the same historical root as *glamor* (via a Scots usage referring to occult learning, and ultimately even enchantment). For some decades, the *g-word* has practically been taboo—and ironically, the restriction is nowhere more doggedly enforced than among language specialists. The current (distorted in our view) situation is rooted in several well-meaning movements: the so-called *whole language* approach to reading as well as a narrowly defined trend in composition research, and subsequent developments in second language teaching that we will cover in this chapter. Under the influence of these, many schools have virtually abandoned all meaningful treatment of grammar. In fact, in our masters' and doctoral programs, we have now seen over a decade of practicing English teachers who have never had a basic course in grammar, a lacuna that only reinforces their phobia. With just the word causing such malaise, it comes as little surprise that teachers are confused about how to treat language structure in their classrooms, whether for mother tongue speakers or language learners. But, there has been a resurgence of interest; today, a quick search yields a bewildering array of trends and conflicting ideas related to grammar, with roots centuries old. Still, even today, no one can seem to agree on what a pedagogical method is best (our answer is, "It depends."). This chapter contains three main sections. In the first, we present a brief historical overview of positions on teaching language. In this section, we suggest that the long history of language teaching, particularly in the past three decades, can be boiled down to a battle between two guiding ideas: *form* and *meaning*. In the second section, we touch on some thorny issues that further cloud the-already-murky competition between the two and that further explain why definitive answers have been so hard to find. Finally, in our concluding section, we make some suggestions for resources and ideas that may guide language teachers in developing their own practice. We will argue that there is no one-method-fits-all answer, but that teachers can experience the excitement of developing their own stance and practice based on familiarity with the issues we cover in this chapter.

HISTORY: TWO TRENDS AT LOGGERHEADS

Grammar Translation

The oft-reviled *grammar-translation* method is also known as the *classical method,* as it originates from the instruction of Latin and Greek to foster intellectual development (Brown, 2000). Before the nineteenth century, most language learners were individual scholars who needed reading knowledge in order to interpret texts. Generally speaking, they were highly educated men and women, trained in classical grammar, and able to apply this knowledge to whatever new language they were studying. This approach, *grammar translation*, worked well for self study by a relatively small elite class, but not for teaching groups in a classroom setting. So, nineteenth century writers of instructional texts like Ahn (1864) and Ollendorff (1848) attempted to make the traditional ways of language learning fit the needs and context of schools. The resulting method was called *grammar-translation* because it kept the basic framework of teaching grammar and using translation exercises. High priority was given to accuracy; the spoken language was neglected; and special status was given to exemplified sentences at the expense of connected text.

Reform Movement: The Roots of Modern Communicative Competence

Almost as soon as these texts appeared, reformers spoke out against the teaching of grammar in isolation from texts and the excessive use of translation in teaching (Howatt and Widdowson, 2004); these reformers championed the use of connected text and a focus on meaning. Also, near the end of the nineteenth century, under the influence of phoneticians, speech and orality began to take a primary place in teaching methodology. However, challenges arose with the new pedagogy: Texts needed to be interesting and coherent, yet still served the purpose of presenting foreign language grammar, which students were expected to understand inductively (Howatt and Widdowson, 2004). Translation still played a central role; however, echoing a debate still raging today, critics worried about the use of the learner's first language in the classroom (Truscott, 1996; Turnbull, 2001). With the focus on speech and confusion over the value of translation, a new method came to light that has been called the *direct method*. Interestingly enough, this is similar to what is known as the *communicative approach* today. Developed (partly by chance, it is said) by Maximilien Berlitz in about 1880, the direct method sees language as a set of skills that human beings intuitively *know* how to acquire under the proper conditions. The method depends on oral interactions and spontaneity in language use, leaving grammar rules to be *learned* inductively and banning translation. The method was widely heralded into the beginning of the twentieth century, and the name Berlitz is still renowned today; but constraints on budget, time, and classroom sizes lead to its decline as a general approach (Brown, 2000).

AUDIO-LINGUAL AND STRUCTURAL METHODS

With the start of World War II, there emerged a high demand for foreign language teaching of all varieties. To meet this demand, a new method was cultivated that borrowed aspects of the direct method, particularly the focus on speech. Called the *audio-lingual method*, the new approach was based on behaviorist principles: that people could be taught through a system of reinforcement and that language learning was largely subject to *stimulus-response* patterns. This method, used by the senior author at the start of her career, worked on the assumption that the student learned the language directly with no translation. Students memorized short conversations, and then went through exhaustive (and exhausting!) grammar drills where the teacher (or a recorded tape) would provide a pattern sentence, and the student would repeat with variations (Student: *I always forget names* . . . Recording: *my purse;* Student: *I always forget my purse* . . . Recording: *my friend's birthday*; Student: *I always forget my friend's birthday*). These drills were presented with no explicit grammar instruction (Brown, 2000). Out of the audio-lingual method came the institutional popularity of the *structural approach* in the 1940s and 1950s, which also advocated habit formation and repetition and supported the notion of drilling students orally before they began to read and write in the target language. Ultimately, the neglect of context in this approach was challenged by John Rupert Firth. In the 1950s, Firth developed the notion of *context of situation* in which language and social activity were unified (Howatt and Widdowson, 2004).

GENERATIVE AND UNIVERSAL GRAMMAR

Also in the mid-1950s, Noam Chomsky appeared on the scene and dealt severe blows to both traditional grammar and the behaviorist view of language, developing a theoretical framework that became well-known under the term *generative grammar*. In a review of grammatical theories, Matthews (1996) characterizes Chomsky's theory as seeking a set of elegant, simple rules that will *generate* (as the theory's name suggests) the grammatical sentences of a language.

Chomsky believed that languages' *deep structures* shared many abstract properties although these similarities were hidden by the *surface structures* of actual sentences (Chomsky, 1965). In a now famous review of B. F. Skinner's *Verbal Behavior*, Chomsky (1959) produced a set of powerful arguments that ultimately undercut the validity of behaviorist ideas as applied to language.

Although the mechanics and terminology of generative grammar have evolved substantially in a half century (Chomsky, 1981, 1995; Radford, 2004), and the movement has spawned numerous other cognitive approaches, the generative goals and view of language have remained the same (for reasonably accessible, but in-depth discussion, see Smith, 1999 and Piattelli-Palmarini, Salaburu, and Uriagereka, 2009).

Central to Chomsky's thinking is that language is a creative system whose workings are rooted in the brain's capacity, in a set of innate *principles* and *parameters* common to all languages and available to all first language learners, called collectively *universal grammar* (*UG*).

Generative grammar has deeply influenced scholarly understanding of first language acquisition, and has, therefore, raised complex questions about the teaching of second languages. If a child's grammatical system draws on innate factors that are set by experience with the language she hears, what happens later, once the parameters for one language have already been set, and the child, now grown, meets other languages? Applications of this theory have led to some surprising results.

To mention just one, a study by Goad and White (2008), universal grammar was used to explain why Mandarin-speaking adult learners of English were producing articles and tense in ways that could be attributed to neither their first language (L1) nor their second language (L2), but are said to be rooted in UG. In the L1 context, linguists have also proposed notions such as *bootstrapping* by which a child uses her grasp of some one aspect of language (say prosody or syntax) to acquire another, such as meaning (Hohle, 2009). In sum, generative grammar has opened a host of new questions about second language learning (e.g., Cook and Newson, 2007; White, 2003), many of which have yet to be fully understood, let alone answered.

THE COMMUNICATIVE APPROACH

In 1966, while educators were scratching their heads over generative grammar, sociolinguist Dell Hymes coined a new term that immediately caught on among language teachers; the new magic phrase was *communicative competence*; in contrast to Chomsky's *grammatical competence*, which referred to a speaker's command of core areas like morphology and syntax, Hymes (1966) proposed that speakers need *communicative competence*, the ability to use language effectively.

Tired of tedious trends that focused heavily on drills, isolated structures, and sheer memorization and unwilling to return to the old, outdated, and discredited grammar-translation routines, enthusiastic researchers and educators in the 1970s and 1980s adapted Hymes' notion and launched the *communicative movement* in applied linguistics and language teaching. Language, it was claimed, could not be separated from real life usage; in fact, it only really worked in the real world, and classrooms needed to respond more to the needs of students as they tried to acquire language. Communicative language teaching (CLT) was soon in full swing, with an emphasis on context and the connectedness of discourse and a disdain for grammar instruction, recalling the nineteenth century direct method (Howatt and Widdowson, 2004).

Researchers such as Widdowson (1978) enriched CLT by emphasizing the connectedness of discourse. Terms such as *coherence* and *cohesion* (Halliday and Hasan, 1976), with their emphasis on relationships in discourse, became popular. Notions like *speech acts* also took center stage with CLT and its desire to teach a second language by emphasizing a speaker's real-world performance.

Speech Act theory focuses on divergence between the form of an utterance and its intended meaning in context (Smith, 1990). When speech acts arrived on the language scene, so did *pragmatics*, a sub-branch of linguistics that studies how meaning relies on context, general knowledge, and the interpretation of speaker intent. Language users depend on pragmatics to work out ambiguity, and to fill in much of what is not literally said or written.

KRASHEN: THE BEST OF ALL WORLDS?

In the 1980s, a dynamic new figure appeared on the second language scene, who seemed to understand both Chomsky and Hymes; most readers will know the name of Stephen Krashen, who became well-known (and soundly criticized) for five hypotheses: the *acquisition-learning hypothesis*, which distinguishes between *acquiring* a language at an implicit, subconscious level, and *learning* a language through explicit, conscious activity (Krashen and Terrell, 1983); the *monitor hypothesis*, which claims that formal rules can function as a *monitor*, ensuring correctness, e.g., in careful writing (Krashen, 2003); the *input hypothesis*, which states that one acquires language only through comprehensible input (Krashen's $i +1$, where i represents knowledge already acquired and $+1$ represents input that triggers new knowledge) (Krashen, 1985); the *affective filter hypothesis*, claiming that negative emotions can impede language acquisition (Krashen, 2003); and the *natural order hypothesis*, asserting that one acquires the rules of a language in a predictable order (Krashen, 2003). Krashen had it all, it seemed; some aspects of his theory incorporated Chomskian views (the *acquisition/learning* distinction, the *natural order hypothesis*) while others represented a deep nod to the importance of communication and context (*i+ 1, the affective filter*); there was even room for explicit grammar (albeit a limited one) via the *monitor*. And most important for busy educators, Krashen presented his ideas in highly accessible language; of course, it also helped that he was an entertaining speaker who kept audiences spellbound.

Krashen and Terrell (1983) proposed what they called the *natural approach* to teaching language, featuring comprehensible input and absolutely ruling out grammar instruction. Students, they said, can learn a new language in the same way they learned their first language, *naturally,* instead of via explicit rules. The new system was intuitively attractive; it seemed to combine the best ideas around, and was a friendly, if eccentric, cousin to CLT.

STORM CLOUDS ON THE CLT HORIZON

In its many forms, CLT was immensely popular; whole classes of SLA students in our doctoral program in the 1980s and early 1990s professed allegiance to the movement. But, ultimately the pedagogy growing out of CLT and the natural approach did seem to have one serious flaw: In some respects, it did not work. Soon enough, stunned educators (such as the elder author of this article) were introduced to Wes, a Japanese artist living in Hawaii whose charismatic personality won him friends, but whose measured accuracy on relative clauses and verb forms put him at distressingly low levels of grammatical competence (Schmidt, 1983). For example, Wes's score for correct usage of the third person singular was only 21%, while his usage of possessives was even lower: 8% accuracy! Schmidt (1983) elaborates: "Except in routine, formulaic utterances … Wes has no subject-verb inversion in questions … no relative clauses… and no passives…" (p. 149). Immersed in regular language input and highly motivated, Wes should have been a grammatical success story according to the reigning communicative orthodoxy. But, in fact, he was not; and such cases have continued to emerge in the years after Schmidt's study. A detailed recent example is Lardiere (2007), who has traced the language development, and the fossilized language forms, of a learner called Patty. Patty had a high degree of integration into English speaking culture, positive attitudes, high motivation, and good socialization skills. But, she still failed to acquire several key structures in English. Lardiere (2007) compares this pattern with that of a learner of French called BH studied by Schumann, who had a similar background to Patty's, but who trained himself rigorously on linguistic forms: "[I]t is quite clear that the main difference between Patty and BH's outcomes lies in the extent of formal metalinguistic study" (p. 42). BH had spent hours in a language lab, and had engaged in "formal study, including the phonology, morphology, and syntax, of the target language" (p. 42).

CLT: THE HYDRA OF COMMUNICATIVE PRACTICE

Basically, then, the *old* traditional grammar-translation method had been based on faulty assumptions and, even worse, on inadequate models of language. Everyone agreed on that much, it seemed; and many institutions made it their one point of certainty in a broiling sea of pedagogical controversies. In fact, the younger co-author of this article recalls that, in her own training and teaching experience, she was always given the impression that grammar-translation was a kind of professional "mortal sin." She commented recently informally on her classroom experience, in terms that will resonate with many teachers: "I as a teacher was constrained quite a bit by administrators. It was CLT all the way, or poor review!"

But, now, to the dismay of its ardent supporters, CLT and its kin were running into one very important global problem: It did not lead to successful language learning. Still, like the proponents of a favored ideology or the supporters of a beloved political candidate, many clung doggedly to CLT's basic tenets: Communication had to be central; grammar rules had to be shunned. Still, they realized that the fluency so prized by communicative proponents needed to be balanced by the accuracy that, it seemed, called for some kind of (sigh) *grammar* instruction. So, although the dread *g-word* virtually never surfaced, a rash of new ideas appeared over two decades, all of which can be seen as amendments to CLT that accorded some degree of centrality to linguistic form. The result, we will argue, has been a kind of perennial tug-of-war between *meaning* and *form* (or *grammar!*), with multiple approaches falling somewhere along a continuum between the two. Before moving on, we highlight a few selected notions from the plethora of approaches proposed in this spirit.

TASK BASED GRAMMAR AND BEYOND

A typical example is *task based grammar*, which teaches grammatical points, but then immediately applies them to authentic situations where the student would need to use what has been taught in order to communicate. As more interest in this approach grew in the field (Skehan, 1998), Ellis played a prominent role in developing the notion of task based language learning. Here, the student is seen more as a *user* of the language than as a *learner*; she focuses more on the message she wishes to convey than on the form (Ellis, 2003). Ellis emphasizes the importance of factors such as perspective (from whose point of view is the task seen?), and real world authenticity of the task (survival tasks, day-to-day living tasks).

Other amended forms of CLT have appeared, and are too numerous to cite here, beyond a few examples. For instance, CLT seems to be at center stage still in proposals by scholars who are advocating *whole-language learning* in order to teach adults. Scheffler (2008) has continued to support a *natural approach*, but advocates explicit instruction in grammar to some extent when teaching adults. Fitch (2001) insists that adult language learners need to be given grammatical rules, as does Zhonggang Gao (2001). Looking at such writers, one sees a continuum, with the completely *natural* approach at one end, and something like an evolved version of *grammar-translation* (minus the translation) at the other.

LONG'S FOCUS ON **FORMS**

In a seminal essay covering evidence in favor of explicit grammatical instruction, Long (1988) maintained his CLT credentials as he distanced himself from what he termed the undesirable *focus on forms* of traditional approaches, which teach isolated grammatical elements with little attention to context, function, or usage:

> [M]y own view is that a focus on *form* is probably a key feature of SL instruction, because of the saliency it brings to targeted features in classroom input, and also in input outside the classroom . . . I do not think, on the other hand, that there is any evidence that an instructional program built around a series (or even a sequence) of isolated *forms* is any more supportable now, either theoretically, empirically, or logically, than it was when Krashen and others attacked it several years ago. (p. 136)

Whether deliberately or unwittingly, Long had created a new buzzword for amended CLT: "focus on form," which has run the gamut of capitalization practice, from "focus on formS" (Laufer, 2006; Sheen, 2005) to "focus on FORMS" (Nassaji and Fotos, 2004).

A decade later, a collection by Doughty and Williams (1998) featured Long's (1991, 2000) ideas in its title and took *focus on form* as its organizational motif. Still, the editors were obliged to admit that the entries in their collection were highly variable in their adherence to Long's original definition—and that the definition itself left much room for variation. In fact, in their introduction, the editors are compelled to admit that "[t]here is considerable variation in how the term *focus on form* is understood and used" (p. 5), and that at least two contributions to their volume advocated approaches that would be seen as "*focus on formS*" (p. 5). Among the proposals in that collection and elsewhere are the following widely divergent suggestions, all of which qualify as applications of *focus on form*: *recasts* (repeating the learner's erroneous sentence with correction); *error correction* (as in written pieces); and *attending* to form (calling the learner's attention to particular forms; providing an *input flood* rich in a given structure). Numerous ideas have grown from the CLT era. One is *processing instruction*, which advocates exposure to a target grammatical point along with activities that focus on input (VanPatten, 2002). Another that has drawn considerable attention is *interactional feedback*, which emphasizes negotiation between the student and the instructor (Nassaji and Swain, 2000). Yet, another is *discourse based teaching*, which argues for "extensive use of authentic or simplified discourse, including corpus analysis, to supply learners with abundant examples of contextualized usages" (Nassaji and Fotos, 2004, p. 136). Hinkel (2002) argued for this method in helping students master the rhetorical patterns needed to create texts in their L2.

FURTHER COMPLICATIONS

So, who is right? Can't we just test the methods and measure the results? Of course, the answer to that is a resounding *no*, most likely because one needs *both* grammar and meaning and both fluency and accuracy. In this section, so as not to leave the reader blaming these fine researchers for their confusion, we will try to outline additional reasons why the questions at the start of this article are so hard to answer. We have already hinted at how tricky the *grammar-versus-meaning* warfare can get. But, there are other issues, often ignored in the literature that make the whole picture even murkier. We touch on two problem areas; each of which would divide into numerous meandering pathways that we can only hint here.

The Nature and Scope of Grammar(s)

As late as the mid-twentieth century, people pretty much thought they knew what *grammar* was. Good heavens, by the end of the first millennium C.E., the Sanskrit grammarians, the Arabic grammarians, the Greeks, and the Romans had figured all of that out, hadn't they? Every sixth grader in the 1950s memorized definitions for *noun* and *verb*, and drew the notorious Reed-Kellogg diagrams of sentences. So what is the problem? Well, grammar has changed radically and in several ways. Recall the generative ideas where grammar is seen as a set of abstract patterns in the mind or brain of the speaker! Well, if such schools of thought are right (and a half dozen others have arisen after Chomsky), the internal mental *grammar* we use to understand and produce language is nothing like what was described in the traditional rule books. To give the non-specialist reader a sense of the technical concepts involved, recent issues of two important linguistic journals feature articles on *Split Auxiliary Selection, Pseudo-resultative Predicates* (*Natural Language and Linguistic*

Theory, vol. 28, no.1, 2010), *Doubly Filled Comps, Left-branch Extraction,* and the deceptively aquatic sounding *Sluicing* (*Linguistic Inquiry,* vol. 41, issue 2, spring 2010).

Oddly enough, these terms are not just ivory-tower intellectual fantasies: The going theory says that they are labels for what *really goes on* in a speaker's head. And, it takes years for a linguist to learn about these processes—some are still beyond the reach of dedicated researchers who have spent decades trying to decipher them. If these very abstract processes are really the way language works—and remember, that is the idea—then we will have to admit that we cannot teach *grammar* in any direct sense. That is, we cannot explain learners the things their brains must do with language. Sometimes, of course, the resulting *surface* patterns can be described: We say French "puts the adverb after the verb" (*Jacques eats always pizza*); while English puts it before (*Jack always eats pizza*). But, many linguists now agree that what is *really* going on in French and English minds is an abstract process involving the verb, not the adverb; to over-simplify drastically, the French verb kind of jumps up into position while the adverb actually just stays in place (though it ends up *after* the verb). In an ingenious study discussed in Lardiere (2007), Trahey and White (1993) actually gave francophone learners of English surface *adverb-placement* training. The group given this explicit training did better than an *input flooding* group given many examples in that they correctly rejected English forms like **Jack eats always pizza* (the asterisk indicates ungrammaticality). However, there was a trick: They also incorrectly rejected sentences like *John walked slowly across the room,* which are grammatical. They had learned a surface pattern (*don't put an adverb right after the verb*); but they had not mastered the *deeper* grammatical system of English, which distinguishes between a verb with a direct object, like *pizza,* and one with a prepositional phrase like *across the room*—but which cannot be easily put into descriptive terms for learners. By the way, did you do a double-take way back in the section on Chomsky, where we suggested that children learn language *without sufficient input?* Yes, we meant it; the simple fact is that children are never given lessons on what is *not* in their language—they are not given what generativists call *negative input.* This deceptively simple mystery about L1 becomes a nightmare in the L2 situation where learners may *need* to be told explicitly that their familiar L1 patterns do not occur in the L2. This negative input problem can be seen in the adverb-verb placement example given just now (note that we have to somehow tell French speakers, not to use their French word order in English). By the way, the explicit instruction group had lost the correct pattern a year later. In vast numbers of cases, indirect description is impossible—and again, the neurologically sound one, discovered by linguists, would make no sense to a learner. In the first journal listed above, Julie Anne Legate (2010) accounts for the way *how* sometimes replaces *that* in embedded clauses in informal speech (*Joe told me how they tore down that old barn*); using two highly abstract structural notions, Legate explains that the *how* form involves "*a definite DP,* rather than a *simple embedded CP*" (emphasis added). Of course, such an abstract jargon would make no sense to a learner. The point is that the more linguists learn about language, the more the distance has grown between pedagogical and brain based pictures of grammar. Lest you be tempted to pooh-pooh these ideas as the inventions of mad linguists with nothing better to do, consider this: There is clear and growing evidence, reaching back to Selinker's (1972) coining of the term *interlanguage* that learner grammars do develop abstract patterns—and that they can do so independently of either L1 patterns, L2 input, or classroom instruction. To take just one example that has been documented, Russian speakers are said to develop usage patterns for English *the,* which do not exist in Russian or in English. Remember Universal Grammar

(UG)? Well, researchers have hypothesized that UG allows languages to choose between two possible semantic criteria for their article use: Either *definiteness* (where speaker and hearer agree, there is one specific individual being referred to) or *specificity* (where the speaker has one individual in mind, but does not necessarily share this knowledge with the hearer). In English, if Jeannine cannot talk to Rachael, she might say something like *I've got to rush, I have to meet with a student now*! The student in question is *specific*: that is, Jeannine (usually) knows which student she is meeting with; but not *definite*, since the knowledge is not shared by her hearer. So, English does not use *the* to mark specificity, at least in standard formal usage. Russian does not use *the* for anything because it has no such form. Now, (finally), here is the catch: Russian learners of English develop a pattern of *alternating between definiteness and specificity*. The theory is that these speakers, "in the absence of transfer, *have direct access to semantic universals*, and fluctuate between them" (emphasis added) (Ionin, Zubizarreta, and Maldonado, 2008, p. 554). Even where linguistic patterns can be described, problems of a different sort rapidly arise from the sheer volume of knowledge we are gaining about usage. The advent of corpus linguistics has led to an explosion of linguistic information that was previously unknown, for instance on the frequency of collocations, lexical chunks, and familiar groupings of words that Willis (2003) calls *polywords, frames, and patterns* (p. 161). For instance, Willis cites scholarly evidence that certain verbs occur nearly always in the continuous form (like *chat, joke, kid,* and *moan*) (p. 180). Surely, these facts and patterns are part of English *grammar*. But, as the body of corpus based information mushrooms, where do we draw the line in identifying the cool patterns we want to share with learners?

Implicit Versus Explicit Learning: What is Taught Versus What is Learned

Not too long ago, I (Jeannine) was sitting with an advanced doctoral student from an Asian country; we will call her Amy. Amy was explaining something about a form required of her by the university's international office: "I fill out a form," she said; now, I wanted to know if she needed my help with this task, or if she had already done it and was just reporting it to me. After Amy repeated the sentence above several times, I finally stopped and said, in a teasing tone, "Amy, you really *have to* get a past tense." Amy smiled broadly, and said, immediately, "I filled out the form already," emphasizing the verbal ending. She knew the form perfectly well like thousands of L2 users. She just somehow never quite got around to using it most of the time. Willis (2003) shares a telling story of his carefully rehearsed lesson on English *tag questions*; the students were getting every form right, and Willis was convinced they had acquired the form—that is, until he asked them to write some examples in their exercise books, and a student immediately raised his hand: "Please, sir, you've got our exercise books … isn' it?" (p. 4) We have all been through this: We have *taught* the rule; we have *practiced* the pattern; the students know it; and they have been flooded with examples. They can recite the correct form on demand. But, we have a sinking feeling, deep in our hearts based on experience, which we will look in vain tomorrow for the correct form in their next spoken sentence, or in the paper they will write tonight. Here, though the issue looks simple, it is devilishly deceptive, poised at the edge of a craggy intellectual abyss, involving the distinction between *implicit* and *explicit* learning. It seemed so clear when Krashen talked about *learning* and *acquisition*: Learning was what you do on purpose, and acquisition was what you do without conscious intent. Obviously, Krashen was right: Much of language acquisition is implicit. But, Krashen side-stepped two major questions: first, what *are* implicit and explicit learning? And second, how are the two related? On the definition issue: DeKeyser (2003) notes that a number of other dichotomies are often confused with, or have been substituted for, the notions of implicit-explicit learning. These include *intentionality* (*explicit* learning happens when the learner deliberately decides to learn); *automaticity* (achieved when one performs without having to think of the individual steps in a process); and *inductive* versus *deductive* learning (either drawing a rule from examples or reasoning from principles). Unfortunately, the tricky issue of grammar teaching involves every one of these dichotomies. What is more, it has been difficult to find a way to measure implicit and explicit learning (e.g., does explicit learning happen only if the learner can *verbalize* what she has learned?); and there are *very* few classroom studies on the matter. To mention just one of many additional complicating factors, one cannot control what a learner chooses to do. For some time, researchers were fond of the term *incidental* learning, typically applied to vocabulary to mean that the words were simply learned, without deliberate effort, through *extensive reading* (another popular term in the 1990s); however, Alshamrani (2003) unwittingly exemplified a problem with that connection in a study looking at student reading experience, including the possibility of incidental learning; he found that his *incidental learners* were actually exploiting a whole range of strategies on their own—making file cards, looking up words, and making marginal notes—when they met new words. Schilhab (2007) affirms that explicit knowledge is transferable between individuals while implicit knowledge "is not within the perspective of representations" (p. 224). Among other things, Schilhab observes that because implicit knowledge is so dependent on context, it is nearly impossible to explain to others except by example. Of course, since linguistic *knowledge* is predominantly implicit, this again adds to the problem of measuring and talking about it— hence most discussions tend to focus on explicit instruction at the expense of trying to understand the nature of implicit knowledge. Even if one could pin down clear definitions of these terms (a task not even attempted in much writing about grammar instruction), the second major problem would still loom on the horizon: Just what is the relationship between explicit and implicit learning? It is clear that there *is* a relationship; but what of those students who learn a rule explicitly can apply it in a Krashen-monitor style, deliberately and explicitly, but whose intuitive, automatic usage does not reflect the rule? And remember the adverb-placement learners, who seem to have acquired the target structure (sort of), but had lost it a year later? Just what does it take for explicit learning to filter down and influence implicit, intuitive skills—and in a way that lasts?

So Where Are We Now? The Instructor's Manual (At Last!)

If you are dizzy at this stage, we sympathize. The overwhelming plethora of terms, notions, approaches, and ideas available in the literature is simply too much for any of us to manage as teachers. So, this last section of our chapter is meant to address the practical issue of pedagogical choices. Why has it been too difficult to decide on the best approach to teaching language? We believe that there are two primary factors, which are at least partly related. The first involves the need to give up the tempting search for the *right* method, and instead to situate oneself flexibly, taking the best from different methods in each new situation. One practical writer on teaching issues, Scott Thornbury (1999), suggests a number of workable classroom activities involving both form and meaning. Thornbury offers a very clear graphic view of our discussion on the tug-of-war between grammar (form) and meaning. We reproduce his diagram here (p. 23):

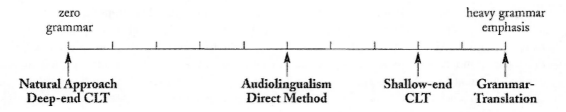

Source: With permission from Scott Thorbury and Pearson Longman, (Copyright 1999).

Using an approach in which the choice of method depends on the situation, the structure or communicative function being taught, the age of the students, and other contributing factors, Thornbury provides a clear discussion of the issues involved in the methodologies on this continuum. It is our position that, given the multiplicities of students, goals, and linguistic features, no method can possibly be *the* right one and that every method probably plays (or can play) some role in successful language learning. After all, in spite of the fall of behaviorism, are we not all just a tad bit behaviorist when we walk around with flash cards and repeat words and phrases to ourselves? And for all the problems with CLT, is it not likely that the communicative *input flood* idea may be the best way for learners to become familiar with frequent collocations and lexical phrases?

The second factor, a related one in fact, simply involves our somehow being willing to rehabilitate the term *grammar*. One courageous researcher (Fotos, 2005), has been able to point out the tug-of-war we have spoken of, and to openly advocate an integration of the two trends, grammar-translation *and* communicative language teaching. In any case, elements of grammar-translation have remained alive and kicking in the wings through decades of methodological warfare—presumably because teachers have always had a residual awareness that structure did somehow matter. (One graduate SLA class that Jeannine taught in the late 1980s included students who unanimously and vociferously declared their allegiance to CLT—but when asked whether they intended to continue teaching grammar in their classes, *all of them*, some rather sheepishly, raised their hands!)

In reviewing a half century's literature, it has become clear to us that some integration of the *best of* multiple methods may be called for in twenty-first century language teaching. Research continues to re-examine earlier positions, and rightly so. For instance, according to Luk and Shirai (2009), many textbooks even today dedicated to second language acquisition (SLA) downplay the importance of L1 transfer in favor of the *natural order* model proposed by Krashen back in 1977. The authors hint that L1 transfer needs much more attention in SLA than it is being given, in the field's tendency to move on to the most popular new trend rather than going back to explore the positive contribution of earlier ideas.

As teachers, each of us will need multiple, flexible positions, not a single static one, on the continuum sketched above. No instructional situation is the same. There are just too many variables when it comes to the students' culture and L1, the situation, the particular combination of L1 and L2, prior L1 and L2 proficiency, class size, time, resources, and the particular structure or communicative goal being taught. The list could go on. We feel that the time has come to accept that there is no one best way to teach a language and that the instructor should be prepared to implement a variety of approaches as the need arises. Instructors need to feel empowered to make their own pedagogical decisions; it is the task of researchers to support that empowerment, rather than to man the barricades in favor of any one rigid pedagogical approach. It may seem dizzying at first; but it can become downright exciting to be making one's own choices from a whole smorgasbord of options, rather than following rigid orthodoxy and fearing the *moral sin* of somebody else's approach.

CONCLUSION

So, what can instructors do to prepare to make these flexible decisions? First of all, readers of this volume, particularly of the two articles on grammar, are taking a necessary step: Seeking an understanding of how different approaches have developed and how they work. As research matures and develops, more teacher friendly answers may be forthcoming—particularly if long-term studies are done, and involve focus on few rather than many forms (Nassaji and Fotos, 2004).

A second essential step is for instructors to learn all they can about English grammar. Even if you have had limited or no grammar instruction, there are excellent, quite comprehensive, grammars available, such as the now-classic Celce-Muria and Larsen-Freeman (1999). A recent addition, Cowan (2008), begins with three chapters addressed to issues such as the rationale for teaching grammar, including one devoted to elaborating on the methods outlined here; the remaining 23 chapters contain a rich store of specific activities correlated with the different approaches. But, many other resources are available; an online search for materials, including visits to publishers' websites, can be a rewarding adventure these days. In any case, we hope every reader of this chapter will make some contribution, small or great, toward welcoming grammar back to its rightful place. In the process, we believe that language teachers will be helping learners to appreciate the wonders of language as well as to learn its many subtle tricks.

REFERENCES

Ahn, F. (1864). *A new, practical and easy method of learning the German language: First and second course in one volume.* London: Trubner and Nutt.

Alshamrani, H. (2003). The attitudes and beliefs of second language students of English regarding extensive reading of authentic texts (Doctoral dissertation). Available from ProQuest Dissertations and Theses database. (UMI No. 3080428).

Brown, H. D. (2000). *Principles of language learning and teaching.* New York: Longman.

Celce-Muria, M., and Larsen-Freeman, D. (1999). *The grammar book: An ESL/EFL teacher's course.* Florence, KY: Heinle and Heinle.

Chomsky, N. (1959). Verbal behavior. By B. F. Skinner. *Language,* 35, 26-58.

Chomsky, N. (1965). *Aspects of the theory of syntax*. Cambridge, MA: MIT Press.

Chomsky, N. (1981). Lectures on government and binding. Amsterdam: Mouton de Gruyter.

Chomsky, N. (1995). *The minimalist program*. Cambridge, MA: MIT Press.

Cook, V., and Newson, M. (2007). *Chomsky's universal grammar*. New York: Wiley-Blackwell.

Cowan, R. (2008). *The teacher's grammar of English: A course book and reference guide*. New York: Cambridge University Press.

DeKeyser, R. (2003). Implicit and explicit learning. In C. F. Doughty and M. Long (Eds.), *The handbook of second language acquisition* (pp. 313-348). Oxford: Blackwell.

Doughty, C., and Williams, J. (1998). *Focus on form in classroom second language acquisition*. Cambridge: Cambridge University Press.

Ellis, R. (2003). *Task-based language learning and teaching*. Oxford: Oxford University Press.

Fitch, D. (2001). Teaching grammar to adults and second language learning research. *Education*, 116(1), 32-34.

Fotos, S. (2005). Traditional and grammar translation methods for second language teaching. In E. Hinkel (Ed.), *Handbook of research in second language teaching and learning* (pp. 673-670). Mahwah, NJ: Lawrence Erlbaum.

Goad, H., and White, L. (2008). *Prosodic structure and the representation of L2 functional morphology: A nativist approach. Lin*gua, 118, 577-594.

Halliday, M. A. K., and Hasan, R. (1976). *Cohesion in English*. London: Longman.

Hinkel, E. (2002). Grammar teaching in writing classes: Tenses and cohesion. In E. Hinkel and S. Fotos (Eds.), *New perspectives on grammar teaching in second language classrooms* (pp. 181-198). Mahwah, NJ: Lawrence Erlbaum.

Hohle, B. (2009). Bootstrapping mechanisms in first language acquisition. *Linguistics*, 47, 359-382.

Howatt, A. P. R., and Widdowson, H. G. (2004). *A history of English language teaching*. Oxford: Oxford University Press.

Hymes, D. (1966). Two types of linguistic relativity. In W. Bright (Ed.), *Sociolinguistics* (pp. 114-158). The Hague: Mouton de Gruyter.

Ionin, T., Zubizarreta, M. S., and Maldonado, S. B. (2008). Sources of linguistic knowledge in the second language acquisition of English articles. *Lingua*, 118, 554-576.

Krashen, S. (1977). *Some issues relating to the Monitor Model*. In H. Brown, C. Yorio, and R. Crymes (Eds.), On TESOL '77 (pp. 144-158). Washington, D.C: TESOL.

Krashen, S. (1985). *The input hypothesis: Issues and implications*. New York: Longman.

Krashen, S. (2003). *Explorations in language acquisition and use*. Portsmouth, NH: Heinemann.

Krashen, S., and Terrell, T. D. (1983). *The natural approach*. Oxford: Pergamon Press.

Lardiere, D. (2007). *Ultimate attainment in second language acquisition*. Mahwah, NJ: Lawrence Erlbaum.

Laufer, B. (2006). Comparing focus on form and focus on forms in second-language vocabulary learning. *The Canadian Modern Language Review*, 63(1), 149-166.

Legate, J. A. (2010). On how how is used instead of that. *Natural Language and Linguistic Theory*, 28, 121-134.

Long, M. (1988). Instructed interlanguage development. In L. M. Beebe (Ed.), *Issues in second language acquisition: Multiple perspectives* (pp. 115-141). New York: Newbury House.

Long, M. (1991). Focus on form: A design feature in language teaching methodology. In K. DeBot, R. Ginsberg, and C. Kramsch (Eds.), *Foreign language research in cross-cultural perspective* (pp. 39-52). Amsterdam: John Benjamins.

Long, M. (2000). Focus on form in task-based language teaching. In R. D. Lambert and E. Shohamy (Eds.), *Language policy and pedagogy: Essays in honor of A. Ronald Walton* (pp. 179-192). Philadelphia, PA: John Benjamins Publishing.

Luk, Z. P., and Shirai, Y. (2009). Is the acquisition order of grammatical morphemes impervious to L1 knowledge? Evidence from the acquisition of plural –s, articles, and possessive 's. *Language Learning*, 59, 721-754.

Matthews, P. H. (1996). *Grammatical theory in the United States from Bloomfield to Chomsky*. Cambridge: Cambridge University Press.

Nassaji, H., and Fotos, S. (2004). Current developments in research on the teaching of grammar. *Annual Review of Applied Linguistics*, 24, 126-145.

Nassaji, H., and Swain, M. (2000). A Vygotskian perspective on corrective feedback: The effect of random versus negotiated help on the learning of English articles. *Language Awareness*, 9, 34-51.

Ollendorff, H. G. (1848). *First adaptation of the new method to teach English: Intended for French speakers*. Paris: The Author.

Piattelli-Palmarini, M., Salaburu, P., and Uriagereka, J. (Eds.). (2009). *Of minds and language: A dialogue with Noam Chomsky in the Basque Country*. New York: Oxford University Press.

Radford, A. (2004). Minimalist syntax (2nd ed.). Cambridge: Cambridge University Press.

Scheffler, P. (2008). *The natural approach to adult learning and teaching of L2 grammar*. IRAL, 46, 289-313.

Schilhab, T. S. S. (2007). Knowledge for real: On implicit and explicit representations and education. *Scandinavian Journal of Educational Research*, 51, 223-238.

Schmidt, R. W. (1983). Interaction, acculturation, and the acquisition of communicative competence: A case study of an adult. In N. Wolfson and E. Judd (Eds.), *Sociolinguistics and language acquisition* (pp. 137-174). Rowley, MA: Newbury House.

Selinker, L. (1972). Interlanguage. International Review of Applied Linguistics, 10, 209-241.

Sheen, R. (2005). *Focus on formS as a means of improving accurate oral production*. In A. Housen and M. Pierrard (Eds.), *Investigations in instructed second language acquisition* (pp. 271-310). New York: Mouton de Gruyter.

Skehan, P. (1998). A cognitive approach to language learning. Oxford: Oxford University Press.

Smith, B. (1990). Towards a history of speech act theory. In A. Burkhardt (Ed.), *Speech acts, meanings and intentions: Critical approaches to the philosophy of John R.* Searle (pp. 29-61). New York: Mouton de Gruyter.

Smith, N. (1999). Chomsky: Ideas and ideals. Cambridge: Cambridge University Press.

Thornbury, S. (1999). *How to teach grammar*. Essex, UK: Longman.

Trahey, M., and White, L. (1993). Positive evidence and preemption in the second language classroom. *Studies in Second Language Acquisition*, 15, 181-204.

Truscott, J. (1996). The case against grammar correction in L2 writing classes. *Language Learning*, 46, 327-369.

Turnbull, M. (2001). There is a role for L1 in second and foreign language teaching, but… *The Canadian Modern Language Review*, 57, 531-540.

VanPatten, B. (2002). Processing instruction: An update. Language Learning, 52, 755-803.

White, L. (2003). *Second language acquisition and universal grammar*. Cambridge: Cambridge University Press.

Widdowson, H. G. (1978). *Teaching language as communication*. Oxford: Oxford University Press.

Willis, D. (2003). *Rules, patterns and words: Grammar and lexis in English language teaching*. Cambridge: Cambridge University Press.

Zhonggang Gao, C. (2001). Second language learning and the teaching of grammar. *Education*, 122, 326-336.

In: Innovation and Creativity in ELT Methodology
Editors: H. P. Widodo and A. Cirocki

ISBN: 978-1-62948-146-3
© 2013 Nova Science Publishers, Inc.

Chapter 13

VISUALLY-BASED GRAMMAR TEACHING

Adriadi Novawan

Politeknik Negeri Jember, Indonesia

ABSTRACT

Visuals or illustrations have been applied widely in support of the language teaching and learning process. Alongside this, this chapter argues for visually-based approach to teaching grammar and maintains that the use of visuals in teaching grammar can help students easily learn particular grammatical rules or features. It begins with a discussion on the need for teaching grammar that underpins the notions of this chapter. Some well-known approaches to grammar teaching are highlighted in order to build an informed foundation for possibilities of using visuals or illustrations that are appropriate to particular grammar teaching situations. Specifically, visuals enhance varied grammar teaching methods: inductive, consciousness raising, and communicative. Finally, the use of visuals is explored in eclectic grammar learning tasks.

INTRODUCTION

Grammar teaching has been hotly debated whether grammar should be taught in language classrooms among language practitioners, researchers, and teachers both in EFL and ESL contexts. Some argue that grammar should not be taught to enable learners to acquire particular grammatical rules as they learned their L1 naturally. In other words, learners learn grammatical rules unconsciously. Others argue that grammar should be taught since it is a mediating tool for learners to express comprehensible spoken and written ideas. Thus, learners should acquire a sufficient knowledge of grammar through instruction inductively or deductively (Widodo, 2010).

In the language postmethod era, teachers need to offer varied ways or methods for teaching grammar to help learners become aware of how important grammar should be learned. The important thing is that how teachers can make use of available language learning resources like visual aids to teach grammar. For this reason, this chapter will pinpoint how grammar is visually introduced to language learners.

THE NEED FOR TEACHING GRAMMAR

In an EFL context, grammar teaching is definitely essential to provide a foundation for learner language acquisition. The absence of grammar instruction may let learners merely perform English skills with frequent grammatical mistakes and be a lack of awareness of how language is learned or sentences are constructed. In other words, grammar instruction contributes to language teaching learning since it can build learners' understanding and awareness of how a set of sentences are formed. For this reason, language teachers need to create enjoyable and anxiety reduced grammar learning tasks in such a way that learners can learn and acquire grammatical rules and encourage them to actively engage in the entire teaching and learning process. Given this notion, grammar should be seen as a mediating tool for spoken and written communication.

Current discussions on grammar teaching focus on the effectiveness and development of grammar teaching approaches and methods. They, apparently, cover criticism on traditional approaches such as grammar-translation and presentation-practice-production, which are more teacher centered, and promote some student centered approaches such as: contextual, communicative, and consciousness raising approaches. "Emerging" theories derived from either combination of those theories or completely innovative frameworks have probably been reviewed and studied for enhancing grammar teaching in a more specific learning context. It is believed that the emergence of the theories in that continued debate is driven by desires of improved grammar teaching practices in language classroom settings. Some authors have addressed grammar teaching issues in relation to language learning and acquisition theories, approaches, and procedures for classroom settings (e.g., Ellis, 2006; Widodo, 2006), which attempted to offer more flexible and contextual approaches for teaching grammar to particular learners with diverse backgrounds. Thus, an alternative way to teach grammar remains a need; one of the way is how language teachers can integrate the use of visuals or illustrations, which are contextual and available locally (e.g., information, cultures, buildings, sceneries, etc.) into grammar teaching. This idea is referred to as *visually-based grammar teaching*.

WHY USE VISUALS IN GRAMMAR TEACHING?

Most of the EFL learners feel that grammar is one of the most difficult English sub-skills to learn. Even though they have learned English grammar since junior high schools, they could not apply what they learned to communicative tasks like speaking and writing. This failure results in a negative attitude towards English language learning and acquisition. It is no wonder that grammar has spooked EFL learners until recently, so the question raised is "how can English teacher create interactive and anxiety reduced grammar instruction when learners are being overwhelmed with such grammar nightmare?" This question challenges language teachers to design interesting, meaningful, and motivating grammar teaching. One of the ways to do so is that language teachers can incorporate visuals or illustrations into grammar teaching.

Visuals can generally be used to (1) attract and maintain learner interest in learning grammar, (2) help learners understand particular grammatical rules easily, (3) illuminate complicated grammatical items, and (4) allow the learners to endure retention on the material taught (Novawan, 2010). Given these benefits, visuals help learners visualize what are being taught to them and stimulate deeper understanding as well as create actual and interesting contexts of grammar learning that facilitate the learners to connect the material being taught to their own lived experience.

Visually-based grammar teaching may be generally believed appropriate for both young learners and adult learners, so the flexibility of using visuals can encourage teachers to choose varied illustrations, which can facilitate grammar learning. For example, drawings, pictures, photographs, cartoons, and stick figures can serve as visual aids, which are best used to teach young learners particular grammatical patterns. On the other hand, the use of other visuals like images or pictures, graphs, diagram, charts, or texts through particular media such as presentation slides, workbooks, and handouts may attract adult learner attention to get involved actively in class activities and consequently improve their understanding on certain grammatical rules taught using different teaching approaches either deductively or inductively. Other interesting visuals, which can be used to teach grammar are such real models or realias as: buildings, zoos, forests, rivers, bookstores, laboratories, and museums. Thus, a variety of visuals can be used to teach learners grammar at different levels, depending on the learning needs and goals. This needs teacher creativity of using illustrations, which best facilitate grammar learning.

VISUALS AND DEDUCTIVE APPROACH TO GRAMMAR TEACHING

A deductive approach to grammar teaching starts from the general to the specific. Rules, principles, concepts, or theories are presented first, and then their applications are treated (Widodo, 2006). This approach has been criticized by varied empirical and theoretical arguments due to its lack of student centeredness. However, it is still useful for particular situations, especially in EFL contexts when suiting particular learner characteristic, cultural background, curricular setting, and material complexity.

Firstly, this approach is preferred by introvert learners who tend to expect clear and sufficient explanation and instruction before working on grammatical rules. Before listening to teacher explanation, such learners are easily de-motivated and afraid of making mistakes. Secondly, a particular cultural background is claimed to have impact on learner learning strategy. Those who have been trained *teacher centered learning* would prefer that teaching is kind of activity of presenting the material, and learning is an activity of listening to the teacher. In addition, a certain language curriculum requires learners to take English proficiency tests like TOEIC, TOEFL, school leaving examinations, or other high-stake tests. These grammar based tests require teachers to emphasize rule-driven learning. Finally, deductive teaching is preferred when grammatical rules taught are too difficult or complex and new for students, so they would prefer learning grammatical rules first, and then practicing such rules into communicative tasks once they have fully understood such rules.

In spite of its advantages, the deductive approach has some disadvantages, including: (1) this approach is claimed to be teacher centered; (2) it gives little impact on learner understanding; (3) it focuses on drilling exercises; and (4) it imposes a negative attitude on the learners—the goal of learning English is merely to know grammatical rules rather than acquire communicative competence. To reduce these weaknesses, visual media can be incorporated into the deductive method of grammar teaching. In this respect, visuals can become important media to attract learners' attention, reinforce teacher presentation on grammar rules, and mediate teacher-learner and learner-learner interactions in a class. Through visuals, teacher presentation can enhance learners' deeper understanding because such aids can stimulate learners to visualize a particular grammatical rule. Visuals can also benefit the class through the presence of situation or context; thereby facilitating practice and production activities and bringing genuine communication to a deductively oriented class.

VISUALS AND INDUCTIVE APPROACH TO GRAMMAR TEACHING

Different from the deductive approach, the inductive approach starts from the presentation of specific examples through either spoken or written manner, and then a general principle or rule can be drawn from them. This approach attempts to highlight grammatical rules implicitly in which learners are encouraged to conclude the rules given by the teacher (Widodo, 2006). Ellis (2006), Felder and Henriques (1995), and Widodo (2006) suggest that inductive teaching makes possible learners get greater degree of cognitive depth, more encouraged to get involved in a class, more self directed, and more exploration in learning English. These possibilities enable the learners not only to learn English, but also to improve personal and interpersonal skills. Thus, inductive reasoning is thought to be an important part in an academic achievement.

Basically, inductive teaching comprises the following steps: (1) the targeted form is presented to learners in a meaningful context; (2) learners are encouraged to recognize grammatical patterns presented in the language sample provided; (3) a teacher explains a grammatical form; and (4) the learners engage in meaningful practice (Paesani, 2005). In the inductive approach, a problem may possibly emerge when learners fail to figure out the forms presented by the teacher due to either too difficult task or the lack of learners' metalanguage. In this case, visuals are useful to give a context so that the learners can grasp what are presented by the teacher. The use of visuals or illustrations can become a clue for the learners to meaningfully identify the rules of specific examples. Visuals can be applied to reinforce teacher explanation and provide a meaningful context for practicing the targeted grammatical items. Therefore, through visualization, such rule discovery practice can be easily done by learners.

VISUALS AND COMMUNICATIVE APPROACH
TO GRAMMAR TEACHING

Communicative approach is considered as a response toward a traditional approach that puts an emphasis on grammar as the core component of teaching-learning process and is awakening of communicative competence (Kumaravadivelu, 2006; Richards, 2001). Communicative competence refers to "the capacity to use language appropriately in communication based on the setting, the roles of the participants, and the nature of transaction" (Richards, 2001, p. 36). This approach is believed to be relevant to language learning system and the nature of language, which is for communication among the society, and characterized by the presence of negotiated interaction, learner autonomy, and integrated or multi-skills instruction (Hinkel, 2006; Kumaravadivelu, 2006). The communicative approach can be adapted to language skills and sub-skills teaching, including grammar teaching. This idea implies that a teacher should apply varied tasks in a class, including: situation based, visually-based, genre based, problem based, community based, and competence based. In spite of this wide range of models and teaching materials compatible with integrated language teaching in the communicative approach (Hinkel, 2006), classroom settings can fail to create opportunities for genuine interaction (Kumaravadivelu, 2006) since learners have an insufficient or limited grammar skill—the ability to construct chunks of functional expressions.

Furthermore, particularly in an EFL context, the effect of communicative approach is not as significant as its popularity due to the complexity of instructional and materials design and learner understanding towards utterances that lead to lower participation and anxiety. Since one of the requirements for the communicative approach is the presence of interactive communication between a teacher and learners and between learners and their peers, it is important to ensure that the learners grasp teacher spoken discourse or utterances. In this case, visuals can serve as essential media to help learners cope with meaning focused activities and mediate interaction during the teaching-learning process.

VISUALS AND CONSCIOUSNESS RAISING (CR) APPROACH TO GRAMMAR TEACHING

CR is believed to be important to teach learners with explicit knowledge of English. It does not aim at enabling the learners to work on grammatical rules correctly, but it can affect language acquisition indirectly and build learner awareness of how grammar is constructed (Widodo, 2010). Ellis (2002) argues that CR is an attempt to equip the learners with an understanding of a specific grammatical feature—to develop declarative rather than procedural knowledge of it. The emphasis of CR is on learner comprehension towards specific and isolated grammatical patterns. Thus, the role of visuals in CR tasks is important for the success of consciousness raising oriented grammar activities and tasks. Whether inductive or deductive, a teacher can design CR based tasks through visual media or presentation (e.g., pictures and texts, diagrams, charts, and tables). In designing CR oriented tasks, the teacher can employ any visuals that can generate learner awareness of the grammatical features taught.

Many models have been developed by some experts. An example is that Ellis (2002) suggests *problem solving task*, which employs a table as a visual aid to discriminate the use of *for* and *since*. Firstly, learners are given information about when three people joined a company using a table consisting of the name, date joined, and length of time. The teacher gives four examples of sentence using *for* and *since* based on the data given to let them identify when such time signals are used. The learners' understanding is then checked through giving a correct or incorrect identification task embracing four sentences. The learners are required to make up the rule to explain when *for* and *since* are used. Finally, they are asked to make their own sentences (in restricted number) using isolated, but actual context.

DESIGNING BLENDED VISUALLY-BASED GRAMMAR TASKS

Debates and controversies in approaches to grammar teaching have led to the advent of eclecticism in class practices. Griffiths and Parr (2001, pp. 248-249) highlight that "ELT classes have moved away from dogmatic to more eclectic position indicating by its attitudes and willingness of recognizing the potential merits of a wide variaty of possible teaching methods and approaches." This implies that an eclectic approach tries to meet a need for language learning, which is locally based and designed for particular learners with certain goals in a given amount of time. In short, in the eclectic perspective, language teachers should be fully aware of diverse learners' characteristics and backgrounds in particular language learning contexts. Many experts or authors propose procedures adopting an eclectic approach to grammar teaching.

For example, Widodo (2006, pp. 131-138) has proposed a step-by-step procedure for grammar teaching. In this procedure, he suggests five-step grammar activities, including: (1) rule initiation, (2) rule elicitation, (3) rule familiarization, (4) rule activation, and (5) rule enrichment. This procedure makes use of blended grammar teaching approaches and methods, such as CR, inductive, and communicative. Adapted from Widodo's procedure for grammar teaching, I would like to connect such a procedure with the concept of visualization. It is essential to remember that some grammatical rules cannot be taught through visuals. For this reason, teachers need to weigh whether visual media can be applied to teaching certain grammatical items.

1. Rule Initiation

In this activity, a teacher sets up induction activities intended to build up learner knowledge of the rule without telling them directly, but presenting examples of rule discovery learning. For example, in teaching *present continuous tense*, a teacher can present a picture or photograph (on a slide or poster) and ask some leading questions to the learners regarding the picture or photograph (see Table 1). This visual is useful to attract the learners' attention and make sense of teachers' oral questions to encourage learners' participation in a class.

Table 1. Teacher presentation of leading questions in rule initiation activity

Look at the photograph and take turns asking the questions below with your peer(s).

- What are they doing?
- What is the woman with a white dress and black pants doing?
- What is the man in the back corner of the room doing?
- What are the women doing?

Table 2. Teacher presentation of answering the questions in rule initiation activity

- They are discussing something.
- The woman is looking at one of the women.
- The man is taking a photograph of the meeting.
- The women are sitting on the chairs.

In response to those questions, the learners are required to answer orally in complete sentences by focusing their attention, firstly, on meaning (or idea) through the picture and teacher's questions, and secondly, on form through figuring out how to express their idea in answering the teacher's questions. This activity is also important to counter learners' wrong belief that learning grammar is merely "to know the rule," and such an activity can help the learners build their confidence in communicative classroom activities.

At the end of this step, the teacher can tell the learners what a grammatical item they are learning. Afterwards, the teacher presents the model in the form of sentences in *present continuous tense* using any media (e.g., slide presentations or blackboards) to help the learners internalize what they have figured out previously (see Table 2).

2. Rule Elicitation

At this stage, the teacher elicits the functions of the rule. This rule elicitation activity is directed to confirm and negotiate what the learners noticed or learned in rule discovery activities. In this rule elicitation activity, the teacher can present verb form, functions, and time signals of *present continuous tense* using a table, chart, or diagram.

In the presentation of *present continuous tense*, a table is appropriate to clarify particular grammatical items such as verb form, function, and possible time signals in sentences (see Table 3).

A chart or a visual organizer is appropriately used to illustrate *present continuous tense* concept hierarchically (see Table 4). A diagram also suits the presentation of *present continuous tense,* which is time frame and process based to clarify the characteristics of actions in *present continuous tense* (see Table 5).

Table 3. A table of "present continuous tense" presentation

Functions	Verb Forms	Time Signals
# 1 To show an action that is happening at the time of speaking	Vena is reading a novel	Now
# 2 To show an action that is happening around now	Jeni is writing her paper	These weeks
# 3 To show future of planned action	They are taking the national examination	next year

Table 4. A chart of present continuous tense presentation

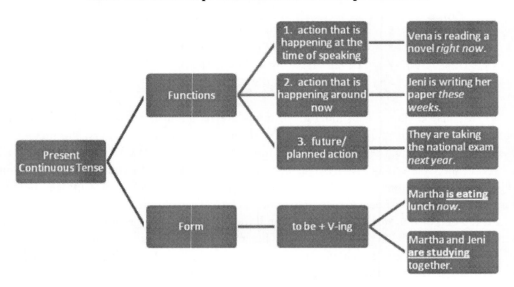

Table 5. A diagram of "present continuous tense" presentation

3. Rule Familiarization

Rule familiarization is intended to make the learners accustomed to the grammatical features taught. After being noticed to the rule, written based exercises are needed to support deeper understanding. In this rule familiarization activity, Widodo (2006) suggests six different tasks to train the learners with the targeted grammar rule: (1) written question input, (2) correct verb form completion, (3) sentence transformation, (4) sentence composition, (5) error recognition and correction, and (6) rule function based sentence composition. In this case, the teachers can create their own tasks in accordance with the target structures and learner need. At this step, visuals can be used as decorative or non-decorative figures. For example, in written question input task (see Table 6), a series of different photographs can be displayed to the learners followed by the question(s) to encourage them to write the answers.

In Table 7, stick figures are used to facilitate the learners in completing the sentences using correct verb form of *present continuous tense*. Either individual or collective feedback can be given at the end of the task. Teaching media such as worksheets, workbooks, or handouts are absolutely needed to help learners learn the item effectively.

Table 6. Written question input task using photographs

Answer the questions below based on each photograph using complete sentences using present continuous tense.

What is the woman doing?	What is the baby doing?
....	....
What are the girls doing?	What is the man doing?
....	....

4. Rule Activation

Rule activation is an important activity following the rule familiarization activity where the learners' comprehension on the grammar items taught is checked, and the learners can practice the rule learned.

The teacher can employ varied tasks such as: situation based sentence production, role play, and game tasks. Shortly, at this stage, communicative based tasks both written and oral are possibly integrated to increase learner awareness of the rule learned. Table 8 is an example of rule activation task using photographs.

Table 7. Correct verb form completion task using stick figures

Complete the sentences below using correct verb form of present continuous tense based on the following stick figures.

The boy _____ the flowers.

The girl _____ the floor.

He _____ his boat.

They _____ tennis.

Table 8. Rule activation task using photographs

Write a sentence expressing what is happening on each photograph.

5. Rule Enrichment

The purpose of this activity is to maximize internalization process and expand the learners' knowledge on the grammatical rule or pattern taught. The teacher can employ pattern identification that is text based task and inter-pattern comparison task (Widodo, 2006). Pertaining to the text based task, the teacher can make use of visual texts in which ideas are visually presented. In the inter-pattern comparison task, the teacher can select pictures or photographs, which contrast one another in terms of ideas. Thus, both text based task and inter-pattern comparison task are geared to help learners reflect on the grammatical rules learned and find out how the rules correspond to other related grammatical ones in genuine communication such as in writing.

CONCLUSION

This chapter has presented an idea about how grammar is visually taught. This suggests that debates in grammar teaching should move away from the investigation of best single method to grammar teaching into how the incorporation of more than one approach suits a particular teaching context. Incorporating a visually-based, eclectic approach into grammar teaching becomes invaluable for best teaching practices that call for empirical studies in different teaching contexts. It is also necessary to suggest that teachers can apply visually-based grammar teaching based on the nature of grammatical rules taught, learner learning style, learner ability, and learner language proficiency while taking into account pedagogical principles of particularity, practicality, and possibility (Kumaravadivelu, 2006). More importantly, language teachers should be fully aware of how grammar can be integrated with other skills like listening, speaking, reading, and writing; at the same time, they consider the concept of visualization.

REFERENCES

Ellis, R. (2002). Grammar teaching practice or consciousness-raising? In J. C. Richards and W.A Renandya *(Eds.), Methodology in language teaching* (pp. 167-174). Cambridge: Cambridge University Press.

Ellis, R. (2006). Current issues in the teaching of grammar: An SLA perspective. *TESOL Quarterly, 40*, 83-107.

Felder, R. M., and Henriques, E. R. (1995). Learning and teaching styles in foreign and second language education. *Foreign Language Annals, 28*(1), 21-31.

Griffiths, C., and Parr, J. M. (2001). Language learning strategies: Theory and perception. *ELT Journal, 55*, 247-254.

Hinkel, E. (2006). Current perspectives on teaching the four skills. *TESOL Quarterly, 40*(1), 109-131.

Kumaravadivelu, B. (2006). TESOL methods: Changing tracks, challenging trends. *TESOL Quarterly, 40*(1), 59-81.

Novawan, A. (2010). The use of visual aids in ELT materials. In H. P. Widodo and L. Savova (2010). *The lincom guide to materials design in ELT* (39-54). Muenchen, Germany: Lincom Europa.

Paesani, K. (2005). Literary texts and grammar instruction: Revisiting the inductive presentation. *Foreign Language Annals, 38*(1), 15-24.

Richards, J. C. (2001). *Curriculum development in language teaching.* Cambridge: Cambridge University Press.

Widodo, H. P. (2006). Approaches and procedures for teaching grammar. *English Teaching: Practice and Critique, 5*(1), 122-141.

Widodo, H. P. (2010). Consciousness-raising (CR) approach to teaching English grammar. *Modern English Teacher, 19*(2), 29-32.

In: Innovation and Creativity in ELT Methodology
Editors: H. P. Widodo and A. Cirocki

ISBN: 978-1-62948-146-3
© 2013 Nova Science Publishers, Inc.

Chapter 14

TEACHING ENGLISH THROUGH CONTENT AREAS

Tom Salsbury
Washington State University, US

ABSTRACT

This chapter overviews the teaching of English through content areas, also known as content based instruction (CBI) or content and language integrated learning (CLIL). The chapter argues for a balanced emphasis on content and language objectives and provides guidelines to teachers in writing measurable objectives. Objectives are based primarily on curricular goals and/or state standards, ESL standards, or other benchmarks that a teacher uses. The author explains how objectives align to both assessments and learning activities. The author also argues for the importance of contextualized instruction and scaffolding in the development of learning activities. The author details activity types to illustrate these pedagogical concepts. The activities simultaneously develop content area knowledge and language skills. A vignette of a university level content based course concludes the chapter.

INTRODUCTION

Worldwide interest in the dual focus on language and content teaching at all levels of instruction has increased enormously in the past two decades (Stoller, 2004). This chapter outlines principles and strategies for teaching foreign language through content area instruction. This is also known as *content based instruction* (CBI) or *content and language integrated learning* (CLIL). The chapter is written for foreign language teachers wishing to develop courses that include a focus on content. It is also written for content or discipline area teachers seeking to incorporate a focus on foreign language development. This chapter draws heavily from current literature in sheltering instruction techniques (Echevarría, Vogt, and Short, 2008) as well as specific strategies aimed at making content comprehensible to learners of a foreign language. The materials presented are neither aimed at a specific target language (e.g., English), nor are they designed for a particular level of language proficiency, content area, or level of education. The first part of the chapter guides the reader through the process of establishing a balanced emphasis on content and language objectives as well as measuring student achievement on those objectives in ongoing, in-class assessment. The argument presented in the chapter is that clearly stated and measurable objectives are the foundation for successful content based instruction. These objectives are based primarily on curricular goals and/or state standards, ESL standards, or other benchmarks that a teacher uses. The second part of the chapter details a selection of highly engaging activities to develop language skills in reading, writing, listening, and speaking while simultaneously teaching to a particular content area such as math, science, or history. The chapter concludes with a vignette of a content based course at the university level.

WRITING AND ASSESSING OBJECTIVES

Collaboration to Determine Course Goals

Lesson planning begins "with the end in mind" (Rothenberg and Fisher, 2007, p. 56). In other words, instruction starts with what students need to know at the end of a lesson or unit and then works toward that knowledge through learning outcomes or objectives, assessment of those objectives, and activities to develop the knowledge that is assessed throughout the lesson. The *what* in what students need to know at a particular grade level is found in learning standards. These standards are developed by educational and professional boards at state, national, and international levels. In the United States, for example, state boards of education develop and publish learning standards in content areas. In addition to content standards, boards of education also publish language development standards for English language learners that are aligned with content area standards (see also the revised ESL standards in Pre-K-12 published by TESOL). Standards are often long and complex. In a content based language course, content teachers may find themselves teaching a language for which they have had limited training. Likewise, language teachers may teach a content area in which they too lack formal training or experience. Thus, collaboration across disciplines is the key to familiarizing oneself with the content and language standards used to develop a course. Teachers use the expertise of their colleagues to help plan the course and write lessons. For example, an English as a foreign language (EFL) instructor interested in developing a content based course in mathematics at the secondary level first works with the mathematics teacher to learn the mathematics standards at that particular grade level. Close collaboration across disciplines is vital to content teachers as well. For example, a chemistry teacher at the secondary school level interested in developing a course to be taught in English as a foreign language (EFL) collaborates closely with the English language teacher to learn what the EFL standards or goals are for that year or level of study.

Developing Content and Language Objectives

Many authors stress the importance of clearly identifying content and language objectives that are measurable and achievable (Echevarría, Vogt, and Short, 2008; Egbert and Ernst-Slavit, 2010; Rothenberg and Fisher, 2007). The lesson objectives are shared with the students, and for this reason, should be written in age appropriate language. Objectives guide the assessment and activities of the lesson. Egbert and Ernst-Slavit (2010) suggest that teachers first write the content objectives. This is done using a predictable formula that students and teachers recognize. The first part of the formula is a phrase such as *Students will be able to* (abbreviated as *SWBAT*). This is followed by a measurable outcome or action verb which in turn is followed by a statement of the content to be learned. For example, the content objectives for a secondary level science lesson might read:

- *SWBAT demonstrate knowledge of how Natural Selection can cause a species to change over time.*
- *SWBAT predict one adaptation of a species given a theoretical habitat.*

The objective begins with the abbreviated phrase *SWBAT* followed by a measurable action verb (*demonstrate* and *predict*) which is then followed by the content to be learned.

Teachers implementing content based language courses also formulate language objectives to share with their students. Language objectives are both process and product oriented, and they address both receptive and productive language skills (Echevarría, Vogt, and Short, 2008). Language objectives address reading, writing, listening, and speaking. They address academic language skills, functional language skills, higher order thinking skills, grammar, vocabulary, and any other language that is necessary for achieving content objectives (Egbert and Ernst-Slavit, 2010). When developing language objectives, it is helpful to make a list of the language needs of a lesson based on those lesson's content objectives. Teachers also refer to the language development standards such as the TESOL standards or other language development standards. In content based language courses, the language to be taught emerges from the content. For example, suppose a secondary mathematics teacher has designed a lesson on *fractions* to be taught in her content based language course. Using the school curriculum and/or state standards for math at this level, the teacher decides to instruct students on *equivalence* and *reducing fractions*. The standards also specify that students be able to apply *fractions* to everyday situations. From this, the teacher writes the following content objectives:

- *SWBAT represent and identify equivalent fractions.*
- *SWBAT write a fraction equivalent to a given fraction.*
- *SWBAT simplify fractions using common factors.*
- *SWBAT explain the meaning of equivalence.*

The next step is to determine what language needs emerge from the content. If the class is to be conducted in a lecture or presentation style, the focus will be on receptive skills such as listening, along with vocabulary, particularly passive vocabulary knowledge—i.e., words that students recognize, but do not necessarily use (Nation, 2005). In contrast, if the teacher opts to engage small groups in problem solving tasks, the language needs to emerge from the content lesson will include productive skills, such as speaking. Students will need to use and explain certain mathematical terms to other members of the group. Teachers may also be interested in developing interpersonal skills in the target language, which would be reflected in the language objectives. The language that emerges from a content lesson depends heavily on a particular teaching and learning style, the language tasks in which students engage, and the specific areas of language development that a teacher has identified to be in need of work. Egbert and Ernst-Slavit (2010) suggest that teachers first list the language needs for a lesson. The following list was created by the mathematics teacher above:

- *Listen to the teacher's instructions;*
- *Listen and work with other students;*
- *Define vocabulary for the lesson;*
- *Use correct grammar in a write up;*
- *Use different strategies to write; and*
- *Use different strategies to read math word problems.*

The language needs that emerge from the content are not all addressed in a single lesson. Echevarría, Vogt, and Short (2008) recommend that teachers view language objectives as parallel to the language development process. For example, language objectives might build from one lesson to the next, such as students learning to use the writing process (e.g., brainstorming, drafting, reviewing, editing, and publishing). The emphasis on language development is balanced between receptive and productive skills, vocabulary development, grammar development, functional language, pronunciation, register, and other features of language development. Language development curricula or standards as well as the collaboration of foreign language teachers are both valuable resources when writing language objectives. Language objectives are written using the same formula as content objectives: a phrase such as *Students will be able to (SWBAT)* followed by a measurable action verb and then a clear statement of the language to be learned or practiced. The following are examples of language objectives:

- *SWAT correctly use the key vocabulary terms: triangle, angle, acute, and obtuse when working in small groups.*
- *SWBAT explain the strategy they used to solve a multiplication story problem.*
- *SWBAT spell the following financial terms: hedge fund, recession, and mortgage.*
- *SWBAT use simple past tense in a scientific report.*
- *SWBAT present a persuasive argument for the mandatory use of seat belts in automobiles.*
- *SWBAT orally agree and disagree appropriately in small group work.*
- *SWBAT demonstrate comprehension of an oral lecture.*
- *SWBAT revise the organization of an essay based on teacher and peer feedback.*
- *SWBAT ask well-formed questions.*

Assessment

Content and language objectives guide the development of a content based language course and are aligned to assessments of student learning. Effective assessments are both authentic and ongoing. Ruddell and Ruddell (1995) suggest principles for implementing authentic assessment as follows:

1. Assessment should be based on observations of students as they engage in authentic learning tasks.
2. Assessment should be tied directly to the instructional goals and teaching.
3. Assessment should be continuous based on observations over a substantial period of time.
4. Assessment should take into consideration the diversity of students' cultural, linguistic, and special needs.
5. Assessment should be collaborative providing opportunities for students to evaluate their own work.
6. Assessment should be multidimensional, that is, based on a variety of observations, in a variety of situations, using a variety of instruments.
7. Assessment should be based on current research and theory concerning language, literacy, and knowledge constructions.

(Peregoy and Boyle, 2005, p. 113)

General examples of authentic assessment include observation, portfolios, inventories (such as the use of a specific skill in a single observation), conferences or interviews, self assessments, and student surveys (Peregoy and Boyle, 2005). Data from assessments are used to plan subsequent lessons. As we explore activity types in the next section of the chapter, we will also see how these activities are tools for ongoing, in-class assessment of language development.

ACTIVITIES

This section of the chapter addresses creative and innovative ways to develop language skills while simultaneously teaching a content lesson. The notion of context embeddedness (Cummins, 1981) and scaffolding instruction form the theoretical framework for this presentation. In his model of academic language, illustrated in Figure 1, Cummins argues that the role of the instructor is to balance the cognitive load of a lesson, portrayed on the vertical axis, with the context embeddedness of a lesson, portrayed on the horizontal axis, most disadvantaged in content learning. Lesson activities fall within one of the four quadrants to a greater or lesser degree. Activities that are neither cognitively demanding nor embedded in context present the least educational benefit to students. These are illustrated in Quadrant C in Cummins' model. Alternatively, an activity may have a low cognitive load, but high context embeddedness (in Quadrant A).

On the other side of the spectrum, classroom activities are more commonly characterized by high cognitive demand and low context embeddedness (in Quadrant D). Example activities in this quadrant are listening to lectures or reading textbooks with no visual aids, writing an essay, or solving a word problem in mathematics. Teachers desire high levels of achievement from students in cognitively demanding content. Certainly, lectures and written texts are a highly efficient means in which to convey new and challenging content. Similarly, essays, standardized tests, and presentations can be an efficient way in which to assess student knowledge of this content. However, these are also mediums in which language learners are most disadvantaged in content learning.

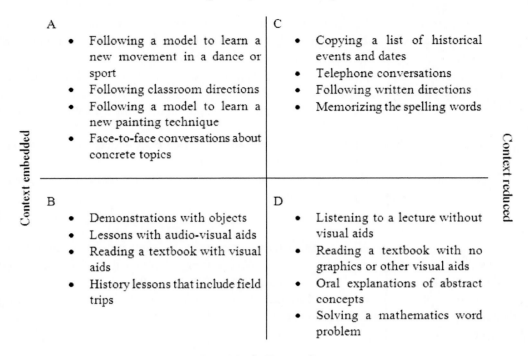

Figure 1. Cummins's (1981) model of academic language and task difficulty.

An alternative way is to provide scaffolding instruction through the introduction of varying amounts of context. Classroom activities of this type are illustrated in Quadrant B in Figure 1. The term *scaffolding* can be defined as a process that enables a child or novice to solve a task or achieve a goal that would be beyond his or her unassisted efforts (Wood, Bruner and Ross, 1976). The term applies to both content and language learning. In a more general sense, scaffolding is used in models that focus on the social construction of knowledge. The most well-known of such models was developed by the Russian psychologist, Lev Vygotsky. In his model, learning takes place at a level just beyond the level at which a learner can complete a task independently. Vygotsky (1978) called this space the Zone of Proximal Development (ZPD). There is a difference between the actual developmental level of a learner where learners are able to complete tasks without scaffolding, and the Zone of Proximal Development where learners are unable to complete tasks without scaffolding. The help or scaffolding is provided by a more capable peer, which may be a teacher, a classmate, or others. As students develop, so does their Zone of Proximal Development. Thus, the larger goal of instruction is to provide relevant tasks to continually move students forward in their ever expanding Zone of Proximal Development (ZPD).

One of the primary instructional strategies for teaching language through content areas is embedding cognitively demanding material in highly contextualized lessons, represented in Quadrant B in Figure 1. In teaching language through content areas, context embeddedness is realized in multiple ways, such as peer-peer interactions, visuals, modifying texts, highlighting key vocabulary, accessing prior knowledge, personalizing knowledge, graphic organizers, experiential learning, or interacting with real objects. What all of these and the following strategies have in common is that they provide assistance to language learners in making important connections between language and content. These aids move students through their ZPD and address both language development and content learning.

Contextualizing instruction makes use of objects (realia), visuals, and manipulatives in order to provide a direct link between the concepts being explored and the language used to explore them. The more concrete the object, visual or manipulative, the greater the contextual information that students have available to aid in comprehension.

Advance Organizers

Advance organizers are brief presentations made prior to a lesson that teaches particularly abstract concepts (Ausubel, 1963). The goal of advance organizers is to link prior learning and experiences to the new material, and such organizers are often cited as an effective means to scaffold challenging content for language learners. It is important to use familiar terms and concepts that all the students know because the purpose of the advance organizer is to link these familiar terms and concepts to the new material.

The first step to implementing an advance organizer is to identify the main concepts or understandings of the new material. Next, the teacher designs ways in which to connect prior knowledge to the new material or concepts. The advance organizer will be used by the students as a framework to understanding what they are learning. The teacher presents the advance organizer and then teaches the new material with reference to the advance organizer. Assessment of the activity is ongoing using observations and anecdotal notes to ensure that students make the desired connections between the new concepts and their previous learning. Visuals and objects are particularly helpful in designing advance organizers.

A common type of advance organizer uses visual and graphic displays to show the relationships between key points of a lesson. These are called *graphic organizers* and have been widely researched as effective tools to improve student performance (Deshler and Schumaker, 2006; Vogt and Echevarría, 2008). Basic types of graphic organizers include T-charts, cycle charts, story stars, network trees, KWL charts, Venn Diagrams, compare/contrast charts, and many more. Graphic organizers vary depending on the content area; thus, interested readers would benefit from a quick search on the Internet for multiple examples of graphic organizers in their specific content area. Graphic organizers can also be developed by students for the purposes of summarizing texts or other content lessons. They allow for the graphical representation of student learning used as an assessment of reading comprehension, listening comprehension, or the comprehension of a content lesson. As such, graphic organizers can be an alternative to reading and listening comprehension questions.

Attribute Charting

A related visual strategy to emphasize attributes of key concepts is to chart those attributes. Attribute charting or semantic feature analysis (Peregoy and Boyle, 2005) is a way for teachers to support both content and language learning by making the relationships between concepts clearly visual so that they may be more easily compared and contrasted orally and in writing (Herrell and Jordan, 2008). A simple illustration of attribute charting at the elementary level is with animal classification. In the far left column of the chart, the teacher lists the animals to be classified (e.g., *dog, chicken, tuna, bat, dolphin, snake*, etc.). In the top row of the chart, the teacher lists animal attributes (e.g., *has hair, lays eggs, has wings, feeds milk to its young, is cold-blooded, has gills, has lungs*, etc.). For each animal in the far left column, students indicate which attributes in the top row of the chart apply. A check can be used to indicate an attribute that the animal has and a minus can be used to indicate an attribute that does not apply to that animal. Additional symbols may be introduced such as question marks if a student does not know or plus signs if the attribute is strongly associated with that animal.

Attribute charting can function as an advance organizer to link prior knowledge of a topic with the new knowledge. At higher educational levels, the attribute chart may be used to introduce provocative topics as a spring board for class discussion and debate. For example, a high school history teacher might use an attribute chart to classify historical and contemporary conflicts between nations. Attributes such as *seeks justice, fights for freedom, removes oppression, necessary to win a conflict*, and *murderer* can be used to classify the concepts of *warrior, soldier, terrorist*, and *non-violent resistor*. Students explore their own biases on the topic of conflict between nations before proceeding with the course readings and other instructional materials. This type of activity is particularly useful in classes with diverse languages and cultures.

The attribute chart is a valuable tool for introducing and comparing/contrasting new concepts. It is also a valuable tool to promote language development. The attribute chart allows language learners to organize vocabulary by semantic category; thus, it is a tool for vocabulary development. In addition, the chart may be used to organize writing, prepare debates, and provide structure to small group discussion. Assessment of both content and language development will align with the objectives for the lesson. If the language objective for the lesson is to use the new vocabulary in writing, the assessment of the written product will analyze how students use the new words in their piece. The attribute chart provides a visual scaffold for the students' vocabulary use.

Jigsaw Reading

Jigsaw reading is a collaborative reading strategy that is helpful to language learners when reading for information (Gibbons, 1993). The activity builds on an information gap so that there is an authentic reason to communicate. Teachers gather multiple texts on a single topic so that students may choose (or be assigned) from a range of reading levels. The focus of jigsaw reading is on content learning (reading for information), reading and writing development, and oral communication skills. Ideally, students read a text that is slightly above their current reading ability (within their Zone of Proximal Development). They collaborate with other members of the class who have read the same text in order to clarify meaning and summarize information. They then work with members of the class who have read different texts in order to share their knowledge of the topic as well as to learn new information on the same topic from their classmates. Information can be shared in myriad ways, such as written summaries, oral reviews, and visual representations in graphic organizers or other means. Jigsaw readings are a useful strategy to differentiate instruction to multiple reading abilities, language proficiency levels, and learning styles.

The first step to implementing a jigsaw reading activity is to collect a variety of texts at different reading levels on a single topic. The second step is to arrange the class into heterogeneous groups of three to four students based on reading level. Depending on the general level of the students and goals of the teacher, a variety of strategies can be used to guide student reading on the topic. For example, Herrell and Jordan (2008) suggest the use of a KWL chart. This is a simple graphic with three columns. Students work together before reading to list what they know about the topic and then what they want to know about the topic. After reading, the group write what they learned about the topic. This can first be done individually and then as a group. Another column (S) may be included for students to write what they still want to learn about the topic.

Other types of graphic organizers may also be used. Students can either be given a graphic organizer to complete while they are reading, or they can be assigned the task of summarizing their text using a graphic organizer of the students' design. The use of a graphic organizer to summarize and share information shifts student output from writing to oral communication. The language objectives for the lesson determine the manner in which students summarize and share their information.

Ongoing assessment of the students' collaborative work may take many forms. Teachers should assess that all students are contributing to the group product and that the group is accountable to each individual student. Teachers also assess how well individual students are reading their assigned or chosen text.

A SAMPLE CBI COURSE FOR ENGINEERS

The final section of this chapter illustrates the alignment of content and language objectives, assessments, and activities in a short vignette of a content based English course at the university level. The teacher, Mr. Suksmith, was an English professor who designed a content based English course for engineering students at a Mexican university. The teacher collaborated with colleagues in the engineering college to familiarize himself with the core curriculum. He and his colleagues decided to focus on an English course to support instruction in mechanical engineering, one of the core engineering courses. The engineering faculty provided Mr. Suksmith with the required text along with supplemental texts that were used in the course. The required text and all supplemental readings were written in English.

Mr. Suksmith did not have any formal training in mechanical engineering. Thus, he and his colleagues in the engineering college selected fundamental and more concrete concepts from the course to include in the content based English course. Because 80% of the reading materials in the students' programs of study were written in English, Mr. Suksmith and his colleagues determined that reading strategies would be one of the goals of the course. Based on the school curriculum for both language and content development, the course addressed basic content learning in mechanical engineering and reading strategy development in English.

The following lesson is from a unit on *tension* and *compression* understood in the context of building materials used in constructing homes, offices, and other structures. In a previous lesson, the students watched two video segments on *building skyscrapers*. The purpose of the video segments was to contextualize the concepts of *tension* and *compression* at their grandest scale: the construction of skyscrapers. The students completed a graphic organizer while watching the video segments.

In the next lesson, Mr. Suksmith wrote the following content and language objectives. The objectives were written on the whiteboard and displayed throughout the lesson:

Content objective:

SWBAT apply the concepts of tension and compression to different types of constructions.
Language objective:
SWBAT read for comprehension using peer support.
SWBAT use a formal language register to present a poster.

Mr Suksmith had been systematic in selecting the objectives for this lesson. He planned to implement a jigsaw reading activity, have students summarize their reading in a graphic organizer, and then have students share what they learned through a formal in-class poster session. In preparation for his class, Mr. Suksmith listed the many language needs of his content based language lesson including reading comprehension, communicating in small groups, organizing and writing words and phrases in a graphic organizer, vocabulary knowledge, control of a formal register when speaking, and listening comprehension in peers' oral presentations. Mr. Suksmith knew that he could not assess all of these language related tasks in one lesson. Thus, he wrote content and language objectives based on what he knew he could assess.

Mr. Suksmith opted to assess content learning and reading comprehension through the graphic organizer activity and language through a poster presentation activity. These assessments align with the objectives for the lesson. In order to assess students efficiently and fairly, he developed rubrics for group and individual assessment. As an added twist to this lesson, he had elicited from the students categories they wanted to include in the rubrics. Students had had a voice in how they would be assessed. He and the class collaborated in developing rubrics that he would complete. They also collaborated to develop rubrics that the students would complete in a self and peer assessment. The group rubric assessed whether the group could successfully identify the concepts of *tension* and *compression* as they applied to different types of constructions in their reading. The student product that he assessed was each group's graphical organization of their assigned reading. The second assessment applied to students' control of register in oral presentations. Students would be assessed individually by the teacher, by peers, and by the student himself/herself in a self assessment. Mr. Suksmith would later compare his assessment results to the results from the peer and self assessments in order to address any discrepancies.

In designing his jigsaw reading activity, Mr. Suksmith chose texts at slightly different reading levels (secondary and university level texts). Rather than give the students the entire text to read, he selected relevant sections from longer chapters in the textbook and supplemental texts that were provided to him by his engineering colleagues. Another modification to the texts was highlighting key vocabulary words to scaffold reading. The texts had been scanned to a pdf file before they were modified and highlighted. They were made available to the students in hardcopy and electronic format.

Mr. Suksmith put students in heterogeneous groups by reading level. In other words, he put strong and weak readers together in the same group. He routinely changed groups and tried various grouping strategies in his class. Each group of students was given a different modified text to read; all members of the group read the same text. The students' task was to read their assigned text individually and then work together to create their own graphical representation of the main points of the text along with supporting details. Mr. Suksmith gave the students sample graphic organizer templates, but they were free to modify the template or design their own. The students had the rubric on which they would be assessed, so they knew what basic elements they needed to include in their graphic organizer and had to show evidence of reading comprehension. While the students worked together on their graphic organizers, Mr. Suksmith moved from group to group. In this lesson, he was most interested in observing students teaching each other in Spanish or English, and particularly whether the stronger readers were scaffolding the content and language for the weaker readers.

Classes at Mr. Suksmith's university met daily for one hour. Thus, the objectives and activities for this lesson carried over to the next day. Students finished their graphic organizers either in class or outside class. The next day, they came with their graphic organizers, ready to participate in a formal in-class poster session. The purpose of emphasizing formality was because students were preparing to use English in professional settings. The class reviewed phrases for introductions and closings in semi-formal settings as well as appropriate body language, eye contact, and other social cues. One group member's task was to remain with the poster to explain the graphic organizer to visitors. The other members of the group visited their classmates' posters. Their task was to learn how the key concepts of *tension* and *compression* applied to other types of construction issues. They were given a graphic organizer on which to take notes. After each poster that the students visited, they assessed the presenter using the rubric that the class developed. The group members switched roles after 10 minutes and then again after another 10 minutes so that each member had an opportunity to present the group poster. Mr. Suksmith also circulated around the room and assessed the presenters while they interacted with their visitors.

After the lesson, Mr. Suksmith looked at his data from the content and language assessments in order to plan the next lesson. The next lesson would involve the students using their notes from the poster session in a follow-up, summary writing activity. Mr. Suksmith would need to review the major concepts displayed on the posters, but he could focus this review by using his assessment data to prepare a lesson that would cover concepts that were most problematic for students. Thus, the assessment data are used to help in the preparation of a future lesson.

CONCLUSION

Content based language instruction is a challenging, yet exciting innovation in language teaching. This chapter has outlined the important issues surrounding choosing and writing both content and language objectives. The chapter has served as an introduction to the major concerns of aligning authentic, ongoing assessments and activities with the objectives of a lesson. Those wishing to explore these issues in more depth will find a wealth of materials to aid in the development of creative and engaging lessons. The primary aim of this chapter has been to emphasize the importance of balancing content instruction with language instruction in order to better ensure student development in both content and language.

REFERENCES

Ausubel, D. (1963). *The psychology of meaningful verbal learning*. New York: Grune and Stratton.

Cummins, J. (1981). The role of primary language development in promoting educational success for language minority students. In C. F. Leyba (Ed.), *Schooling and language minority students: A theoretical framework* (pp. 3-50). Sacramento, CA: California State Department of Education.

Deshler, D., and Schumaker, J. (2006). *Teaching adolescents with disabilities: Accessing the general education curriculum*. Thousand Oaks, CA: Corwin Press.

Echevarría, J., Vogt, M. E., and Short, D. J. (2008). *Making content comprehensible for English language learners: The SIOP model*. Boston, MA: Pearson.

Egbert, J., and Ernst-Slavit, G. (2010). *Access to academics: Planning instruction for K-12 classrooms with ELLs*. Boston, MA: Allyn and Bacon.

Gibbons, P. (1993). *Learning to learn in a second language*. Portsmouth, NH: Heinemann.

Herrell A. L, and Jordan, M. (2008). *Fifty strategies for teaching English language learners (3rd ed.)*. Upper Saddle River, NJ: Merrill Prentice Hall.

Nation, I. S. P. (2005). Teaching and learning vocabulary. In E. Hinkel (Ed.), *Handbook of research in second language teaching and learning* (pp. 581-595). Mahwah, NJ: Lawrence Erlbaum.

Peregoy, S. F., and Boyle, O. F. (2005). *Reading, writing and learning in ESL: A resource book for K-12 teachers (4th ed.)*. Boston, MA: Pearson.

Rothenberg, C., and Fisher, D. (2007). *Teaching English language learners: A differentiated approach*. Upper Saddle River, NJ: Merrill Prentice Hall.

Ruddell, R. B., and Ruddell, M. R. (1995). *Teaching children to read and write: Becoming an influential teacher*. Boston, MA: Allyn and Bacon.

Stoller, F. L. (2004). Content-based instruction: Perspectives on curriculum planning. *Annual Review of Applied Linguistics*, *24*, 261-283.

Vogt, M. E., and Echevarría, J. (2008). *99 ideas and activities for teaching English learners with the SIOP Model*. Boston, MA: Allyn and Bacon.

Vygotsky, L. (1978). *Mind and society: The development of higher psychological processes* [M. Cole, V. John-Steiner, S. Scribner, and E. Souberman, Eds., trans.]. Cambridge, MA: Harvard University Press.

Wood, D. J., Bruner, J. S., and Ross, G. (1976). The role of tutoring in problem-solving. *Journal of Child Psychology and Psychiatry*, *17*, 89-100.

In: Innovation and Creativity in ELT Methodology   ISBN: 978-1-62948-146-3
Editors: H. P. Widodo and A. Cirocki   © 2013 Nova Science Publishers, Inc.

Chapter 15

CORPORA IN ENGLISH LANGUAGE TEACHING

John Spiri

Tokyo University of Agriculture and Technology, Japan

ABSTRACT

Corpora have a variety of potential uses in English language learning. Some corpora are huge and represent both written and spoken forms of a major native dialect such as British English while smaller corpora are being created for specialized purposes. Meanwhile, via computers and the worldwide web, these corpora can be utilized by anyone with basic computer skills and an Internet connection. The uses of corpora are not limited to vocabulary acquisition, but also include study of grammar and pronunciation. Material writers can also make use of corpora to make research based choices regarding which words are most appropriate to include in their texts.

INTRODUCTION

While *corpus* is often defined simply as *a body of texts*, its composition represents an aspect of a language. The British National Corpus (BNC), perhaps the best known and most widely utilized corpus, can be seen as representative of British English because it covers a wide range of factors: gender, class, age, region, medium, and other factors. The BNC achieves this wide ranging representation of a regional aspect of the English language by its enormity: over 100 million words. Meanwhile, while the Brown corpus is the oldest for American English, the BYU-Corpus of Contemporary American English has far surpassed it both in terms of number of words (over 360 million), search, and downloaded features offered on the website. Other corpora, as we shall see, can be representative of a targeted segment of a language by careful design. "A corpus *must* represent something," (emphasis added) as O'Keeffe, McCarthy, and Carter (2007) note, "and its merits will often be judged on how representative it is" (p. 1). A section on *Specialized Corpora*, will provide some examples of the ever growing variety of corpora being built and utilized by researchers, teachers, and learners of English and often made available on the worldwide web.

A corpus can be applied to English language education in myriad ways. One particularly useful product of the corpus is the word frequency list which, by showing the rank of words based on how often they are used, provides learners an idea of which words ought to be learned first, and thus afford them more methodical ways to approach vocabulary study. Via word frequency lists, students can gain greater awareness of which words are most useful, and study these words intentionally, leaving lower frequency words for later in their studies. In particular, the first 2000 words are important to learners because "these will enable the learner to recognize about 80% of any normal text" (Milton, 2009, p. 47). Further, this chapter will briefly describe uses of word frequency lists.

In addition to word frequency lists, corpora have led to the availability of online concordance programs. These concordance programs allow users to gain deeper knowledge of the ways words are used in a particular corpus and have various applications for teachers, researchers, and learners. Further, this chapter will explore some of the ways concordance programs enhance teaching and learning. For example, they can be utilized to gain a greater understanding of pronunciation and grammar; they can even be utilized to analyze the evolution of language, at least over the past 100 years; and of course, researchers can refer to concordance data and apply it to their research studies related to word meaning and usage.

Finally, corpora can be exploited for material design, guiding the material writers in their quest to present vocabulary in a manageable and efficient sequence. The availability of online corpus programs may aid any materials writers. Then, this chapter will introduce one such website and demonstrate possible applications.

APPLICATIONS OF CORPORA

The corpus itself is a pool of information about a language or aspect of a language from which a variety of insights can be made. McCarten (2007) lists several aspects of a language that teachers and learners can understand more deeply by making use of corpora. Such aspects include: "frequency, differences in speaking and writing, contexts of use, collocation, grammatical patterns, and strategic use of vocabulary" (p. 3). Largely due to the groundbreaking work of vocabulary researchers (e.g., Paul Nation), the word frequency list has become well-known in a variety of language learning contexts. Frequency lists and information about the other aspects of language that McCarten articulated are becoming ever more accessible due to the Internet, vocabulary websites, and powerful programs. This chapter will touch on some of the ways corpora output can be utilized.

SPECIALIZED CORPORA

While the BNC and the BYU-Corpus of Contemporary American English are generalized while focusing on British and American English respectively, corpora can be formulated for more narrowly defined purposes. One of the most interesting such corpora is the *TIME* magazine corpus. With words taken from the popular American magazine *TIME*, this corpus contains more than 100 million American English words from 1923 to date. Users of this corpus can get a sense of the development of American English as words come in and out of fashion. In some cases, the changes reflect societal events and trends such as the Vietnam War and the lexicon of its counterculture (i.e., *hippie* and *acid*), or technological developments such as *internet* and *ipod*. Grammatical developments such as the popularization of the *-aholic* suffix may also be researched and analyzed. The corpus also allows for searches for word usage by periods, and a comparison of which words might be used more in, for example, the 1950s compared with the 2000s.

Another example of a specialized corpus is the University of Michigan's online corpus, MICASE, which contains 1.8 million words of spoken academic English. These words were transcribed mainly from lectures, but include academic discussions, student presentations, lab sessions, tutorials, dissertation defenses, and interviews—basically any verbal act that occurs in an academic setting. Users of this corpus, which would include materials writers and EFL professionals among others, will get search results that reflect academic communities. The MICASE website includes downloadable PDF documents containing exercises based on actual exchanges made on the corpus material. For example, one such PDF contains a brief description of the academic situation, three members of a math study group complaining about their homework, and a transcript of the conversation followed by a number of general and specific questions. Many of the site's sound files are freely available for listening and downloading online as well.

The TAT900 is even more focused, a specialized list made expressly for Japanese students at Tokyo University of Agriculture and Technology (TAT). Faculty members utilized English language materials taken from TAT's entrance examinations from 1996 to 2008, scanning them using OCR software to create a core corpus of 10568 tokens (word instances). In addition, passages from 34 textbooks utilized in upper level reading classes were similarly compiled, providing another 401187 tokens, and then analyzed according to frequency by using Ant Conc, a text analysis tool. The researchers, then, did analyses for common words found among the following: the TAT entrance examination list, the TAT textbook list, the general service list (GSL), and the academic word list (AWL).

In this way, faculty members at TAT could create and utilize a specialized vocabulary list that is most relevant to students studying at their university. TAT English instructors encourage students to become familiar with and drill the list of words via self study. Then, first year students in selected classes are given a test towards the end of the semester, which is 10% of their final grade. This system having just been implemented in April 2010 will likely undergo improvements (such as finding a way to help a wide range of mostly adjunct faculty members successfully convince students to study the words on their own time), but it is noteworthy for the attempt to create a list from specially tailored corpora and then create a vocabulary learning program appropriate for a single institution. This targeted research has been implemented in a practical way for all incoming students at TAT, a model for other institutions to consider.

Even more specialized corpora such as a business letter corpus and the works of several poets such as P. B. Shelley have become available online. One new corpus worth mentioning given the emergence of English as the lingua franca is the VOICE corpus, the Vienna-Oxford International Corpus of English. Like other corpora, it is a "structured collection of language data," but is unique in that it contains over one million words spoken by non-native speakers available at http://www.univie.ac.at/voice/page/index.php.

WORD FREQUENCY LISTS

Waring (2000) has articulated four uses of word frequency lists: as a learner reference, as a teacher resource, for materials writing, and for decontexualized learning. As a reference, teachers and learners can simply check the rank of a word to know its usefulness. As for decontexualized learning, the potential ways include all methods of drilling including handmade word cards, vocabulary notebooks, or online quizzes. Since the effectiveness of intentional study of vocabulary has been established (Hunt and Beglar, 1998, p. 8), word frequency lists can only make learners more informed about which words to drill. As awareness of the uses of word frequency lists and the value of intentional study of vocabulary grows, so does the number of printed resource materials, including textbooks. *Learning English Vocabulary*, which some teachers use as the main classroom text (personal correspondence with Barker, July 22, 2010), is one good example. It contains the 2000 most common English words, based on the BNC, with definitions in Japanese and sample sentences in English, as well as other grammatical descriptions. In contrast to an in-class textbook, Spiri (2010) describes *Word Quest*, composed of an in-class series of quizzes which learners progress at their own pace, combined with opportunities for online drilling of high frequency words.

UTILIZING ONLINE CORPORA VIA CONCORDANCE PROGRAMS

The worldwide web offers an amazing array of ever-improving opportunities to learn vocabulary and better understand corpora. Anderson and Corbett (2009) note that "students of language and linguistics can make considerable inroads into linguistic study solely by using freely available corpora, provided that they know where to look, have an appreciation of a few basic notions, and know how to maximize the potential of language corpora, with all their idiosyncrasies and differences" (p. 2). The most obvious way that online corpora can assist learners is by giving them the opportunity to deepen their knowledge of vocabulary. The word frequency list, as noted previously, allows learners to know which words are most useful and hence most worthy of their time and attention to study intentionally. Concordance programs provide learners with another way to deepen their word knowledge.

Concordance Programs

Concordance programs allow users to see the varied way a word is used in context. Users may input a word and a moment later be provided actual instances of the word being used, in context, from the corpus, as shown in Figure 1 below.

Students who are introduced to online concordance programs will be provided another tool to research and deepen their vocabulary knowledge. Below is a sample series of instructions for students along with a suggested word to search for (*attach*):

1.   Go to http://corpus.byu.edu/bnc/;
2.   Under *DISPLAY*, make sure *LIST* is chosen;

3. Type a word you would like to learn more about in the box. It can be a word from class, a word related to your major, or any other word;

4. Click the word after it appears on the right;

5. Write a few interesting or useful ways it is used on the handout; and

6. Repeat the process for a couple more words (e.g., the word *attach*, a word chosen from a class activity).

One drawback of English language learners utilizing concordance data in this way is that lower level learners will surely struggle to make sense of the sentences, phrases, and fragments; all of which are from native speaker texts. This fact may be seen as an advantage for higher level learners who desire to access authentic materials. In addition, most electronic dictionaries provide ample examples of carefully chosen sample sentences, making it less likely that learners who possessed such a dictionary would have a need for concordance data. At any rate, concordance data provide the opportunity for deep analysis of a word and its varied uses within a particular corpus. A further advantage of concordance programs compared with electronic dictionaries is that they allow for a wider range of searches. For example, any sort of collocation or idiom can be input and analyzed the same as can be done for individual words. Yet, another advantage of online concordance programs is that they can allow the user to do grammatical analysis. For example, on the BYU-BNC website an advanced search allows the user to separate noun usages from verb usages (words that double as both nouns and verbs such as *ferry* or *play*), which are particularly useful for English, a language that has so many words that double as both nouns and verbs.

1	FM2	S_meeting	, yes. Otherwise, as it says. on the top, Remember to **attach** all receipts and note all mileages. This claim will not be paid in the
2	J97	S_meeting	meeting when we have got all the other's together as well because again they may **attach** things, just that you've got your information and know what's been deci
3	JN7	S_meeting	do is guarantee any travel at their normal travel agent, do the business, **attach** the voucher to the B S P Well he'd have to process his direct
4	KM4	S_meeting	refer to job descriptions. Yes, it says on the thing that you can **attach** a job description to the back, but I should say that probably they want
5	CH1	W_newsp_tabloid	do n't rely on older children to look after them. 2) Don't **attach** fragrant blocks to the toilet rim. Children chew them. 3) Put bleach
6	CH1	W_newsp_tabloid	booking form and return it with the full payment due. You will need to **attach** three Daily Mirror tokens to take up the special offer. You can also visit
7	CH1	W_newsp_tabloid	Dates Complete the booking form, and send with full payment due. You must **attach** three separate Daily Mirror Tokens, printed this week, to take up the special
8	CH1	W_newsp_tabloid	"I was desperately waiting for the magic word "Cut" so I could **attach** myself to the wires before falling," he says. "But it did
9	CH6	W_newsp_tabloid	jumper is killed A YOUNG bungee jumper plunged to his death --; after forgetting to **attach** the rope. Spectators watched in horror as the 19-year-old daredevil sr
10	K4N	W_newsp_other_science	legal loophole that enabled the device to be sold, even though it is illegal to **attach** one to a telephone in the UK. Miss Lamb, of Worsley Crescent,
11	A6F	W_ac_polit_law_edu	possible, however, to classify most British political leaders according to the relative importance they **attach** to these values. In the inter-war years Stanley Baldwi
12	ABP	W_ac_polit_law_edu	; and, so long as it can be identified, the rights of the beneficiaries will **attach** to the fund into whatever form it may have been converted by him. If
13	ABP	W_ac_polit_law_edu	this : thus food and shelter are included in the definition. The court may **attach** to its grant such conditions as it sees fit. The maintenance ordered may be
14	EB2	W_ac_polit_law_edu	held to be guilty of theft by reason of conduct to which no moral obloquy could reasonably **attach** . These considerations suggest that conceptual analysis in crimi
15	FE1	W_ac_polit_law_edu	to construe the actual words enacted by Parliament so that in no circumstances could the court **attach** to words a meaning that they were incapable of bearing. He

Figure 1. Sample concordance output for the word "attach".

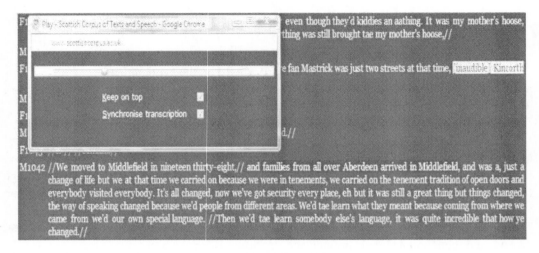

Figure 2. Sample output from spoken corpus of scottish english.

Of course, the same principle applies to analyzing usage of particles or determiners, conjunctions, or interjections.

Analyzing Pronunciation

The analysis of English via corpus availed to learners is not limited to written texts. Since spoken text is included in corpora, conversation discourse can also be analyzed with a concordance program. An exceptionally advanced corpus for spoken analyses is the SCOTS. Via the SCOTS website, a user can choose *Spoken* only (making sure the *Written* box is unclicked). The search condition can simply be a letter such as *r* that will provide the user with a number of documents that include words ending with *r*. By choosing one word or letter, users can see the transcript of a natural conversation. For one example taken from a BBC document, old-timers from Aberdeen were reminiscing about word usage for clothing, a category, which has notable regional differences (see Figure 2 below). A man identified as M1042 explains how "those things worn on your feet during P.E." were known as *jammies*, among a number of other regional words. In a coincidentally similar archaic or regional dialect word, the same speaker explains that, as a child, he would ask his mother for *jammy*, which is bread with either jam or butter (*ye didnae get baith* meaning *you did not get both*). The exchange can be heard via a quick time popup window while following a text, which automatically highlights the phrases being spoken. The exchange is both fascinating and educational for anyone who has an interest in the Scottish dialect, especially related to that particular region. Undoubtedly, useful sites such as this will become more widespread and include American, Australian, Indian, and other English dialects in the near future.

Analyzing Accents

One online project conducted and made available by George Mason University can be found at their Speech Accent Archive http://accent.gmu.edu/. This site aims to inform users of issues related to English phonetics and phonology. Individuals from all over the world who choose to participate in this project speak the phrase below in their native accent:

Instructions for English Speakers Participating in the Speech Accent Archive

Please call Stella. Ask her to bring these things with her from the store: Six spoons of fresh snow peas, five thick slabs of blue cheese, and maybe a snack for her brother Bob. We also need a small plastic snake and a big toy frog for the kids. She can scoop these things into three red bags, and we will go meet her Wednesday at the train station.

Each speaker's accented English was transcribed phonetically and made available to users of the website. For example, the speaker from Ireland saying the above passage was phonetically represented by the characters in Figure 3 below:

[pʰliz kʰɑl stelɔ ask ɚ ɾɔ bɹɪŋ
ðɪʂ θɪŋz wɪθ ɚ fɹɔm ðɔ stɔɚ
sɪks spũːnz əy fɹeʃ sno pʰiːz
fɑɪv tʰɪk slabz ɔ blu tʃʰiz ʔɛ̃n
meɪbi ɔ snæk fɔ̃ ɔ bɹʌðɚ bɑb
wi ʌlso nir ɔ smɑ̃ːl pʰlæsɪk
sneɪk ɛ̃n ɔ bɪg tʰɔɪ fɹɔg fɔ ðɔ
kʰɪdz ʃi kɔ̃n skup ðiz θɪŋz ʔĩntu
θɹi ɹɛd bægs ɛ̃n wi wɪl go mɪr
ɚ wɛ̃nzeɪ æt̚ ðɔʔ tʰɹeĩn
steɪʃɔ̃n]

Figure 3. Phonetically represented output of irish english.

While the standardization of the spoken phrase may be useful for comparison purposes, it can at the same time be seen as a weakness for its lack of spontaneity. Some speakers can be heard laboring to read the passage correctly, which might have affected their natural pronunciation. The Scottish Corpus of Texts and Speech (SCOTS), by contrast, addresses that drawback by including the spontaneous spoken utterances of a large number of individuals from inside as well as outside Scotland. In addition, the speakers represent a wide range of social classes, ages, and places of birth. Utterances are available as not only audio form, but also audio-visual files from the SCOTS website http://www.scottishcorpus.ac.uk/.

Analyzing Grammar

The usefulness of concordance results need not be limited to semantics (lexical). The grammatical function of a word can be examined either explicitly via a teacher made exercise, or by learners having an awareness of this application of concordance results. For example, a search can be refined for a target word such as *record* along with a particular part of speech (POS), with approximately 50 POS tag choices ranging from nouns, verbs, and adjectives to more specific categories such as a *plural common noun*. Searches can also be refined to consider collocations, with a collocate (such as *to*) anywhere from 0-9 positions before or after the target word (*record*). Analyzing the results of a search will not only make certain patterns clearer to learners, but also deepen their understanding of grammatical items such as prepositions and determiners. With even more advanced searches, noun, verb, and adjective phrases; clauses; or other types of grammatical constructions may be searched and analyzed as well. Anderson and Corbett (2009) note that until recently, researchers had to rely on intuition or deal with a "long and arduous process to compile and search substantial bodies of data" (p. 2). An intuitive approach was not only necessary considering the lack of analytical tools until recently, but actually promoted with Chomsky's emphasis on competence, knowledge of a language and its grammatical structures, performance, and the ways the language is actually used. While some might still claim that intuition based on knowledge is the best approach for researchers, the value of powerful concordance programs, readily available to everyone with an Internet connection, cannot be understated. They state that "given the proven insights that corpus data have given us into the behavior of words and phrases, it is now difficult for any grammarian to dispense with the immensely powerful tools that corpora represent for the study of language."

CORPORA INFLUENCING MATERIAL DESIGN

This section will explore the ways corpora can be utilized by material developers to make course books and other English language learning materials. The analysis of text to determine word frequency has potential applications for materials writers. As McCarthy (2004) notes, "A corpus can be a very rich resource for writers of textbooks and other teaching materials because it gives us a detailed view of how real people speak and write in everyday situations" (p. 6). After analyzing the relative difficulty of words in a textbook draft, overly difficult words can be replaced or translated or defined. Vocabulary exercises may be added to focus on those words. Corpus analysis can even inform writers of the relative difficulty of grammatical items in a textbook. By taking advantage of websites dedicated to corpus analysis, textbook writers can, with relative ease, see which words of a passage are most or least often used. One of the most useful vocabulary profiler website is Tom Cobb's http://www.lextutor.ca/ (Loucky and Spiri, 2007, p. 108). One way to analyze data will be described below, followed by a discussion of potential pitfalls and tough decisions that the materials writers face. A materials writer merely has to paste text into a window on the website and press the submit button to receive an in-depth vocabulary profile of the text. In the example below, a 520 word passage, which is the draft of a reading for a chapter of a writing textbook, was analyzed yielding a report (see Figure 4 below).

As noted above, the passage has 84.24% coverage for the first 1000 words, with 6.75% for the next 1000, 2.25% for academic vocabulary; and 6.75 words being off-list. There are two factors in particular that mitigate the problematicity of considering all off-list words as unknown or extremely difficult words. First, as the diagram below shows, all proper names are included in this percentage. Thus, for all students, even students in Japan, the words *Japan, Tokyo, London*, and *John* would all appear off-list despite the relative certainty with which the material writer can feel that they are known. Even when the proper nouns are more obscure, like the writer's hometown *Herkimer* (see Figure 5 below), a reader of reasonable skill could readily detect that the vocabulary represents a place name and continue reading without losing comprehension or time.

In addition, some of the off-list vocabulary, denoted in red, would probably not be difficult for students in Japan who, because of shared culture, are familiar with either the Japanese equivalent of the word (*ko-chi* for *coach*) or the word itself (*baseball*).

Home > VocabProfilers > English (Alt-arrow-left to preserve settings) > Output

EDIT-TO-A-PROFILE SPACE

WEB VP OUTPUT FOR FILE: Untitled

Words recategorized by user as 1k items (proper nouns etc): NONE (total 0 tokens)

	Families	Types	Tokens	Percent		
K1 Words (1-1000):	154	187	449	84.24%	Words in text (tokens):	533
Function:	...	...	(260)	(48.78%)	Different words (types):	243
Content:	...	...	(189)	(35.46%)	Type-token ratio:	0.46
> Anglo-Sax	...	...	(116)	(21.76%)	Tokens per type:	2.19
+Not Greco-Lat/Fr Cog					Lex density (content words/total)	0.51
K2 Words (1001-2000):	23	26	36	6.75%		
> Anglo-Sax:	...	...	(19)	(3.56%)	Pertaining to onlist only	
1k+2k				(90.99%)	Tokens:	497
					Types:	219
AWL Words (academic):	5	6	12	2.25%	Families:	182
					Tokens per family:	2.73
> Anglo-Sax:	...	...	(7)	(1.31%)	Types per family:	1.20
Off-List Words:	2	24	36	6.75%	Anglo-Sax Index:	80.89%
					(A-Sax tokens + function / onlist tokens)	
	182+?	243	533	100%	Greco-Lat/Fr-Cognate Index: (inverse of above) 19.11%	

Figure 4. Vocabulary profiling software statistical output.

Another factor for materials writers to consider when analyzing vocabulary usage data is the context. For example, for the above passage, the pre-reading photograph featured a woman playing tennis. For this reason as well, *tennis* would not necessarily be considered a difficult word for students. Furthermore, every time that a word or a form of the word appears it gets counted as an off-list word. Thus, in the above example, *tennis* might appear several times, driving the percentage of off-list words up even though it should be readily understandable even the first time.

The main advantage of running passages through vocabulary analysis programs such as the one above is not necessarily to strictly follow the results (by, for example, striking out all the off-list words), but rather to provide the material writers with guidance so that they can then consider the usefulness of each word given the students, users, context, and purpose.

While many textbooks may be influenced by some sort of word frequency analysis, rarely is the impact of such analysis made explicitly clear to users of the textbooks. One seldom utilized option would be to directly communicate the word frequency results to students so that they could see for themselves via color coding, the various frequency, and approximate difficulty levels of each word. Most textbook writers choose to isolate the difficult or key words for students to complete activities about and focus on intentionally.

In contrast, by simply making students aware of where the words stand on a word frequency list, they could then make better informed decisions about which words they want to focus on and learn intentionally.

Decisions about whether and how to study and/or drill certain words would be left up to the individual student and teacher, leaving more room for different learning styles. In this way, students could then know that it is strongly recommended to thoroughly understand the base level 1000 words while becoming aware of the advantages and potential drawbacks of such lists.

Figure 5. Vocabulary profiler output with color coding for word frequency.

SUGGESTIONS FOR CLASSROOM APPLICATION

There is no shortage of teacher resource books dedicated to provide teachers with ideas and resources for teaching vocabulary in the classroom. Nation's *New Ways of Teaching Vocabulary*, Morgan and Rinvolucri's *Vocabulary*, and *Working with Words* by Gairns and Redman are just three established examples. For practical principles, however, McCarten (2007) makes the following thorough list of suggestions for teachers: Focus on vocabulary, offer variety, repeat and recycle, provide opportunities to organize vocabulary, make vocabulary learning personal, do not overdo it, use strategic vocabulary in class, and help students become independent learners in and out of class. Teachers can best apply these principles and access resources after considering their unique teaching situations and student needs.

Because of the fact that corpora have only relatively recently been developed, information about utilizing corpora in the classroom is not so voluminous. O'Keeffe, McCarthy, and Carter (2007) have explained the basics of corpus linguistics and how corpora might be utilized in the classroom. Anderson and Corbett (2009) provide many practical activities for readers of their book with step-by-step directions and objectives for accessing and utilizing online corpora.

Many of these activities can be adapted by teachers to create classroom activities regarding anything from frequency word vocabulary, borrowed words, grammar, world Englishes, collocations, or any other language related topic mentioned in this chapter. Both large and small scale corpora are still being built, as are corresponding websites with more powerful and detailed searches, so the probability of rapid change and advance is high, making it an exciting field for teachers and researchers to explore, but difficult to keep up with. For example, just between the time this chapter was written and went to print, the BYU corpus website http://corpus.byu.edu/ for registered users noted five additions including the following two: (1) the Corpus of *Historical* American English (COCA) of more than 400 million words was put online and (2) frequency lists were expanded to include the top 60,000 lemmas (headwords).

CONCLUSION

This chapter has discussed the utilization of corpora for materials writing and accessing online corpora for language study and research. It has briefly described a number of exciting new corpora that are now available on the worldwide web, and ways such corpora can be exploited with tools such as concordance programs. As more and more online corpus linguistic tools become available, users such as language learners, teachers, and researchers are provided greater opportunities to deepen their understanding of the English language. Thus, they can offer learners informed corpus oriented language instruction, which help the learners acquire language skills like vocabulary and grammar in context, for example.

REFERENCES

Anderson, W., and Corbett, J. (2009). *Exploring English with online corpora*. New York: Palgrave Macmillan.

Hunt, A., and Beglar, D. (1998). Current research and practice in teaching vocabulary. *The English Teacher*, January 7-12.

Loucky, J., and Spiri, J. (2007). Systematic ways of teaching, studying and testing high frequency vocabulary online. *Language Forum: A Journal of Language and Literature, 33*, 101-114.

McCarten, J. (2007). *Teaching vocabulary: Lessons from the corpus, lessons for the classroom*. Cambridge: Cambridge University Press.

McCarthy, M. (2004). *Touchstone: From corpus to course book*. Cambridge: Cambridge University Press.

Milton (2009). *Measuring second language vocabulary acquisition*. Bristol, UK: Multilingual Matters.

O'Keeffe, A., McCarthy, M., and Carter, R. (2007). *From corpus to classroom: Language use and language teaching*. Cambridge: Cambridge University Press.

Spiri, J. (2010). Developing corpus oriented English materials. In H. P. Widodo and L. Savova (Eds.), *The Lincom guide to materials design in ELT* (pp. 177-188). Muenchen, Germany: Lincom Europa.

Waring, R. (2001). *Second language vocabulary: The word lists page*. Retrieved August 7, 2010, from http://www.robwaring.org/vocab/wordlists/vocfrequses.html

In: Innovation and Creativity in ELT Methodology
Editors: H. P. Widodo and A. Cirocki

ISBN: 978-1-62948-146-3
© 2013 Nova Science Publishers, Inc.

Chapter 16

TEACHING ENGLISH THROUGH CALL

Tilly Harrison
Warwick University, England

ABSTRACT

The average English teacher is faced with an increasing number of choices for the introduction of technology into the classroom. The different technologies have different "affordances" or opportunities for action and perception; not all of which are necessarily useful for language learning. The chapter traces the concept of affordance through the history of CALL to the present, emphasizing the importance of context in terms of learner and task. The changing hardware of the modern classroom offers opportunities, but the expectations of the students are a challenge in an age where learning becomes more and more mobile. By focussing on affordances that benefit language learning, teachers of English can ensure that they remain effective and relevant as the world changes.

INTRODUCTION

With the advent of personal computing and the Internet, the environment for learning, including the environment for learning languages, changed dramatically. However, in many parts of the world, the classroom environment has stayed relatively unaffected by these resources, and those who harness them may be seen as, at best, pioneering, at worst rash tinkerers with untried methods. This chapter is about Computer Assisted Language Learning (CALL) in English language teaching (ELT).

That is, it will look at ways that technology (since now the word *computer* applies to much more than the set box on a desk) has been and is being used to enhance the learning of English, particularly in a classroom environment.

A New Environment

As one of the tools in the hands of a teacher of English, computers have gone from being too remote and inaccessible to use to a natural and seamlessly integrated part of the daily experience of students and teachers. We not only use technology more often and more easily, but also find it in more aspects of our lives. In an increasing number of classrooms, the majority of students have a mobile phone in their pocket.

However, these devices are no longer just telephones; most are capable of taking photographs, recording sound, and storing video; and many can now access the Internet. In effect, they are mini computers. More and more students have laptops, printers, and access to the Internet at home. Very few expect to give hand-written work to their teacher or communicate by letter. How does teaching and learning languages differ in this technology-rich environment?

The focus on the word *environment* is intentional since the theoretical framework on which this chapter will be based stems from the work of the ecologist, J. J. Gibson, who first introduced the concept of *affordance* in the context of describing how humans perceive the world around them. This term has been much debated in the field of learning technology, and it has a number of interpretations.

However, the idea it represents offers a useful way to categorize and conceptualize the opportunities which modern CALL brings to the classroom. For me, an understanding of this concept provides the average English teacher with a powerful means of assessing and critiquing the plethora of emerging technologies, and a rationale for using *old school* CALL (also called Structural CALL by Warschauer and Healey, 1998 or Restricted CALL by Bax, 2003) where this is still evidently effective. As such, I will briefly define the term before going on to relate it to ELT in particular.

The Concept of Affordance

Originally for Gibson (1986), *affordances* were the opportunities for action and perception which humans can discover in their physical environment – solid ground affords us the opportunity to walk; fire affords the opportunity to cook; and a path affords the opportunity to proceed without obstacles. It is important to notice that for Gibson, an item and its affordance were bound together in a context where humans were discovering relevant uses or meanings.

It would be meaningless to abstract a particular affordance from its use in its expected context: Walking does not happen unless there is solid ground; cooking does not happen without heat, etc.

Equally, affordances assume an actor or perceiver, but they exist whether they are acted on or perceived. So, although affordances seem to be simply *functions*, they are context bound, human specific, and practical. As far as CALL is concerned, there has not been a specific taxonomy of affordances as such, but implicitly in notions of the Computer as Tutor or Tool or Stimulus (Warschauer and Healey, 1998), we see that the role of the computer in language learning can be seen as offering "opportunities for action and perception." These actions and perceptions, which lead to language learning merit close attention.

AFFORDANCES IN ICT

In the ICT literature, the affordances of technology were abstracted and listed by Conole and Dyke (2004) who identified the following: (1) accessibility, (2) speed of change, (3) diversity, (4) communication and collaboration, (5) reflection, (6) multi-modality and non-linearity, (7) risk, (8) fragility and uncertainty, (9) immediacy, (10) monopolization, and (11) surveillance. This seems to be a useful starting point, but I do not feel it makes best use of the concept for pedagogical purposes. The context and user specific aspects of an affordance are crucial. What teachers need is to know which types of technology exactly will afford, which benefit, and in what circumstances. Further, they need to know whether such benefits seem to coincide with current theories of language learning – there may be a number of affordances in a particular use of technology, but crucially, does it afford language learning?

Teasing out the aspects of ICT that can be proved to enhance reading, writing, speaking, listening, and vocabulary learning or grammar knowledge and use (the "differences that make the difference" as Kenning, 2010, puts it) is the *holy grail* of CALL research. To date, only a small proportion of studies have robustly made a case for technology over and above any other kind of teaching or communicative context. Many seem to be replicating the classroom or teacher input, which in an ideal world, the student would be able to access without the intervention of technology. However, the problem for CALL researchers is that the technology changes faster than painstaking research can cope with (Levy, 2007). What may be found to be useful one year could be obsolete later on.

EARLY CALL – SPEED AND RECORD KEEPING

From the beginning of CALL in ELT, the affordances of computer use allowed opportunities to practice language in different ways. Initially, CALL was associated with bespoke programs for vocabulary or grammar drilling, which took the kind of material that was used in the classrooms of the time, and turned them into activities that required a computer. Sometimes, the difference was simply speed – you could fill in the gap or answer a multiple choice question, and the computer afforded an instant answer. A paper based version of the same exercise could give you the same result (a book after all has many useful affordances!), but the novelty of the computer was that it was instant and that the correct answer could be embellished with sound or a cute graphic. A computer could also add up your score for you and remember your previous score – again not impossible to replicate, but the immediacy and convenience gave this affordance novelty value. The capacity for tireless repetition (unlike human teachers) was another affordance, which enabled learners to work at different paces. However, all of these could be replicated without technology, which is perhaps why many teachers were not easily convinced of the utility of CALL.

FEEDBACK AND CUSTOMIZED INPUT

Further, along in the development of computer programs for CALL, it was realized that more attention needed to be paid to feedback. Simply giving instant feedback did not necessarily help students understand their mistakes. Customized exercises with teacher created feedback allowed students to undertake tasks that a book could not easily replicate. With authored programs, teachers created customized responses for each answer so that when a student chose wrongly, they had the opportunity to learn and improve. The affordance in question is the automization of customization – the class teacher can choose the text and write the responses according to the students' needs, and the computer patiently offers these responses as many times as needed – freeing the teacher from tedious repetition, but not from the need to prepare and update such exercises. Technology, in the long run, did not seem to save time, nor were these programs better than direct feedback from a teacher on a one-to-one basis – they simply replicated and automated it.

THE AFFORDANCES OF COMPLETE CLOZE

One of the first language teaching programs to truly harness the computer's unique attributes was the idea of total text deletion (or *Complete Cloze*) where the letters of a given text are replaced by blobs. The student is left with the punctuation and shapes of the words (the number of letters each has), but on guessing one word correctly, all instances of that word are immediately restored. As more words are correctly guessed, the student's linguistic ability, particularly understanding of discoursal features, is challenged and tested. Although ways to replicate this in the classroom were suggested (Rinvolucri, 1984), unusually the inspiration for this activity (the original idea was that of Tim Johns as discussed by Davies, 2007) flowed from the computer back to the classroom rather than vice versa.

Teaching Suggestion:
Language Learning Concepts: Noticing – reflection on discourse features/negotiation of meaning
Technology Affordances: Total text deletion, correct guesses replace all instances, sound, and video
Process: (lower intermediate – adaptable up to advanced level), students have been studying giving directions and have just watched a video of a dialog between someone who is lost and a helpful passer-by. On the computer, they are challenged in pairs to reconstruct the words of the dialogue from a complete cloze. Depending on the level of the students, they may or may not be allowed access to the video as they do this. With unlimited access to the sound, the students practice noticing unstressed words and focus on understanding speech at natural speeds. Repeated focused listening helps embed the pronunciation and intonation. Without access to the sound, the focus is more on predicted (or remembered) sequences, likely vocabulary, and clause level grammar. With repeated trial and error, the pair negotiate options and in the process explore and stretch the limits of their own knowledge and that of their partner.

Text reconstruction uses the affordances of the computer to change the appearance of texts, search, and replace instantly as well as to jumble texts. When such a puzzle is used by learners in pairs or groups, the whole activity affords deeper processing of vocabulary and sentence structures as attempts are made, and failures and successes are discussed (Hewer,

1997). As such, it offers a number of promising links to second language learning theory through the *noticing* and negotiation of meaning and discourse that take place. However, these affordances depend greatly on the total context – the text chosen, the ability of the students, their interest in this kind of activity, the relevance to their regular curriculum, the teacher's role both as initiator and facilitator, and other classroom specific sociocultural factors. A CALL *formula* such as this is most successful (commercial versions of this idea still sell well) where teachers can easily perceive its affordances for their own context, perhaps through personal experience of its use via CALL training.

AFFORDANCES OF WORD PROCESSING

However, alongside these customized and authored programs, which were arguably having little impact on most classrooms, other important uses of technology were quietly changing the way that people wrote and communicated. The affordances of the word processor are now taken for granted – we expect to be able to cut and paste or search and replace. Those with more proficiency happily track changes, add comments, graphics, and even interactive elements.

Teaching Suggestion:

- *Language Learning Concepts: Noticing–negotiation of meaning-collaboration-motivation*
- *Technology Affordances: Editing features of a word processor, search and replace, printing*
- *Process: (Beginner to Upper Intermediate) in pairs, students work on a computer filling in gaps in a word processing document. The prompts can be dictated or supplied within the text, depending on the level of the students. Students need to supply the name of a male, the name of a female and a place in the sentence "One ………… (adjective) day …………… (male) met ……………… (female) in /on / at ………………………… (place)." All students then move to the next computer, read the existing text, correcting it if necessary, and then add the opening of the conversation between the couple. The teacher supplies the prompts "He said to her: "I'm hungry …… "She said to him: "………" and the students work together to supply the dialog. As soon as all have finished, students save the file and move around to the next computer, reading, and correcting as before. The teacher then supplies the prompt: "They went to a restaurant called …………… and ordered …………… The waiter said: "…………………" The students then move on to the next computer and are asked to finish the "story" in as interesting / surprising a way they can. The finished texts can be printed and given to the original pairs. All students can then "act out" the short, self penned plays. As a focus on pronouns, a variation of this activity is to ask the students at the end to exchange the male and female roles and search and replace the relevant pronouns (he / she / him / her / his / her / etc.). The creativity allowed within this highly structured activity typically engenders great amusement, while allowing "safe" rehearsal of known language and practice with new structures.*

All of these attributes have pedagogic potential although they are not always thought of as CALL. Though classroom resources are limited, teachers with access to a word processing program can set tasks, which enhance English language learning. This could be by either a focus on form (change this text from the present to the past and add the omitted verbs to this text), discourse features (re-arrange these paragraphs or sentences in the correct order and separate this text into two different texts), or creativity (students add their own ideas to a partially dictated text) (see Slaouti, 2000, for these and other ideas about the uses of word processing for ELT). The fact that this technology was already well-known and widely available made this approach to computer use more easily adopted into classrooms and could be seen as an early manifestation of *normalization* (Bax, 2003) where technology ceases to be the focus, but becomes invisible in the total language learning context.

AFFORDANCES OF COMPUTER MEDIATED COMMUNICATION (CMC)

The other change that migrated from every day life into the classroom was communication via email. Although the affordances of email were easily recognized for personal communication, and early adopters were quick to suggest its use for language learning, it took teachers a little longer to realize that something so *mundane* could, in fact, be harnessed for language learning. What were the advantages exactly? Emails afford the ability to send and receive written communication quickly. However, there is enough delay in the written mode to allow redrafting, so learners can edit their contributions before committing them to the target audience. This affordance (which is also true of synchronous communication) offers language learners an ideal middle ground between talking (which requires speed and fluency) and traditional writing (which requires accuracy and is generally a slow medium of communication). The other major affordance is connection to anyone with email anywhere in the world. Although the use of penpals had offered a similar connection, the new idea of *keypals* had the potential for faster and more dynamic communication. Linked to communication by email was the developing field of *chat* (synchronous computer mediated communication), which seemed to harness even more effectively the affordances of identity creation and confidence building as well as language practice through negotiation of meaning that genuine communication in the target language can give (Warschauer and Kent, 2000). Again, however, the task and context are the keys. In Pelleterini's study of negotiation using Synchronous Network based Communication, she found that of the 5 tasks given to her students, those that were difficult, but with fewer possible outcomes, (such as checking with a partner differences in a set of similar pictures) generate more negotiation. She also found that the requirement to compose a shared text encouraged reflection and focus on form. She writes:

> Synchronous Network based Communication language tasks should be goal-oriented, with a minimum of possible outcomes, and they should be designed in such a way that all participants are required to request and obtain information from one another for successful task completion . . . this study suggests that if the language goal is to promote an even higher level of learner focus on grammatical forms, those tasks that require learners to produce and then reflect on the language produced might be fruitful avenues to pursue.

(Warschauer and Kern, 2000, p. 83)

So, although here the computer provides the medium for the required communication, the task itself has the key affordances of action and perception that are useful to the students.

Teaching Suggestion:
- *Language Learning Concepts: Negotiation – authentic audience – autonomy*
- *Technology Affordances: Synchronous computer-mediated communication (chat or web conferencing), access to the Internet*
- *Process: This activity presupposes that students are not physically close to each other. As such, it suits a homework activity where the students live at a distance, or an activity on a distance learning course. In pairs, the students are given the task of creating a text together, which contains a given number of deliberate mistakes. The text will then serve as a stimulus for further work by another pair (or keypals) to unravel the truth and untruth in the text. The students may need to negotiate the topic (facts about their town, a famous person, or an endangered species, for example) if this is not supplied by the teacher as part of the existing curriculum. They will then need to find suitable sources of information (keeping track of these as helpful hints for their quiz) and agree which facts to keep and which facts to change. The simultaneous use of a chat program and a wiki, or a web conferencing facility where individuals can see each other's desktops would be suitable technologies for this task.*

MULTIMODALITY

One of the affordances often cited as unique to computers is the ability to offer a multimodal (and multimedia) environment for learning: sound, graphics, video, texts, and the means of interaction with these resources cannot easily be combined in any other way. Programs, which offer teachers the opportunity to use their own texts, pictures, video, and a variety of exercise types with customized feedback are still popular – the best known of these is the freely downloaded *Hot Potatoes* (Holmes, 2010). With the advantage of being web based, *Hot Potatoes* brings the affordances of immediacy and customizability within the grasp of most teachers. It affords a number of other opportunities, which cannot be replicated on paper. Multimodality becomes an option, linking sound to sight (text or pictures), sequencing of text or graphics. The effect on motivation of multimedia has been well-documented (e.g., Kim and Gilman, 2008), particularly for vocabulary, which benefits from a range of input (Nation, 2001).

However, far beyond the fairly static merging of graphics or video or audio into texts or exercises, the Internet now offers users a huge range of options for do-it-yourself animation creation. Virtual worlds such as Second Life go even further, allowing a learner to script in real time the dialog of an avatar with other learners' (and teachers') avatars and have a fully animated experience on the Internet. Perhaps, *scripting* seems too strong a word since the interaction is real to some extent. Moreover, the opportunities for input, output, and negotiation are extremely rich once the interactants are comfortable in the virtual environment and can use it appropriately.

CLOSED SYSTEMS

So, often in CALL, attractive opportunities have been trumpeted and undoubtedly exist, but the more practical details of what the *context* must be for those affordances to be exploited are vague or unrealistic. Many projects that report to be successful turn out to be closed systems, which cannot be easily replicated by ordinary teachers. This is particularly true of commercial software where there has been considerable investment in a certain *package* for language learning. A recent example (Liu and Chu, 2010) is a study of a course in which teenagers were issued with mobile devices and given tasks to do in the form of *ubiquitous* games where they interacted with peers and with the mobile, recording their responses to questions as spoken answers. A unique aspect of this set up was that the students were out of the classroom and that the mobile device could, by scanning a barcode, give the students contextually relevant material (if they were in the library, the practice conversations were relevant to libraries). The results showed clearly that on all levels the learners in the experimental group had enjoyed and benefited from the experience. The teachers and researchers involved had clearly harnessed the affordances of the technology for language learning in that context effectively. However, the benefits are not generalizable since it relies on a bespoke combination of hardware and software. In the following, I will attempt to describe some of the technologies, which are currently freely available and their affordances for particular aspects of ELT.

AFFORDANCES OF WIKIS AND BLOGS

I will start with a personal story of experimentation with technology and an evolving understanding of the concept of *affordance*. Teaching a class of undergraduate Chinese students in a UK university, I became increasingly alarmed at the small size of their vocabulary when they arrived − often falling below the 3000 word threshold necessary for intermediate English, let alone the fairly advanced academic texts they needed to read. I wanted to find a way of encouraging them to focus on vocabulary learning and hit on the idea of requiring them to hand in every week a word that they had come across in their reading. Obviously, this should help each individual with their ongoing vocabulary expansion, but I wanted it to become a resource for the whole class. I began by typing up the slips of paper on a web page so that the week's words were visible to all (using the Internet's affordance of accessibility), but this was time consuming and ultimately unsustainable. At this point, the concept of a *wiki* or editable web page offered the very affordance I needed − the opportunity for each member of the class to contribute to a shared space. I had not used a wiki before other than to read *Wikipedia*, nor was I aware of other wikis being used as a vocabulary collection, but it seemed the ideal solution to my problem. The homework requirement became that of making a page in the wiki for the student's new word, complete with context sentence, definition, comment, picture, and whatever else they felt would make it memorable. Later, I asked them to add concordance lines grouped by collocation extracted from Collins Wordbanks online. Now, each year, I start a new wiki for vocabulary collection. However, my reading about wikis led me to feel that something was missing − the affordances generally discussed were those of collaboration, cooperation, and co-ownership of the space, and I did not notice this as an aspect of the *micro-pedia* that my students created. I realize now that an affordance can exist, but is not necessarily taken up just because the technology is available. The task and teacher input are arguably more important than the technology. However, the lack of *community spirit* in the class wiki did not detract from its usefulness as a shared resource – the technology truly offered something I could not have done otherwise (The project is discussed in more detail in Harrison, 2007). Blogs are another way that the average Internet user can now have a presence and a *voice* without knowing anything about web page creation. They differ from wikis in that contributions are sequenced (dated like diary entries) and can generally only be edited by the author. They lend themselves to use as a vehicle for personal opinions, and as such blog writers have become a powerful, one could even say democratizing, force in the modern era. The fact that blogs allow comments from strangers means that the *conversation* can continue, creating a micro-community of contributors on the topic in hand. For learners, as with native speakers, the uptake of this technology (a personal blog in the language they are learning) can depend on the confidence and personality of the individual. There may be many opportunities for communication and self publication on the Internet, but this does not mean that learners will all wish to participate equally enthusiastically. It is vital to have an appropriate task and adequate support.

Teaching Suggestion:
- *Language Learning Concepts: Writing for an authentic audience, writing with purpose, autonomy*
- *Technology Affordances: Accessibility of the Internet, free blog sites, personal publishing, editability of wikis, graphics from text (word clouds)*
- *Process: Students are first made into teams of about 4 or 5, either randomly or by self selection (if such groups already exist so much the better). As follow up to a class activity, each class member is asked to write a personal, individual response to a given topic on a blog, such as their first impressions of school/their favorite music/their dreams of the future. These are open for comment by anyone in the class or beyond, but are not corrected. A nominated member of the group reads and summarizes the contributions of the group perhaps with the support of some scaffolding language such as "Most of the group felt……… A few……… Some ……… One person ………" At higher levels, this is practice in synthesizing information from different sources, which is a useful academic writing skill. The summary is posted on a wiki, which can be edited by other group members. The teacher can also edit this piece of writing more freely since the text is not a personal account but a factual report of the groups' ideas. The class wiki can then feed into further discussion of trends in the whole group. Another way of showing this is to put the text of the blogs and the wiki into Wordle.net, which will create a graphic picture from the text making the more frequent words larger.*

MISCONSTRUED AFFORDANCES (PODCASTING)

Working on ways to harness the affordances of technology (and any other language teaching resource) is necessarily a personal journey for teachers, who have particular needs and issues to deal with. My journey has taken many twists and turns. I was happy with the way the wiki was working to raise awareness of vocabulary learning in my students, but I wanted ways to make it more useful and accessible to other members of the class. Again, a new development presented itself – the concept of podcasts (audio files that are available on the Internet) as a way of enriching the class vocabulary pages. The affordances of this technology, particularly the subscription element of podcasting, seemed to me to offer wonderful possibilities – I envisaged each student making a recording of their word in collaboration with native speaking friends, uploading it to their page, and their friends subscribing to the class recordings and so getting 30 one minute *injections* of vocabulary every week. I prepared a script for their native speaker collaborators, which asked them to end the short recording with their own opinion of the word, or what for them would be a natural context for it. All this seemed to offer great potential for making each word salient and memorable.

However, I did not realize that for my students, the requirement to ask a native speaker to make the recording (despite the availability of small MP3 recorders on loan) was too heavy a burden, they were just too unsure of themselves in the UK context to dare approach their flatmates for a favor. The project foundered until I recruited two volunteer British undergraduates who patiently made several recordings in one sitting. Eventually, I dropped the expectation that the wiki vocabulary page should have a link to a podcast. Again, the affordance and its uptake are totally context dependent. Teachers should feel able to experiment and at times fail while all the time seeking affordances that are practical and effective in their context.

WEBQUESTS

CALL is not of itself a language teaching *method*. However, individual uses of technology do seem to support a number of language learning theories. Where a teacher is seeking to use a more constructivist approach in their teaching, emphasizing collaboration between peers, supporting learning through a supportive environment of scaffolded tasks, and encouraging more learner autonomy, there are now many online activities whose affordances complement these ideals. One of these is the WebQuest – a specific approach to pedagogic use of the Internet initially designed by Bernie Dodge in collaboration with Tom March.

Dodge defines the WebQuest as "an inquiry oriented lesson format in which most or all the information that learners work with comes from the web" (Dodge, 2007). The key features of the concept are that it should be carefully structured and requires learners to collaborate, research, and crucially transform material that the teacher has pre-selected on the Web. It is NOT a *Web search* since learners should spend time using information, not looking for it. As March (2010) points out, the sound teaching strategies used in WebQuests (he lists nine including Motivation Theory, Schema Theory, and Constructivism) are not particularly new. However, educational establishments have generally been slow to adopt them. The affordance of access to the Web and web page creation with hyperlinks has facilitated teacher adoption of the approach, and it is now a concept that is used worldwide for all levels of student and all topics.

For ELT, WebQuests offer the same motivational affordances as well as exposure to selected parts of the Web for reading and listening practice. The scaffolding inherent in the approach allows teachers to mediate authentic materials with access to online dictionaries and glossaries. Of the many uses of CALL that I have introduced teachers to as a teacher trainer, the WebQuest is the approach that catches their imagination most. Its flexibility means that any online resource can become part of the task, so it can become a way of exploring the affordances of other online technologies (March, 2007) such as blogs, wikis, chat, audio conferencing, or virtual worlds such as Second Life. The key is the appropriate task for the context.

Teaching Suggestion:
- *Language Learning Concepts: Collaboration – authentic task – negotiation – autonomy – constructivism (learning through connecting to existing knowledge)*
- *Technology Affordances: Connection to the Internet and thus resources for facts/opinions/advice/instructions/etc., web page template (for WebQuest) and hyperlinks*
- *Process: There are many WebQuests available on the WebQuest.org site and although the vast majority are designed for mainstream U.S. schools, with a little extra support a good number can be adapted for language learning. As an example, the following WebQuest is adapted from Stranded by Nicolene Golas. It is designed as a support for the book Lord of the Flies and as such would suit a literature oriented class although it is not necessary to have read the book. Students are introduced to the topic on the Introduction page of the WebQuest: "Congratulations! All of (insert name of teacher or class)'s class have won an all expenses paid vacation to the Bahamas!"*

Warning!
"The engine has caught fire and the plane has crashed down in uncharted waters! You have all made it safely onto land and upon exploring the surrounding area, you have found the plane control panel intact over by the rocks. Further inspection has led your group to find that the plane computer is able to receive an Internet signal!"

At this point, the students can be introduced to an online dictionary to check any word or phrases which they may not know (e.g., all expenses paid, uncharted, intact, further inspection, etc.).

The task is then given to the students:
In your groups, you will use the Internet to retrieve viable information for your survival. You will use the Internet with the information found. You will create a survival brochure for others who could potentially become stranded in the event that you are rescued.

The process outlines the steps to this task. The students are assigned different roles in the group. These could be according to the book characters, for example, one student could be Ralph, the leader, assigning tasks to the other characters who support him in different ways. Or the students could be given roles according to particular areas of research (e.g., Habitat Hunter, Food Forager, Animal Agent, and Weather Wizard).

The final product is described in detail:

The brochure should include:

- *An attractive cover with an attention grabbing title and appealing graphics throughout the brochure.*
- *Survival tips that include: how to build/find shelter, what to eat, what is safe to eat, what animals are indigenous to the island, and what kind of climate one can expect on the island.*
- *The back of the brochure should include all of your resources.*

(If using the book) Above your resources, your group is to include a list of suggestions for the characters in the Lord of the Flies as to what they could have done differently while on the island now that your group has done the research and have become educated on the topic of survival.

The websites required for the task are already chosen and grouped under headings (Survival Tips, How to Survive, Images, Tropical Climates, How to make a Brochure) so that the students do not waste time looking for resources, but can quickly get straight to the task in hand. Where extra language support is needed, the teacher should be available to offer suggestions either in person or online. Students work together and individually to produce the final product. On the WebQuest website under Evaluation, there is a suggested chart for ways to assess the students' work – this could be adapted according to the focus of the class. Finally the project is rounded off with a happy ending:

Great News! A rescue ship has spotted the wreckage from your flight and you have been rescued. Everyone will be able to read your survival brochure and benefit from its contents! GREAT WORK!!! We are glad to have you home SAFE and SOUND!

WEB 2.0

Internet development continues to race ahead with new ways of connecting people and creating new communities and new ways of interacting. The affordances of social networks such as Facebook, Twitter, and Flickr can, in the right context, provide English learners with the opportunity for genuine interaction within a community, and access to native speakers outside of the classroom. The *personal learning network* (PLN) that such technologies afford can affect the dual purpose of learning the language while learning the focus subject of the discussion. At this point, the teacher's role may be simply to encourage such an autonomous environment, assuming the learners are old enough to use such sites responsibly.

HARDWARE IN THE CLASSROOM

In the classroom, too, the range of technical options now offered to teachers creates special affordances that can be exploited or ignored. Document visualizers can be used simply for presentation, but the affordance of real time display and sharing of small items means that students' written work can be shared and annotated. The interactive whiteboard allows dynamic new ways of presenting material, but its other affordances for student participation in learning can sometimes be ignored. Early adopters and enthusiasts may try to pass on their own uses of a technology, but ultimately a teacher needs to feel their way from affordances that they know will be effective in their context (which includes their own teaching style) to new approaches. Adopting a new technology is in effect creating a whole new *ecology* in the classroom. It is little wonder that teachers are often cautious about potentially radical changes.

Mobile Learning

However, in the last decade or so radical changes have taken place in the world outside the classroom, and inevitably, the external environment will eventually impact that inside. Of the major changes we are seeing, the most radical for educationalists is the advent of the affordances of mobile learning. Students now have instant access to each other and the world from the *computer* in their pocket. The use of the mobile phone for learning English was hampered from the start by the small size of the screen for texts of any substantial length. The more laborious input of text was another factor that seemed to rule this technology out for any meaningful language learning activities. Nevertheless, there have been some successes for vocabulary learning and personal or group blogging (see Kukulska-Hulme and Shield, 2007 for an overview and Appendix B in that publication for a list of affordances of mobile devices for language learning).

However, modern tablet devices seem to herald a new era of mobile learning since the functionality of the portable device has exploded. The iPad, for example, offers connection to the Internet and email, an A5 size screen for reading and inputting texts, touch control that frees the user from keyboards and mice, tilt sensitivity, GPS positioning, clear graphics, sound, and access to any number of *apps*; many of which are language learning related. Although many of these, at the moment, look like old-fashioned *flash card* drills, they come with sound and extreme ease of use (a finger swipe to sort through them). However, educational packages of all kinds are available to download in science, astronomy, history, and other disciplines, so learning English through other content is easier than ever. Games also proliferate, many of them with Web 2.0 features to connect the player to a virtual community. The touch screen can even split in two so that two people can sit opposite each other, and each participates in a task (for example, playing a piano duet). The range of affordances of this device is stimulating software developers to think of more and more intelligent ways to exploit them. For teachers, a classroom where all students have such a device is as yet a long way off, but the push for more mobility in learning is real. We should be ready to seek out the affordances of mobile technology and using them to help our students learn *anytime* and *any where*.

Conclusion

To make the concept of affordance relevant to modern day CALL, it is necessary for teachers to be able to abstract the opportunities available to them from the technology at their disposal and relate it to their particular students in their particular context (both the classroom and curriculum). I strongly believe that so far no single *innovation* in CALL can be generalized across all contexts. The way one teacher harnesses a particular affordance may not be possible in a different context and/or may not have the same result. However, as teachers come to notice and appropriate the concept of affordance, they will also grow in the confidence to select and experiment with what will be relevant to them and what will create for their students the optimum environment for language learning.

REFERENCES

Bax, S. (2003). CALL— past, present and future. *System*, *31*, 13-28.

Conole, G., and Dyke, M. (2004). What are the affordances of information and communication technologies? *ALT-J, Research in Learning Technology*, *12*, 113-124.

Davies, G. (2007). *Total cloze text reconstruction programs: A brief history*. Available in Word DOC format at the ICT4LT website [http://www.ict4lt.org/en/index.htm]

Dodge, B. (2007). *WebQuest.org*. Retrieved September 19, 2010, from http://webquest.org/

Gibson, J. J. (1986). *The ecological approach to visual perception*. London: Lawrence Erlbaum.

Harrison, T. (2007). Experiences of using Wikis to support students' learning. *Warwick Interactions Journal 30 (2)*. Retrieved September 19, 2010, from http://www2.warwick. ac.uk/services/ldc/resource/interactions/current/abharrison/harris

Hewer, S. (1997). *Text manipulation: Computer-based activities to improve knowledge and use of the target language*. London: CILT.

Holmes, M. (2010). *Hot potatoes*. Retrieved September 19, 2010, from http://hotpot.uvic.ca/

Kenning, M-M. (2010). Differences that make the difference: A study of functionalities in synchronous CMC. *ReCALL*, *22*(1), 3-9.

Kim, D., and Gilman, D. (2008). Effects of text, audio and graphic aids in multimedia instrcution for vocabulary learning. *Educational Technology and Society*, *11*, 114-126.

Kukulska-Hulme, A., and Shield, L. (2007). *An overview of mobile assisted language learning: Can mobile devices support collaborative practice in speaking and listening?* Paper presented at the EUROCALL 2007 Virtual strand. Retrieved September 19, 2010, from citeseerx.ist.psu.edu/viewdoc/download?doi=10.1.1.84.1398andrep

Levy, M. (2007). Research and technical innovation in CALL. *Innovation in Language Learning and Teaching*, *1*(1), 180-190.

Liu, T-Y, and Chu, Y-L. (2010). Using ubiquitous games in an English listening and speaking course: Impact on learning outcomes and motivation. *Computers and Education*, *55*, 630-643.

March, T. (2007). Revisiting WebQuests in a Web 2 World. How developments in technology and pedagogy combine to scaffold personal learning. *Interactive Educational Multimedia*, 15, 1-17. Retreived November 30, 2010, fromwww.ub.es/multimedia/iem

March, T. (2010). *What WebQuests are (really)*. Retrieved September 19, 2010, from http://bestwebquests.com/what_webquests_are.asp

Nation, I. S. P. (2001). *Learning vocabulary in another language*. Cambridge: Cambridge University Press.

Rinvolucri, M. (1986). *Grammar games*. Cambridge: Cambridge University Press.

Slaouti, D. (2000). Computers and writing in the second language classroom. In P. Brett and G. Motteram (Eds.), *A special interest in computers: Learning and teaching with information and communications technologies* (pp. 9-30). Whitstable, Kent: IATEFL.

Warschauer, M., and Healey, D. (1998). Computers and language learning: An overview. *Language Teaching, 31,* 57-71.

Warschauer, M., and Kern, R. (Eds.). *Network-based language teaching: Concepts and practice.* New York: Cambridge University Press.

In: Innovation and Creativity in ELT Methodology
Editors: H. P. Widodo and A. Cirocki

ISBN: 978-1-62948-146-3

Chapter 17

APPROACHING THE TASK OF GENERATING LANGUAGE LEARNING TASKS: USING SPECIFIC QUESTIONS TO GENERATE WELL-DEVELOPED TASKS

Sharon K. Deckert
Indiana University of Pennsylvania, US

ABSTRACT

The purpose of this chapter is to present considerations of task creation that are consonant with a postmethod understanding of second language acquisition and learning. In particular, the purpose of this chapter is to provide language teachers with a series of questions that can be used to evaluate whether a proposed activity has the qualities of a well-developed task. It also provides discussions of each of these questions to further support the teachers in consciously making informed decisions about designing tasks that take into account the particular context and needs of language learners. The chapter also addresses considerations for classroom research.

INTRODUCTION

This chapter is basically intended to provide language teachers or instructors a conceptual framework of how task creation is made in relation to a postmethod understanding of second language acquisition and learning. In other words, this chapter addresses a series of questions that language teachers or instructors can use to assess or weigh whether a particular proposed activity has the merits of a well-developed task.

As Richard and Rodgers' (2001) outline of many of the historic language teaching methods and approaches indicates, methods and many of the traditional approaches to language teaching have been based on particular assumptions about the nature of language and of language learning. Critiques of many of these methods and approaches, however, have argued that these methods failed to provide for a wide range of individual contexts for language learning. For example, in his critique of historical methods, Kumaravadivelu (2001, 2006) argues that the *myth* of method is the result of an inherently flawed assumption—there is a *best method* for teaching any group of language learners. He argues that this assumption did not take into consideration language learners' particular contexts, needs, and goals, for example, and that it fostered an environment in which research was not part of classroom practice. It is important in any discussion of tasks to make it clear that using tasks in a language learning context is not itself a method. Tasks are tools that language teachers can use to encourage learners to engage language in relevant ways. As Skehan (1996) has noted, it is possible to identify both a strong and weak form of task based instruction. He argues that the strong form would view tasks as the *unit of language teaching* and that everything else would be subsidiary to this. He adds that in a weak form of task based instruction, tasks could be seen as a "vital part" of a language classroom, but they would also be only a part of a larger pedagogy (p. 36).

One basis for considerations of language learning is recognition that learning a language is, in major part, a socialization process. Watson-Gegeo (2004), for example, argues that "linguistic and cultural knowledge are *constructed* through each other" and that "language acquiring children and adults 'are active in selecting agents in both processes'" (p. 339 emphasis in original). In learning a second or other language, it is also important to consider that language learners are developing multicompetence in relation to language use (Cook, 1992; Hall, Cheng, and Carlson, 2006). As an act of resistance to terms such as *non-native* speaker or learner, I will refer to individuals gaining multicompetence in language as individuals who are becoming increasingly multicompetent—as multicompetent language users. In addition to creating a focus on the positiveness of becoming a second or other language speaker, this orientation allows for both considerations of how multicompetent speakers actually use language and understandings of how these considerations can be used when developing language tasks.

DEFINING *TASK*

With the advent of postmethod arguments, discussions about the need to provide language learners with classroom based language learning opportunities have often focused on the notion of tasks. Before discussing the creation of task based language activities, however, a working definition of *task* that differentiates it from other types of activities must be developed. In Skehan (1996, 1998) based on the work of Candlin (1987), Nunan (1989), and Long (1989), Skehan (1998) provides five criteria to define a task. In this definition, "a task is an activity in which:

- meaning is primary;
- there is some communicative problem to solve;
- there is some sort of relationship to the real world;
- task completion has some priority;
- the assessment of the task performance is in terms of task outcome." (p. 95)

To clarify this definition, Skehan (1998, p. 95) presents Willis' (1996) complementary clarification explaining characteristics of activities that would not fit the given definition of task. Five of these characteristics include: "… tasks:

a) do not give learners other people's meanings to regurgitate;
b) are not concerned with language display;
c) are not conformity-oriented;
d) are not practice-oriented;
e) do not embed language into materials so that specific structures can be focused upon."

So, although most of us (English teachers or instructors) would consider tying our shoes to be a kind of task, if we use the parts of this definition as a set of criteria, we find that tying shoes does not qualify as a task. It may have a relationship to the real world, and its completion would have some real priority. We can trip if we do not tie our shoes. If we are feeling particularly creative, we might even be able to say that tying shoes can be assessed in terms of task outcome.

For example, not tripping over our shoelaces could be said to be a positive evaluation of having tied them. However, tying shoes does not meet two fundamental criteria of tasks. The focus of the task is not on meaning, and tying shoes does not present some communicative problem to solve.

We can expand this discussion by considering how the task changes if we ask multicompetent language users to *teach* one another to tie their shoes. This activity would meet the criteria that meaning was somehow primary in the sense that language users would have to engage in exchanges that were meaningful—the understanding of the process of tying shoes. Task completion would still have priority, and the assessment of the task performance would be whether the language users could successfully tie shoes. There are, however, at least two difficulties with this activity meeting the criteria of task. First, the focus of this activity is on a physical process rather than on solving a communicative problem. Second, this rather simple example has brought up a new consideration. While it was argued that tying shoes, has some sort of relationship to the real world, we must now ask: *does the act of one language user teaching another language user to tie shoes have a relationship to the real world of these individual language users?* In other words, *under what conditions would the act of teaching and learning to tie shoes be an actual part of the lives of these particular language users?* In relation to Kumaravadivelu's (2006) notion of *Particularity*, the answer to this question is directly related to the age and needs of the language users. For four-year olds, teaching one another to tie shoes might be a task related to real world activities. For most of the older language learners, however, learning to tie shoes typically no longer has a meaningful relationship to some sort of activity in the real world. While we might be able to label this as an appropriate language task for young learners, we would not want to label it as an appropriate task for older learners.

This one example, then, shows that these criteria, while seemingly simple, provide for complex discussions of creating tasks within a postmethod environment that considers particular users and their contexts. Therefore, this is the definition of task that will be used throughout this chapter.

CREATING TASKS—USING A SEQUENCE OF EVALUATIVE QUESTIONS

Obviously, due to space considerations, this chapter cannot discuss every theoretical aspect related to creating language learning tasks. Instead, what this section provides is a practical series of questions that can be used to enable anyone who is designing a task to consciously consider the qualities of the task being designed. The questions will allow a task designer to evaluate the potential tasks in relation to two major focuses. First, the questions can be used to explore whether an activity under development fits the criteria of a well-developed task. Second, the questions can lead to discussions of whether the practical application of a given task actually accomplishes the expected goal or goals of that task.

What is the Task that You are Asking Learners to Do?

As obvious as it may seem, this first question asks task creators to consciously consider the specific actions that they are asking language learners to do. Quite often in teaching instructors to focus on tasks, I find that they come back with activities that are really a complex sequence of tasks. Let me use a concrete example here. In one activity, I support language learners as they put together a half-hour news broadcast video. If the criteria of a task are applied to this activity, it quickly becomes incredibly complex. News broadcasts exist in the real world, so the activity as a whole seems to meet the criteria that a task should resemble real world activities. However, this can be described in a more detailed way. First, it is important to notice that this activity is really made up of a sequence of individual tasks. Among other things, the language users must:

- analyze a certain number of news broadcasts to find out what their typical structure is;
- negotiate who will take responsibility for which sections of the broadcast;
- collect news from various sources;
- write the news sections for which they are responsible;
- have their news sections edited by other members of the group;
- practice reading their news for an audience;
- perform in front of a camera; and
- edit and copy the video.

As noted, this activity is really made up of a sequence of activities, and each of these pieces can be evaluated separately as a task. Notice, for example, that each separate task has a different relationship to how meaning acts as a primary goal. The communicative problems are different for each task. The relationship to real world activities is slightly different for each task. For example, while it might not be part of most learners' lives to analyze a news broadcast, it is typically a part of language socialization to analyze the parts of an event (see Hymes, 1974, 1986). On the other hand, it is quite typical of most multicompetent language users' lives to read news from several sources. Also, notice that each element of the complex sequence of tasks has some priority since it is necessary for the completion of the next task. Finally, notice that the assessment of each task in the larger sequence is different. The function of this first question, then, goes beyond the obvious one of being clear about what language users are asked to do. This question also functions to challenge task creators to recognize that what they are trying to develop as a task may, in fact, be a sequence of tasks, and each of these tasks has its own relationship to the task definition. Developing each separate task in relation to task criteria provides the task creator with a clearer understanding of the entire activity as it is being designed.

What *Meaning* Do You Think Language Users will Be Focusing on as They Work through this Task?

Applied linguists writing about tasks foreground the importance of creating tasks that require language learners to focus on the meaning of the task. A contrasting example might be useful here. In a structuralist approach to language learning, language learners were frequently asked to complete fill-in-the-blank grammar exercises in which each sentence in the activity was written merely to get the learner to recognize some grammatical patterns. They might be asked to fill in the *correct* verb form to agree with the sentence subject in both person and number. There are two points to be made in terms of these types of activities. First, they help reinforce a language hierarchy in which versions of English other than the *Standard* can be judged as incorrect. Second, and more directly relevant to this discussion, such fill-in-the-blank activities often contained sequences of decontextualized sentences that sacrificed a focus on meaning for a focus on form. The relationship to meaning and form will be further discussed in this chapter.

This question is included here to remind the task creator that from the perspective of the language user, solving a task requires some negotiation of meaning rather than a specific focus of repetitive practice of some language element. As Nunan (2004) has pointed out, tasks are different from typical classroom language exercises, because "tasks have a non-linguistic outcome" (p. 2). In creating a task, a language teacher should have a clear understanding of the meaning language users will focus on during the task. Consider, for example, a literary reading task in Hanauer (2001). In this task, language users were asked to read a poem in pairs and negotiate a paired-group understanding of the meaning of the poem. From a meaning perspective, it is clear that the task prompted language negotiation related to the individuals' focus on the meaning of the poem. As Hanauer points out in his article, however, the exercise also initiated awareness in the language users that certain language forms were necessary to consider as part of the understanding and negotiation of meaning. So, while a primary consideration in constructing a task is one of creating a task in which participants must focus on meaning, a task can also be used to create an implicit focus on form. Research has shown a difference in the types of focus depending on whether language users are given time for strategic planning. See, for example, Nitta's 2008 review of the literature on this topic.

What Communicative Problems are Language Users Asked to Solve?

The types of tasks we as language teachers or task creators are developing are inherently communicative. Essentially, we are dealing with the creation of communicative language tasks. This does not mean, however, that we are suggesting that the use of tasks is the equivalent of a syllabus that operationalizes the communicative language teaching (CLT) approach. Nunan (2004) explains the distinction between the two as one between a broad philosophical approach represented in CLT and the realization of this philosophy as represented in the development of tasks.

The focus of this question is to reinforce the idea that tasks are not only focused on meaning. The communicative criterion of the definition of a task also requires that task participants negotiate meaning and overcome some type of difficulty. Not all tasks are created equal in relation to their levels of communication. As Skehan (1996) discusses, tasks can be analyzed in relation to their code complexity, cognitive familiarity, and communicative stress. Code complexity includes linguistic complexity, vocabulary load, redundancy, and density. He breaks cognitive complexity into the subcategories of cognitive familiarity, which includes familiarity of topic, discourse, genre and task, and cognitive processing, which includes considerations of information organization, clarity and sufficiency of information, and information type, among others. He includes as part of communicative stress notions of time limits and time pressure, speed of presentation, number of participants, length of texts used, type of response, and opportunities to control the interaction.

Research also indicates that participant structures (Philips, 1983; Pica, 2000) play a significant role in the communication within task groups. As Storch (2002) has noted, while learners working in pairs can scaffold each other's performances, not all pairs will work collaboratively. She argues that language user pairs fall into one of four categories: collaborative, dominant/dominant, dominant/passive, and expert/novice. Of these four types, her research found that "… scaffolding is more likely to occur when pairs interact in a certain pattern; either collaborative or in an expert/novice pattern" (p. 147). As Jenks (2007) notes, there is a difference in pair performance and collaboration based on how information is distributed within the pair. For example, if one member has more information than the other, this member is more likely to spend more time communicating due to the need to share the missing information. If, however, both members have access to the same information, "their interactional roles will therefore require them to collaboratively more the task forward" (p. 619). This question, then, challenges task creators to consider not only the communicative elements of the task, but also the participant structures of the task.

How is This Task Related to Real World Activities?

Considerations of questions such as this one often lead to a somewhat false dichotomy between in-class and out-of-class life activities where it is often taken for granted that out-of-class activities somehow are more *real world* than in-class activities. First, it is important to note that anything we do in a classroom is part of our real lives. As obvious as it may be to say, classroom activities are a subset not a *counter set* of the life activities we experience. It may be accurate to argue that we build different identities and carry out different activities in the classroom than we do in other areas of our lives. However, close thought and reading on this subject can lead to the understanding that this is accurate for every different area of our lives. We carry out different activities and construct particular identities in our jobs, in our various relationships, and in every different aspect of our lives. We create identities that are fluid and context dependent in all of the multiple contexts in which we interact. Classroom events themselves are very real types of language events. Additionally, as Norton's (2000, 2001) work on language learner's identities reinforces, language users bring contextual understandings of themselves, their roles, their identities, and their relationships to language with them into pedagogical contexts.

So, one is left to ask why many discussions of tasks focus on a tasks in relation to real world activities. Nunan (1993) takes a slightly different perspective when he makes a distinction between *target tasks* those that "refer to language use outside of the classroom" and the "pedagogical tasks" that take place in the classroom (p. 1). However, it is also important to note that language use inside a classroom—while quite specialized under some circumstance—is still part of the real lives of language users. One function of this question is to make a distinction between some of the processes that were used to teach language historically and language use that would be encouraged in more postmethod understandings of classroom activities. If we recognize that many methods and approaches relied very heavily on decontextualized language exercises, translation, and repetitious activities, for example, it makes sense that there would be a call for activities that were more like those that occur in *real life*. This question, then, is very much focused on Willis' (1996) arguments, as earlier pinpointed.

It is important to notice that in saying that language should not be embedded in materials in which specific structures can be focused upon, this is not the equivalent of saying that tasks should not allow language users to recognize a need they might have to master a particular form. Again, a quick example might clarify this distinction. In the past, it was quite typical to produce activities in which students were given a sequence of sentences related to prepositions and then asked to analyze the uses of the prepositions. This would be an exercise in which students were forced to focus on a certain form—in this case *prepositions*. In a recent class that I observed, on the other hand, I watched a teacher carry out an information gap city map activity in which pairs of language users shared clues to find a particular character from a story they were working on. During this activity, growing multicompetent language users noticed that they needed to pay attention to particular prepositions so that they could achieve the goal of the activity. The language users' main focus was to carry out the task, which was to find where the main character was in the city. In focusing on the meaning while carrying out their task, however, they became aware that they needed to pay attention to particular prepositional forms to carry out the activity successfully.

The first function of this question, then, is to make the task creator remain aware of avoiding those repetitious, meaning regurgitating, language displaying, and conformity oriented types of activities.

A second function of this question is that it allows for interesting questions related to notions of multicompetence. If we view language learners as individuals who are developing multicompetence, we can ask new questions about tasks. For example, when considering the code switching capabilities of multicompetent language users, we can begin to ask if we are creating tasks that support code switching. We can also ask questions such as *under what conditions does a speaker of one language naturally choose to speak in another language?* One rather obvious answer to this question is when the second language is necessary due to the needs of the speaker's interlocutor. An answer such as this one can lead to tasks that ask language users to interact online with individuals who have in common the language currently being studied. Notice that in this context, *real world* actually takes on the meaning of asking that a task reflects circumstances in which using a particular language would be the natural choice of multicompetent language users. This is a very real life application of these types of questions. One piece of research that examines a question that addresses learners' use of more than one language in a task is Swain and Lapkin's (2000) examination of the role that learners' L1s played relative to the type of task they were doing. They note that, ". . . when used within a pedagogical context, different task types may generally provide greater or lesser need for different uses of the L1" (p. 267).

Obviously, much more research, including classroom research, needs to be done in relation to considerations of code switching and multicompetence, but even questions such as this one can help generate tasks that may have more of a multicompetent language user focus.

From the Language Users' Perspective, What is the Outcome of the Task? From the Task Creator's Perspective, What is the Outcome of the Task?

The criteria that are being addressed by these questions are the notion that task completion should have some priority. However, it is important to notice that task design can be complex in relation to this notion. At a very simple level, language users should see the task as something that needs to be done. In the example of the sequence of tasks that made up the news video activity, each task in the sequence could be seen from the language learners' perspective as something that needed to be done in order for the next step to take place. So, for example, from the language learners' perspective, the task of analyzing the organization of a news program needed to be done so that they could produce a news video that had a similar organizational pattern. From their perspective, then, completing the task had priority because the knowledge gained in the analysis was needed to accomplish their next task. In his discussion of how tasks are different from typical classroom language exercises, Nunan (2004) points out that "tasks have a non-linguistic outcome" (p. 2). Note that this sentence addresses a task's outcome from the language learners' perspective.

From a task designer's perspective, however, this task created a need for the language learners to pay attention to some of the qualities of a speech activity or speech genre. This task, then, provides students with the implicit need to focus on a particular linguistic genre. A major function of the two questions in this section is also to encourage language instructors to recognize that the outcome they describe to language learners may be slightly different from that expected by the task designer.

What *Language Forms* Do You Want Your Learners to Focus on?

As the previous example indicates, although tasks are partially defined as activities in which the focus is on meaning, this does not mean that form is never a consideration when designing tasks. Another example of this focus was seen in Hanauer's (2001) poetry reading task, which was designed to motivate language users to focus on particular poetic forms. In another previous example, it was noted that in an information gap map activity, students became aware that they needed to pay attention to prepositions to make their directions to one another clear. This question essentially reinforces the duality of the previous question. Language learners may focus on task completion at the same time that the task design promotes an implicit focus on form, for example.

How Do You Think Your Task Directs Learners to those Particular Linguistic Properties of the Task?

This question may be very difficult to answer. In fact, it may actually require an element of classroom research to fully explore issues related to how learners are directed to different elements of tasks. This type of research can be as simple as conducting post-task interviews or questionnaires to investigate multiple elements of the task. So, the point of this question for a task creator is to increase the awareness that there must be some element of the communicative task whether it is related to code complexity, cognitive complexity, or communicative stress that creates the need for an implicit focus on meaning.

From Your Perspective, What is the End Product of the Task? From the Learners' Perspective, What is the End Product of the Task?

A major quality of a task is that task completion must have some sort of priority for students. The function of the two questions in this section is to think about how to define a task that language users are motivated to work completely through. In other words, from a language users' perspective, there has to be a good reason for participating in a task. This is another place in which the notion that a task should have a relation to real world activities is relevant. In typical real world activities, we all have particular motivations for participating. We have a goal in mind. This can be as simple as getting to know someone better or gaining a piece of information we need. The words *end product* in this question can be related to something as simple as having gained new knowledge about a conversational partner or getting a piece of information. It can also be as complex as writing a research paper. The main function of these two questions, then, is to challenge the task creator to also consider the possibility that language users may find their own goals, motivations, and results in relation to a particular task.

How Will the End Product Be Assessed?

This question is useful for consideration on at least levels that are directly related to classroom practice. First, in constructing tasks, with their inherent criterion that task completion should be a priority, it is important that language users know much about the completion of the task as possible; this includes any notions of how the task will be assessed. A great deal of work has been done on task assessment (see, for example, Bachman, 2002; Mislevy, Steinberg, and Almond, 2002), but space precludes an in-depth discussion of assessment. One of the first functions of this question is to remind task creators to communicate with language users about the role of assessment, if any, in the task they are pursuing.

The second level that this question can be used to address is the issue of in-class research. From this perspective, it is not the communication of the language users that is at issue, but the efficacy of the task itself. All language instructors can consider doing research on whether the task actually functions in the way in which it was designed to function (see among others Hanauer, 2001; Mislevy, Steinberb, and Almond, 2002).

CONCLUSION

As a final note, it must be acknowledged that in a single chapter, only the briefest of discussions can be made in relation to a set of knowledge and practice as broad as that related to the development, practice, and research of task based language instruction, yet in a postmethod era of language practice, tasks can be a crucial part of classroom practice. The questions included in this chapter are not designed to introduce all of the possible facets of knowledge relative to tasks, but they can be used to provide language teachers or instructors with a hands-on series of explorations that can be used to prompt multiple areas of development as practitioners create tasks to be implemented by emerging multicompetent users of language.

REFERENCES

Bachman, L. F. (2002). Some reflections on task-based language performance assessment. *Language Testing*, *19,* 453-476.

Candlin, C. N. (1987). Towards task-based language learning. In C. N. Candlin and Dermot Murphy (Eds.), *Language learning tasks* (pp. 5-22). Englewood Cliffs, NJ: Prentice Hall.

Cook, V. (1992). Evidence for multicompetence. *Language Learning*, *42*, 557-591.

Hall, J. K., Cheng, A., and Carlson, M. T. (2006). Reconceptualizing multicompetence as a theory of language knowledge. *Applied Linguistics*, *27*, 220-240.

Hanauer, D. (2001). The task of poetry reading and second language learning. *Applied Linguistics*, *22*, 295-323.

Hymes, D. (1974). *Foundations in sociolinguistics: An ethnographic approach*. Philadelphia, PA: University of Pennsylvania Press.

Hymes, D. (1986). Models of the interaction of language and social life. In J. J. Gumperz and D. Hymes (Eds.), *Directions in sociolinguistics: The ethnography of communication* (pp. 35-71). New York: Basil Blackwell.

Jenks, C. J. (2007). Floor management in task-based interaction: The interactional role of participatory structures. *System*, *35*, 609-622.

Kumaravadivelu, B. (2001). Toward a postmethod pedagogy. *TESOL Quarterly*, *35*, 537-560.

Kumaravadivelu, B. (2006). *Understanding language teaching: From method to postmethod*. Hillsdale, NJ: Lawrence Erlbaum.

Long, M. H. (1989). Task, group, and task-group interaction. *University of Hawaii Working Papers in English as a Second Language*, *8*, 1-26.

Mislevy, L., R. J., Steinberg, L. S., and Almond, R. G. (2002). Design and analysis in task-based language assessment. *Language Testing*, *19*, 477–496.

Nitta, R. (2008). Incidental focus-on-form in task-based language teaching: A rationale for strategic and on-line planning processes. *NUCB Journal of Language, Culture and Communication*, *9*(2), 31-42.

Norton, B. (2000). *Identity and language learning: Gender, ethnicity and educational change*. Harlow, UK: Longman.

Norton, B. (2001). Non-participation, imagined communities and the language classroom. In M. P. Breen (Ed.), *Learner contributions to language learning: New directions in research* (pp. 159-171). Harlow, UK: Pearson.

Nunan, D. (1989). *Designing tasks for the communicative classroom*. Cambridge: Cambridge University Press.

Nunan, D. (1993). Task-based syllabus design: Selecting, grading and sequencing tasks. In G. Crookes and S. M. Gass (Eds.), *Tasks in a pedagogical context: Integrating theory and practice* (pp. 55-68). Clevedon: Mutilingual Matters.

Nunan, D. (2004). *Task-based language teaching*. Cambridge: Cambridge University Press.

Philips, S. U. (1993). *The invisible culture: Communication in classroom and community on the Warm Spring Indian reservation*. Long Grove, IL: Waveland Press.

Pica, T. (2000). Tradition and transition in English language teaching methodology. *System*, *28*, 1-18.

Richards, J. C., and Rodgers, T. S. (2001). *Approaches and methods in language teaching*. Cambridge: Cambridge University Press.

Skehan, P. (1996). A framework for the implementation of task-based instruction. *Applied Linguistics*, *17*(1), 38-62.

Skehan, P. (1998). *A cognitive approach to language learning*. Oxford: Oxford University Press.

Storch, N. (2002). Patterns of interaction in ESL pair work. *Language Learning*, *52*(1), 119-158.

Swain, M., and Lapkin, S. (2000). Task-based second language learning: The uses of the first language. *Language Teaching Research*, *4*, 251-274.

Watson-Gegeo, K. A. (2004). Mind, language, and epistemology: Toward a language socialization paradigm for SLA. *The Modern Language Journal*, *88*, 331-350.

Willis, J. (1996). *A framework for task-based learning*. London, Longman.

INDEX

D

Q

R

S